WITNESS TO GETTYSBURG

Other books by Richard Wheeler

In Pirate Waters

Voices of 1776

Voices of the Civil War

The Siege of Vicksburg

Sherman's March

Iwo

A Special Valor

Sword Over Richmond

WITNESS
TO
Gettysburg

RICHARD WHEELER

1817

HARPER & ROW, PUBLISHERS, New York

Cambridge, Philadelphia, San Francisco, Washington
London, Mexico City, São Paulo, Singapore, Sydney

973.7
Whe

Designer: Sidney Feinberg
Copyeditor: William C. Reynolds
Index by Olive Holmes for Edindex

Library of Congress Cataloging-in-Publication Data

Wheeler, Richard
  Witness to Gettysburg.

  Includes index.
  1. Gettysburg, Battle of, 1863—Personal narratives. 2. Gettysburg, Battle of, 1863. I. Title.
E475.53.W55   1987   973.7'349   86-46108
ISBN 0-06-015760-7

    89 90 91 RRD 10 9 8 7 6 5 4 3 2

Contents

160570

Illustrations

MAPS

Preface

YEAR AFTER YEAR the Battle of Gettysburg maintains a unique appeal among readers of history, so I probably do not have to justify the introduction of still another book on the topic. But I would like to point out that *Witness to Gettysburg* attempts something new: a telling of the story, in terms both historical and human, as largely as possible in the words of participants, both military and civilian, both male and female.

Most eyewitness histories are prefaced with a warning that many of the passages, being of popular origin, contain errors and inconsistencies, but this volume is offered as a veracious study. The technical statements have been checked against the official records and the personal stories have been analyzed for credibility. Although most of the book's ellipses indicate the employment of condensation, some were used to eliminate details that appeared to be faulty. In a number of cases it was necessary to include clarifications enclosed in brackets. Arranged chronologically, the accounts are linked together in such a way as to maintain coherence and continuity. I have used this style of narrating history in seven previous volumes, the most recent of which is *Sword Over Richmond*.

Some of the quotes in the present work will be recognized as coming from the Gettysburg battle's better-known eyewitness records, but I have utilized many old books, pamphlets, magazine and newspaper articles, diaries, and letters that never achieved more than transient notice. In order to supplement a personal collection of Gettysburg items, years in the gleaning, I paid visits to the Pennsylvania State Library at Harrisburg, the library of the Gettysburg National Military Park, and the United States Army Military History Institute at Carlisle, where Dr. Richard J.

Sommers referred me to the Robert L. Brake Collection, which was especially useful.

Many of the illustrations, which were taken from *Battles and Leaders of the Civil War* and other publications of the postwar decades, are adaptations of sketches or photographs made at the time of the battle.

WITNESS TO GETTYSBURG

1

Prelude on the Rappahannock

THE TIME WAS mid-May 1863, and the Civil War had entered its third year. In the western theater a Union army under Ulysses S. Grant had begun to encircle fortress Vicksburg, key to control of the Mississippi River, and the Confederate defense was failing. In the East, however, Robert E. Lee's Army of Northern Virginia had just capped a generally successful career against the Union's Army of the Potomac with a victory at Chancellorsville, made spectacular by the fact that the Confederates were outnumbered more than two to one. Chancellorsville took the life of Lee's ablest subordinate, the renowned Stonewall Jackson, accidentally shot by his own men, but the Army of Northern Virginia emerged from the battle a supremely confident team. Lee himself was bolstered in his belief that his ill-accoutered and often hungry troops were truly a special breed, and he became almost contemptuous of a foe whose superior numbers and lavish resources remained largely unexploited under a series of second-rate leaders: Irvin McDowell, George McClellan, Ambrose Burnside, and, now, Joseph Hooker. It was a joke in Lee's army that Hooker, who had made such a poor showing at Chancellorsville, bore the sobriquet "Fighting Joe."

About fifty miles north of Richmond, in campgrounds verdant with spring, the armies of Lee and Hooker lay watching each other over Virginia's southeasterly flowing Rappahannock River, the Confederates on the south bank at Fredericksburg and the Federals on the north at Falmouth. On May 14 Lee rode a train through the greening countryside to the Confederate capital to discuss new operations with President Jefferson Davis. The general, according to a clerk in the War Depart-

Robert E. Lee

ment, "looked thinner and a little pale." Seven weeks earlier, Lee had suffered a debilitating affliction that was probably a mild heart attack. During his three-day conference with Davis, however, he showed all of his old intellectual force, and he petitioned earnestly in favor of a plan he had for carrying the war to the North.

Lee had tried an advance into Northern territory the previous September, only to be repulsed in a fight with George McClellan along the Antietam Creek near Sharpsburg, Maryland. But that invasion had been an impromptu affair, an effort to exploit the Confederate victory at Second Bull Run on August 29 and 30. The new plan was the product of careful consideration. Hooker's presence on the Rappahannock was a threat to Richmond, and Lee wanted to make it necessary for him to withdraw northward to cover his own capital. This would bring the added benefit of easing the agony of a war-ravaged Virginia. At the same time, the Confederate army would be able to supply itself from the rich stores in the towns and farmlands of Pennsylvania. The invasion might startle the North into easing its pressure on Vicksburg; it would at least take the spotlight from Confederate reverses there. And, with Lee's army on Northern soil, the Union's peace advocates might heighten their efforts to stop the war. It was also possible that a Confederate victory in the North would prompt England and France to recognize the Confederacy and send a fleet to its aid. Because the South's cotton was important to the European economy, the two countries were already sending arms and other supplies. All in all, Lee believed, an invasion offered a potentiality for rewards that made the risk worth taking.

Winning his point with the Davis administration, the general hurried back to the Fredericksburg area to prepare his campaign. Recruits were coming in, and the army was building to 75,000 men formed into three corps of infantry and one of cavalry. As the work of organization and supply was speeded, the camps sounded with shouted orders, the subdued thump of marching, the rumble of wagons, and the clop of horses. Few of the troops knew where they were going, but the ranks were swept by enthusiasm and jocularity. "The infantry and cavalry were always casting jokes at one another as they passed," explains John O. Casler, a short, black-haired private in the 33rd Regiment, Virginia Infantry, a part of Jackson's original Stonewall Brigade. "The infantry would ask them how long it took 'them things to grow out of a man's heels' (referring to their spurs). . . . They would reply, 'If it wasn't for them things you'd lose your wagon trains,' intimating they would have to protect them while we retreated. We would ask the North Carolinians if

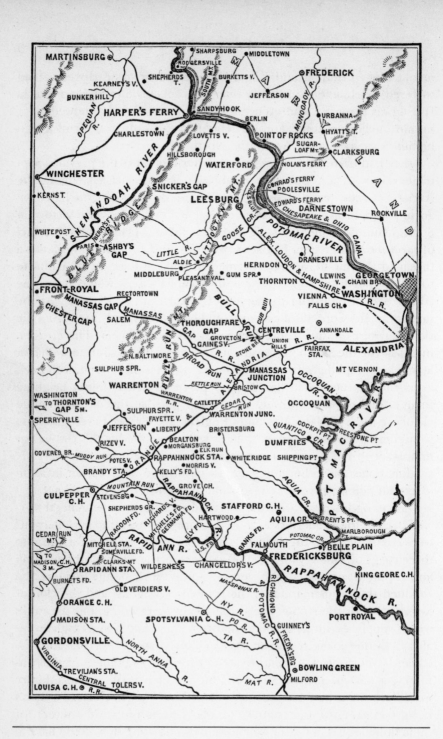

Field of operations in Virginia

they had any 'tar,' and call them 'Tar Heels.' They would reply that they were just out, as they had let us Virginians have all they had to make us stick in the last fight, and call us 'sore-backs,' as they had knocked all the skin off our backs running over us to get into battle. And so it would go, but all in the best of humor, knowing that all did their duty."

The mood in the Union camps at Falmouth was far less airy. From the newspapers that reached them the men learned that their defeat at Chancellorsville was a topic of lamentation in the North. Of course, there was a measure of consolation in the knowledge that they were good soldiers lacking only in inspired leadership. They were aware that the people at home were crying toward Washington, "Abraham Lincoln, give us a man!" Unfortunately the President (who had reacted privately to Chancellorsville by exclaiming, "My God, my God, what will the nation say?") could find no man to offer. He was trying to salvage something with Hooker. "I will make no complaint," he wrote the general, "if for some time you do nothing more than hold the enemy in check by demonstrations, and occasionally by some cavalry expeditions, if they are practicable, while you are getting your army in good condition. However, if you clearly think that you can renew the attack with success I will not hinder you." Hooker's army was smaller now, diminished not only by casualties but also by enlistment terminations; but he still had about 100,000 men divided into seven corps of infantry and one of cavalry. Eager to redeem himself, the general intended to press his campaign against Richmond as soon as possible. But he was forestalled.

The opening phase of Lee's plan called for one corps of infantry to remain temporarily at Fredericksburg facing Hooker across the Rappahannock, while the other two, quietly utilizing the cover of the terrain on the southern side of the river, began marching northwest toward the Blue Ridge Mountains, their first destination Culpeper, about thirty miles from Fredericksburg. The cavalry moved out before the infantry. In charge of this corps of about 10,000 men was thirty-year-old Major General James Ewell Brown ("Jeb") Stuart, a legend in the Confederacy and a source of wonderment in the North. Irrepressibly lighthearted and classically dashing, Stuart was perhaps overfond of publicity, but he deserved the notice he was given. His feats included two raids entirely around the Union army, both made while McClellan commanded in 1862. Lee relied on Stuart to screen the movements of the Confederate infantry and to gain information on the movements of the enemy.

Among Stuart's staff officers was young Major Heros von Borcke, a gigantic, lushly mustached Prussian aristocrat who had resigned a cav-

Joseph Hooker

alry commission in Berlin in order to cross the Atlantic and embrace the Confederate cause. Von Borcke rode with the first troopers to reach Culpeper. "Our tents," he relates, "were pitched in a beautiful spot, overshadowed by magnificent hickory and tulip-poplar trees, and surrounded by broad clover fields where our horses were richly pastured, and through which the pretty little river, Mountain Run, rolled its silver waters between picturesque banks and afforded us the chance of a magnificent cool bath and plenty of sport with the rod and line. Our cavalry were in the highest spirits and were kept in constant and salutary activity by incessant drilling and other preparations for the impending campaign." On May 22 Jeb Stuart, who had a passion for pageantry, held a review. It was only a small affair, since only 4,000 of his troopers had reached the scene. Stuart planned to conduct a more elaborate review, with General Lee attending, when the campaign was further advanced.

By June 1, even before Lee got his infantry moving, General Hooker knew that something was stirring. His spies and the Confederate deserters who crossed the river informed him that Lee had ordered his troops to prepare for a campaign that would involve long marches beyond the range of the South's railway transportation. This word was followed by a report that Lee intended to invade Maryland. Because of the uncertainty of the situation, Hooker could make no immediate response, but an alert was established. According to Captain Henry N. Blake of the 11th Regiment, Massachusetts Volunteers: "Every object south of the Rappahannock was scanned by many eyes. The troops were ordered to keep constantly on hand rations for three days."

Lee's march from Fredericksburg to Culpeper began on June 3. Leading the way was the 1st Corps under big, strong-limbed, full-bearded James Longstreet, Lee's "old war horse," his most trusted subordinate now that Jackson was dead. Longstreet's columns were followed by those of Lieutenant General Richard S. Ewell's 2nd Corps. Ewell was a nervous-mannered man with a bald head, protuberant eyes, and a jutting nose, the combination giving him a curious birdlike appearance. He had lost a leg at Groveton in August 1862, and he left Fredericksburg riding in a buggy, a pair of crutches beside him; but he was prepared to take to the saddle, strapping himself upon it, when the action started. Left behind for the present to face Hooker was the 3rd Corps under Lieutenant General Ambrose Powell (A. P.) Hill, a slender, weak-framed man who was chronically ill yet maintained the will to be a furious fighter.

On the morning of June 4 the Union observers at Falmouth noted

Jeb Stuart

that many of the enemy's tents had vanished, but there was no intelligence of a general movement. Before noon the next day Hooker telegraphed Lincoln in Washington: "This morning some more of their camps have disappeared. The picket line along the river is preserved, and as strong as ever. . . . As I am liable to be called on to make a movement with the utmost promptitude, I desire that I may be informed as early as practicable of the views of the Government concerning this army. . . . I am instructed to keep 'in view always the importance of covering Washington and Harpers Ferry [on the Potomac River at the northern end of the Shenandoah Valley], either directly or by so operating as to be able to punish any force of the enemy sent against them.' In the event the enemy should move, as I almost anticipate he will, the head of his column will probably be headed toward the Potomac, via Gordonsville or Culpeper, while the rear will rest on Fredericksburg. After giving the subject my best reflection, I am of opinion that it is my duty to pitch into his rear. . . . Will it be within the spirit of my instructions to do so?"

The President wired back at once, saying that he was turning the message over to the War Department for a response by Major General Henry W. Halleck, General-in-Chief of the Union Armies. Lincoln added that he himself was doubtful that Hooker should cross to the south side of the Rappahannock to attack Lee. "If he should leave a rear force at Fredericksburg, tempting you to fall upon it, it would fight in intrenchments and have you at disadvantage, and so, man for man, worst you at that point, while his main force would in some way be getting an advantage of you northward. In one word, I would not take any risk of being entangled upon the river, like an ox jumped half over a fence and liable to be torn by dogs front and rear, without a fair chance to gore one way or kick the other."

General Halleck's wire followed fast on the heels of the President's. "Neither this capital nor Harpers Ferry could long hold out against a large force. They must depend for their security very much upon the cooperation of your army. It would therefore seem perilous to permit Lee's main force to move upon the Potomac while your army is attacking an intrenched position on the other side of the Rappahannock. Of course your movements must depend in a great measure upon those made by Lee."

Lee's march upon Culpeper developed slowly. By this time Jeb Stuart, his entire cavalry command having assembled, had proceeded with his arrangements for a grand review, and the affair matured before

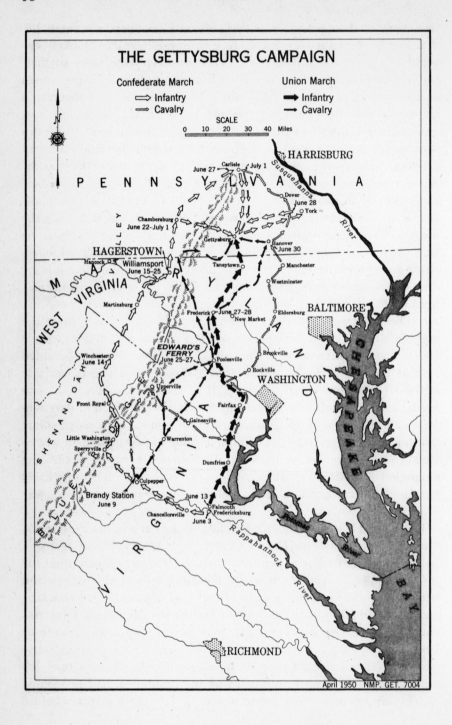

THE GETTYSBURG CAMPAIGN

Lee got there. It was a great success, as Heros von Borcke attests: "In-vitations having been sent out to the whole circle of our acquaintances far and near, the hotels of the town, and as many private houses as had any accommodations to spare, were got ready for the reception of our guests, many of whom, after all, we had to put under tents. Among those we expected on this occasion was General [George W.] Randolph, the former Secretary of War, a warm friend of Stuart's and mine. . . . Gladly eager to give him a proof of my esteem . . . I started off on the morning of the 4th for Gordonsville to meet our friend on his road, and I had the pleasure of bringing him by special train into Culpeper with all honors, our battle flag floating from the locomotive.

"Every train that afternoon brought in fresh crowds of our guests, and we all assembled at the station to receive them and forward them to their destination by the ambulances and wagons we had got prepared for that purpose. In the evening there was a ball at the town hall, which went off pleasantly enough, although it was not, in the language of the reporter, 'a gay and dazzling scene illuminated by floods of light stream-ing from numerous chandeliers,' for our supply of light was limited to a few tallow candles; and when the moon rose we were glad to avail our-selves of her services by adjourning to the spacious verandah.

"As the morning of the 5th dawned bright and beautiful, we com-pleted our preparations and gave the last touch to our arms and equip-ments; and about eight o'clock General Stuart and his staff mounted their horses and made for the plains of Brandy Station. . . . Our little band presented a gay and gallant appearance as we rode forth to the sound of our bugles, all mounted on fine chargers and clad in our best accoutrements, our plumes nodding and our battle flag waving in the breeze. I myself had on a uniform new from head to foot; and the horse on which I was mounted seemed to me in the very perfection of beauty as it danced with springing step upon the turf, its glossy coat shining like burnished gold in the morning sun.

"As our approach was heralded by the flourish of trumpets, many of the ladies in the village came forth to greet us from the porches and verandahs of the houses, and showered down flowers upon our path. But if the smiles and patriotic demonstrations of the daughters of old Virginia were pleasant and flattering to us as mortal men, not less grate-ful to our soldiers' hearts were the cheers . . . which rose in the air as we came upon the open plain near Brandy Station, where the whole cavalry corps awaited us, drawn out in a line a mile and a half long, at the

James Longstreet

extreme right of which twenty-four guns of our horse artillery thundered forth a salute.

"About ten o'clock the marching past commenced. General Stuart had taken up his position on a slight eminence, whither many hundreds of spectators, mostly ladies, had gathered in ambulances and on horseback, anxiously awaiting the approach of the troops. The corps passed first by squadrons, and at a walk, and the magnificent spectacle of so many thousand troopers splendidly mounted made the heart swell with pride and impressed one with the conviction that nothing could resist the attack of such a body of troops. The review ended with a sham charge of the whole corps by regiments, the artillery advancing at the same time at a gallop and opening a rapid fire upon an imaginary enemy.

"The day wound up with a ball; but as the night was fine we danced in the open air on a piece of turf near our headquarters and by the light of enormous woodfires, the ruddy glare of which upon the animated groups of our assembly gave to the whole scene a wild and romantic effect."

It was during the afternoon of this day that General Hooker ordered one of his divisions to throw a set of pontoon bridges across the Rappahannock at Fredericksburg and make a demonstration aimed at developing Lee's intentions. A. P. Hill responded to the incursion by ringing the area with troops, but this told Hooker little. At the same time, however, news reached his Falmouth headquarters that Stuart had been located. The next day Hooker wired Halleck in Washington: "As the accumulation of the heavy rebel force of cavalry about Culpeper may mean mischief, I am determined, if practicable, to break it up in its incipiency. I shall send all my cavalry against them, stiffened by about 3,000 infantry. It will require until the morning of the 9th for my forces to gain their positions, and at daylight on that day it is my intention to attack them in their camps."

General Lee reached Culpeper on June 7. According to Jeb Stuart's adjutant general, the youthful but serious-minded Major Henry B. McClellan (a first cousin of the Union army's George McClellan): "It was not esteemed a matter of congratulation when . . . notice was received that the commanding general desired to review the cavalry on the following day. The invitation could not be declined; and on the 8th of June the brigades were assembled on the same field and passed in review before the great leader of the Army of Northern Virginia." Lee's appearance that day made a lasting impression on Captain John Esten

Richard S. Ewell

Cooke, Stuart's chief ordnance officer, a man of deft expression who, like Heros von Borcke, viewed the war as a romance. Lee could be seen "sitting his horse, motionless, on a little knoll—the erect figure half concealed by the short cavalry cape falling from his shoulders, and the grave face overshadowed by the broad gray hat—while above him, from a lofty pole, waved the folds of a large Confederate flag."

There was a moment during the proceedings when the dignity of the troops was at risk. As recorded in the diary of George M. Neese, a gunner in Captain R. P. Chew's battery of horse artillery: "I was trying to act in the capacity of first sergeant of our battery in the review today, and was riding at the head of the horse artillery mounted on a mule with ears about a foot long. . . . General Stuart spied the waving ears of my mule, and he quickly dispatched one of his aides to Captain Chew with the urgent request to order the mule and me with it off of the field, which was quickly done with neatness and dispatch. I cared very little about the matter, but the mule looked a little bit surprised, and, I think, felt ashamed of himself and his waving ears, which cost him his prominent position in the grand cavalcade.

"No doubt General Stuart is proud of his splendid cavalry, and well he may be, for it certainly is a fine body of well-mounted and tried horsemen whose trusty blades have ofttimes flashed in the red glow of battle's fiery tide and stemmed the deadly wave of war. But my mule, too, has heard the raging battle roar and the dreadful musketry roll and seen the screaming shell tear the sod to smithers around his feet. True, a mule was not built for the purpose of ornamenting a grand review or embellishing an imposing pageant, but as mine so willingly bears the hardships and dangers of the camp and field I thought it not indiscreet to let it play a little act in some of the holiday scenes of war."

Henry McClellan explains that "much less of display was attempted on this occasion, for General Lee, always careful not to tax his men unnecessarily, would not allow the cavalry to take the gallop, nor would he permit the artillerymen to work their guns. He would reserve all their strength for the serious work which must shortly ensue. . . . Longstreet and Ewell had already reached Culpeper . . . and he wished his cavalry to move across the Rappahannock on the following day to protect the flank of these corps as they moved northward."

Even while the review was in progress, Hooker's cavalry corps—numbering, like Lee's, about 10,000 men—was stealing toward the north bank of the river at the fords leading to Stuart's position. Thus far in the war the Army of the Potomac's troopers, although they had ridden their share of missions, had won no special acclaim. They hoped to do better from now on, for they had a new leader, installed after Chancellorsville: Brigadier General Alfred Pleasonton, a man of quick perception and generally good judgment. Pleasonton was thirty-nine years old, small-statured, furtive-eyed, and notably neat and dapper, his uniform including a straw hat worn at a jaunty angle. Although unassuming in manner, he was not above coloring his battle reports to enhance his reputation. Among Pleasonton's subordinate commanders were experienced regulars John Buford and David McMurtrie Gregg, the young but promising Hugh Judson Kilpatrick, and British soldier of fortune Sir Percy Wyndham.

The close of the review at Brandy Station found Lee well pleased with what he had seen. He returned to his headquarters at Culpeper, from which he wrote his wife: "The men and horses looked well. . . . Stuart was in all his glory. . . . The country here looks very green and pretty, notwithstanding the ravages of war. What a beautiful world God in his loving kindness to his creatures has given us! What a shame that men endowed with reason and knowledge of right should mar his gifts!"

After Lee's departure from the review field, Stuart spent the evening hours starting his brigades toward the Rappahannock, about five miles distant, in preparation for his anticipated crossing the next morning. The units moved independently, and all bivouacked well back from the river, but pickets were dispatched to cover the several fords. According to staff officer Henry McClellan: "With everything in readiness for an early start, Stuart himself bivouacked . . . on Fleetwood Hill, so called from the name of the residence there situated. The hill is between Brandy Station and the river, about half a mile from the station, and commands the open plain around it in every direction."

Stuart had no idea that the Union cavalry corps was making its bivouacs on the other side of the river. Pleasonton had ordered his men to move quietly and to refrain from building campfires. Moreover, it rained for a time during the evening and laid any dust that might have risen above the trees and aroused suspicion. The corps was in two columns, the one led personally by Pleasonton, seconded by John Buford, the other under David Gregg. Pleasonton's column faced Beverly Ford, while Gregg's was at Kelly's Ford, about six miles to the southeast. Pleasonton was directly in Stuart's front, whereas Gregg's position offered him a route to the Confederate leader's right flank. But neither Pleasonton nor Gregg was sure of Stuart's location. Both believed he might be as far away as Culpeper, ten miles from the river.

Alfred Pleasonton

Federals and Confederates alike settled down to sleep, and the shadowed stillness of the camps was disturbed only by sentries making their monotonous rounds and by periodic stirrings among the horses. No one on either side suspected that the stage had been set for the greatest cavalry action of the war.

2

Sabers at Brandy Station

THE STORY of the Battle of Brandy Station (or Beverly Ford, or Fleetwood) is begun by a Union trooper, Captain Frederick C. Newhall, who explains that Pleasonton's expedition was "in fact a reconnaissance in force to ascertain for General Hooker's information to what extent the rumors were true that Lee was en route across the Blue Ridge to the Shenandoah Valley, and so, no doubt, to the Potomac and beyond. . . . As an aide-de-camp to General Pleasonton, it was my fortune to be thrown with the Beverly Ford column. . . . It was not yet dawn when General Pleasonton rode to the river bank. . . . The atmosphere at that hour was very hazy, and the group of officers assembled near the general were half hidden from each other by the mist. General Buford was there, with his usual smile. He rode a gray horse, at a slow walk generally, and smoked a pipe no matter what was going on around him, and it was always reassuring to see him in the saddle when there was any chance of a fight."

Pleasonton and Buford were relying on Colonel Benjamin F. Davis to lead the advance with his 8th New York Cavalry, backed by the other regiments that made up the brigade he commanded. In Pleasonton's words: "With Colonel Davis . . . I reconnoitred the ford, and found the circumstances favorable for a surprise of the enemy on the opposite side, in case he was there in force. The north bank of the river commanded the southern, and, with the exception of a few cavalry pickets scattered up and down the river, nothing was to be seen. The roaring of the water over the dam just above the ford would prevent the sound of cavalry from being heard in making the passage of the river, while [the] dense fog . . . extending some distance on the other side . . . would screen from observation any body of troops while crossing. It was decided, therefore, to attack immediately. . . . Accordingly, at five o'clock, Colonel Davis gallantly led the 8th New York Cavalry through the ford."

One of the Confederate troopers with the companies of pickets facing the ford was a nineteen-year-old Virginian named Luther W. Hopkins, who had served a watch during the night but was now asleep in a blanket, with about twenty of his comrades around him, in a woods a few hundred yards back. "I was . . . rudely awakened by the watchman, who shouted that the enemy was crossing the river. We all jumped up and mounted our horses. Our captain was with us. The day was just breaking. The pickets were hurrying up from the river in every direction, firing their pistols to give the alarm. Our captain formed the men in the edge of the woods for the purpose of checking for a few minutes the advancing enemy, so as to give the 10,000 cavalrymen that were encamped . . . in the rear time to saddle and mount their horses and prepare for battle.

"The enemy came pouring up from the river, and we opened fire on them, checking them for the moment. Two of our men were killed, several wounded, and two horses killed. Two couriers had gone ahead to rouse the camp. We soon followed them along the road through the woods, the enemy hard on our heels. I was riding with the captain in the rear. We were not aware that the Yankees were so close to us, and the captain was calling to the men to check their speed. I looked behind, called to the captain and told him they were right on us, and just as I spoke two bullets went hissing by my head. The captain yelled to his men to move forward, and, bending low on the necks of our horses, we gave them the spur. As we came out of the woods into the fields we met the 6th Virginia . . . coming down the road at full gallop."

Riding with the 6th Virginia was another nineteen-year-old, John N. Opie, who was worried about his mount, a headstrong mare. "My horse did what I too well knew she would do—that is, she shot out from the column like a thunderbolt and rushed down the road with the rapidity of lightning. I looked around behind me, and no one was in sight. I pulled with all my strength and vigor; I hallooed, 'Whoa! Whoa! Whoa!' but to no purpose, as her mouth was fixed against her breast. I thought of killing her, but I had nothing but a saber, as, three days before, someone had stolen my six-shooter. . . . I thought of jumping off, but that would never have done. I turned a bend in the road, and there, across my path, was a double line of [Union] cavalry. My hope was that,

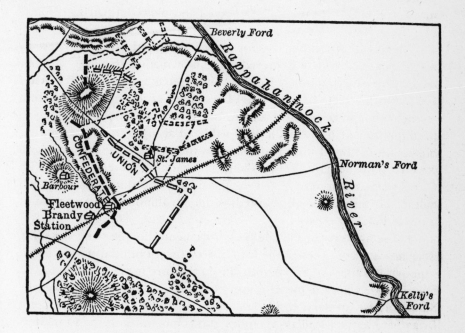

The cavalry fight at Brandy Station

seeing a single horseman, they would understand the situation and not fire; but I suppose they thought it was the devil, as my horse was as black as night and was running at the rate of about forty miles an hour. At any rate, I saw them raise their carbines, then a line of smoke, then a crash; when, heels over head, both horse and rider tumbled through the air and fell, headlong, in a pile on the side of the road. My right leg felt as if paralyzed, but, seeing and feeling no blood, upon examination I found that a ball had struck the toe of my boot and plowed a furrow through the sole.

"I jumped up, still having my saber in my right hand, my horse by my side dead, not having uttered a groan or made a struggle. . . . Four bullets had penetrated her. How I escaped remains a mystery. . . . After I arose to my feet, I heard [our] boys charging down the road. In a moment they were opposite me in the road, when another volley was fired [by the enemy]. A man dropped dead at my feet. . . . I seized his horse and mounted him, and joined in the charge. We broke the 8th New York. Lieutenant [R. O.] Allen had a hand-to-hand encounter with Colonel Davis, whom he killed. . . . Having by this time lost more than half of our men, we were charged by the 8th Illinois and driven out of the woods."

Large numbers of Pleasonton's horsemen, whooping and shouting, were now splashing across the ford, a detachment of infantry wading in support. Pushing the broken 6th Virginia before it, the van was soon a mile inland, where it posed a mortal threat to the camp occupied by Stuart's horse artillery, headed by Major R. F. Beckham. At this point Brigadier General William E. Jones, top commander of the Confederates facing the ford (but now looking uncommanderlike, for he was minus his hat and coat, and his feet gleamed bare in his stirrups), rushed the 7th Virginia Regiment forward to bolster the remnants of the 6th, while one of the threatened guns spoke up defiantly. The combination delayed the Federals long enough to save all of the batteries, along with the camp's transportation. According to Stuart's aide Henry McClellan: "No serious loss occurred save that Major Beckham's desk, in which he had placed the order of march received by him the previous night, was jostled out of its wagon in its hasty retreat, and fell into the enemy's hands, thus revealing to him authoritatively part of the information which he had come to obtain.

"Retiring to the vicinity of Saint James Church, the artillery was placed in position for action, and the whole of Jones' brigade having now been brought forward, the advance of the enemy was still further

A hand-to-hand encounter

checked." Jones' brigade soon had the support of two like units, one led by wealthy South Carolina planter Wade Hampton, the other by W.H.F. ("Rooney") Lee, second son of Robert E. A somewhat perplexed Stuart galloped to the front from Fleetwood Hill. Having learned that the Federals were crossing also at Kelly's Ford, about five miles to his right, Stuart had already sent a detachment in that direction.

The greater part of the Confederate front at Saint James Church faced open terrain stretching toward the woods the Federals had captured and were now using to cover their deployment. Young George Neese, of Stuart's artillery, had a fine view of the ensuing action. "Our cavalry advanced to the edge of the woods, but had to retire immediately, as the woods were full of Yankee horsemen and dismounted sharpshooters. Soon after our cavalry fell back into the field the Yankee cavalry made a charge from the woods. . . . Our courageous cavalry gallantly withstood the enemy's first determined charge, and the field in front of the woods was covered with a mingled mass, fighting and struggling with pistol and saber like maddened savages. At that juncture of the fray the warlike scene was fascinatingly grand beyond description. . . . Hundreds of glittering sabers . . . gleamed and flashed in the morning sun, then clashed with metallic ring, searching for human blood, while hundreds of little puffs of white smoke gracefully rose through the balmy June air from discharging firearms all over the field in front of our batteries.

"During the first charge in the early morn the artillerymen stood in silent awe gazing on the struggling mass in our immediate front, yet every man was at his post and ready for action at a moment's notice; and as soon as our cavalry repulsed the enemy and drove them back into the woods, sixteen pieces of our horse artillery opened fire on the woods with a crash and sullen roar that made the morning air tremble and filled the woods with howling shell. Then for a while the deep diapason roar of artillery mixed with the sharp crash of small arms swept over the trembling field and sounded along the neighboring hills like a rumbling chariot of rolling thunder. We kept up a steady artillery fire for a while, until the enemy in our front disappeared from sight and retired deeper into the woods."

Pleasonton hadn't been driven off; it had become necessary for him to look to his right flank, which Rooney Lee's brigade was trying to swing around in order to gain possession of Beverly Ford. In the fighting that followed, Pleasonton repelled the threat to his line of retreat. But he was inhibited in resuming the offensive by a lack of contact with the Kelly's

Ford column. Dividing his forces had turned out to be a mistake. The plan had been made under the assumption that Stuart was farther from the river. Pleasonton had expected to make a junction with Gregg at Brandy Station before doing any major fighting.

Gregg was now well on the way, but 1,900 of his troops were not with him. He had detached these men, who made up Colonel Alfred N. Duffié's division, on a probe to the left toward Culpeper, and they had come up against two regiments that had been hurried from Stuart's lines to cover his rear. The encounter ended Duffié's availability for Pleasonton's use, for he was long delayed. Among the casualties in the series of brushes was one of Stuart's favorite aides, Captain William D. Farley, who lost a leg to a cannonball, the wound being a mortal one. The Confederate witnesses to Farley's fall included Lieutenant John T. Rhett, who, along with a Captain Chestnut, went to the luckless man's side. Rhett relates: "He was very cool, in fact pleasant and smiling, though evidently in great pain. Just as we were about to send him away, he called me to him, and, pointing to the leg that had been cut off by the ball, and which was lying nearby, he asked me to bring it to him. I did so. He took it, pressed it to his bosom as one would a child, and said, smiling, 'It is an old friend, gentlemen, and I do not wish to part from it.' Chestnut and myself shook hands with him, bidding him goodby and expressing the hope that we should soon again see him. He said, 'Goodby, gentlemen, and forever. I know my condition, and we will not meet again. I thank you for your kindness. . . .' Courteously, even smilingly, he nodded his head to us as the men bore him away. . . . I have never seen a man whose demeanor, in the face of certain, painful, and quick death, was so superb."

General Gregg, making his approach to Brandy Station with about 2,400 men, was substantially aided by luck. The detachment Stuart had sent to intercept him—Brigadier General Beverly H. Robertson's brigade—had been ordered to cover the direct route from Kelly's Ford, and Robertson adhered to the letter of his instructions, merely watching as the Federal column swung around his right flank by another road, one leading toward the right-rear of Stuart's position. Robertson did bestir himself to send a courier toward Fleetwood Hill, where he believed Stuart to be.

Upon his departure from the hill to take personal command of the defense against Pleasonton and Buford, Stuart had left Henry McClellan in charge of the Fleetwood headquarters. In McClellan's words: "Every scrap of the camp was removed toward Culpeper . . . and there remained nothing on the hill except the adjutant [McClellan] and his couriers. A 6-pounder howitzer from Chew's battery, under charge of Lieutenant John W. Carter, which had been retired from the fight near the river because its ammunition was exhausted, was halted at the bottom of the hill, a circumstance which proved to be our salvation.

"Perhaps two hours had elapsed since Stuart had mounted for the front when an individual scout from one of Robertson's North Carolina regiments reported to me that the enemy was advancing from Kelly's Ford, in force and unopposed, upon Brandy Station, and was now directly in our rear. Not having personal acquaintance with the man, and deeming it impossible that such a movement could be made without opposition from Robertson's brigade, I ordered the scout to return and satisfy himself by a closer inspection that he had not mistaken some of our troops for the enemy. In less than five minutes the man reported that I could now see for myself. And so it was! Within cannon shot of the hill a long column of the enemy filled the road, which here skirted the woods. They were pressing steadily forward upon the railroad station, which must in a few moments be in their possession. How could they be prevented from also occupying the Fleetwood Hill, the key to the whole position?

"Matters looked serious! But good results can sometimes be accomplished with the smallest means. Lieutenant Carter's howitzer was brought up and boldly pushed beyond the crest of the hill; a few imperfect shells and some round shot were found in the limber chest; a slow fire was at once opened upon the marching column, and courier after courier was dispatched to General Stuart to inform him of the peril. It was all-important to gain time, for should the enemy once plant his artillery on this hill it would cost many valuable lives to recover the ground, even if that could at all be accomplished. We must retain this position or suffer most seriously when enclosed between the divisions of Buford and Gregg.

"But the enemy was deceived by appearances. That the head of his column should have been greeted with the fire of artillery as soon as it emerged from the woods must have indicated to General Gregg the presence of a considerable force upon the hill; and the fact that his advance from Kelly's Ford had been entirely unopposed, together with his ignorance of what had transpired with Buford, must have strengthened the thought that his enemy, in force, here awaited an attack. In point of fact there was not one man upon the hill beside those belonging to Carter's howitzer and myself, for I had sent away even my last courier, with an urgent appeal for speedy help. Could General Gregg have known the true state of affairs he would, of course, have sent forward a squadron to take possession; but appearances demanded a more serious attack, and while this was being organized three rifled guns were unlimbered [by Gregg], and a fierce cannonade was opened on the hill.

"My first courier found General Stuart as incredulous concerning the presence of the enemy in his rear as I had been at the first report. . . . Stuart turned to him and ordered him to 'ride back there and see what all that foolishness is about.' But simultaneous with my second message—which was delivered by young Frank Deane, of Richmond, Va., one of my confidential clerks and, in the field, one of our most trusted couriers—came the sound of the cannonading, and there was no longer room for doubt. The nearest point from which a regiment could be sent was Jones' position [at Saint James Church], one and a half miles distant from Fleetwood. The 12th Virginia, Colonel A. W. Harman, and the 35th Battalion, Lieutenant Colonel E. V. White, were immediately withdrawn from his line and ordered to meet this new danger. But minutes expanded seemingly into hours to those anxious watchers on the hill, who feared lest, after all, help could not arrive in time. But it *did* come."

The help included the regiment to which John Opie belonged, the 6th Virginia, which had been badly hurt in the action at Beverly Ford but had retained its morale. The 6th had been dispatched in the wake of the first two units. Opie relates: "So great was the danger that we were marched . . . in a sweeping gallop; consequently, when we reached the enemy our horses were blown and the ranks completely disordered. Harman's regiment charged by fours, but the head of the column recoiled under the heavy fire of the Federal artillery and cavalry. They, however, reformed, and, being reinforced by the rest of the regiment, our regiment at the same time coming up, White's battalion being already on the ground, we made a simultaneous charge, breaking the Federal cavalry and charging through the guns."

During these moments Stuart was expanding his efforts to meet the emergency. Leaving Rooney Lee's brigade to continue the contest with Pleasonton and Buford, the general rushed everyone else toward Fleetwood Hill. As might be expected, the movement was fraught with disorder. Some of the regiments collided and intermingled, and the resulting din was dominated by stentorian orders colored by swearing born of frustration. Among the movement's odder sights was artillery gunner George Neese trying to maintain a suitable pace astride his faithful mule. "The dust in the road was about three inches deep, and in our hurried movement my mule fell down and rolled over me, and I over him, both of us wallowing in three inches of dust, and for once I and my mule favored and looked alike so far as color was concerned. By the time I got my mule up and I was mounted again the battery had disappeared in a thick cloud of flying dust."

The three Confederate units fighting alone at Fleetwood Hill were now in critical trouble, for Gregg had his attack organized. In the fore was Sir Percy Wyndham's brigade, composed of men from Maryland, New Jersey, and Pennsylvania. "Colonel Wyndham," relates Pennsylvania trooper William P. Lloyd, "formed his brigade in column of regiments in the open field east of the railroad station, and, heading the 1st New Jersey in person, ordered the whole line to move forward and charge the enemy. . . . On our right Kilpatrick . . . was hurrying his brigade into position. His regiments, as fast as formed, moved forward with flags and guidons flying. . . . The field now presented a scene of thrilling interest. Whole brigades of cavalry in column of regiments moving steadily . . . to the attack on our side, while the enemy's cavalry stood in glittering ranks awaiting the assault. . . . With undaunted firmness our lines moved forward; first at a steady walk, as they had nearly a half mile to advance over an open plain, then quickening their pace to a trot; and again, as the space between the battle fronts rapidly shortened, the gallop was taken; and, as the crowning act in the inspiring scene, when we had closed on the enemy until scarcely fifty paces intervened, the order to charge rang along our front."

The narrative is assumed by another Pennsylvania trooper, William F. Moyer: "In an instant a thousand glittering sabers flashed in the sunlight, and from a thousand brave and confident spirits arose a shout of defiance which, caught up by rank after rank, formed one vast, strong, full-volumed battle cry; and every trooper, rising in his stirrups, leaned forward to meet the shock, and dashed headlong upon the foe. First came the dead, heavy crash of the meeting columns, and next the clash of saber, the rattle of pistol and carbine, mingled with frenzied imprecations, wild shrieks that followed the death blow, the demand to surrender and the appeal for mercy—forming the horrid din of battle. For a few brief moments the enemy stood and bravely fought; and hand to hand, face to face, raged the contest; but, quailing at length before the resistless force of our attack and shrinking from the savage gleam and murderous stroke of our swift descending sabers, they at length broke and fled in confusion."

Stuart's aide Heros von Borcke was a part of this action. He de-

Brandy Station's climactic collision

scribes his personal flight: "A great hulking Yankee corporal, with some eight or ten men, immediately gave chase after me, calling on me to surrender and discharging their carbines and revolvers in my direction. Not heeding this summons, I urged my horse to its highest speed; and . . . clearing [a] fence at a part where it was too high for them to follow, I soon left my pursuers far behind. I had not galloped many hundred yards further, however, when I overtook Captain [Benjamin S.] White of our staff, who had received a shot-wound in his neck and was so weak as scarcely to be able to keep himself up in the saddle. Having to support my wounded comrade, whom I was determined to save, retarded my pace considerably, and several times the shouts and yells of the Yankees sounded so close at our horses' heels that I gave up all hope of escape. Suddenly, however, the Yankees gave up the pursuit."

The pursuit was abandoned all along the line, for Gregg's men had noted that new foemen were coming up in large numbers. Stuart soon had all of Jones' and Hampton's regiments ready for action. The time was about noon. During the next hour and a half the fighting was marked by charges and countercharges, both major and fragmentary, with the advantage seesawing. The confusion was riotous. As explained by a Union trooper in Percy Wyndham's 1st Maryland Regiment: "The choking dust was so thick that we could not tell 't'other from which.' Horses wild beyond the control of their riders were charging away through the lines of the enemy and back again. Many of our men were captured, and escaped because their clothes were so covered with dust that they looked like graybacks."

"At first," says Confederate observer George Neese, "it was doubtful as to who would succumb and first cry *enough;* but eventually the enemy began to falter and give way under the terrible strokes of the Virginian type of sabering. Yet the enemy fought stubbornly. . . . They rallied twice . . . and heroically renewed the struggle for the mastery of the heights, but in their last desperate effort to regain and hold their position our cavalry met the onset with such cool bravery and rigid determination that the enemy's overthrow and discomfiture was so complete that they were driven from the hill, leaving three pieces of their artillery in position near the crest . . . and their dead and wounded in our hands." As Gregg continued to fall back, Neese goes on to explain, "squadrons and regiments of horsemen were charging and fighting on various parts of the plain. . . . Away to the southeast General Hampton had his South Carolinians in splendid battle line. . . . Clouds of dust, mingled with the smoke of discharging firearms, rose from various parts of the field, and the discordant and fearful music of battle floated on the thickened air."

The running fight was soon discontinued. Confederate officer Henry McClellan sums up: "Thus ended the attack of Gregg's division upon the Fleetwood Hill. Modern warfare cannot furnish an instance of a field more closely, more valiantly contested. General Gregg retired from the field defeated, but defiant and unwilling to acknowledge a defeat. He reformed his division on the same ground on which he had formed it to make the attack."

It was at this point that Gregg was rejoined by the column under Duffié. The reinforcements did not tempt Gregg to undertake another offensive, for he had learned that Confederate infantry units from Culpeper were being hurried to the area. The general turned his forces toward Saint James Church for a junction with Pleasonton and Buford, who were still involved with Rooney Lee.

By this time, according to Pleasonton's aide Frederick Newhall, "all that was necessary to the purposes of General Hooker had been fully accomplished; the information required had been secured with unmistakable accuracy from personal observation and from the official documents captured on the field. . . . There was nothing to demand any further effort on General Pleasonton's part, and in view of the approach of the enemy's infantry he determined to recross the river without further delay. He ordered General Gregg to retire by way of Rappahannock Station [about two miles southeast of the Beverly crossing] with the whole of the Kelly's Ford column, thus bringing those troops within supporting distance of the other column on its return to Beverly Ford. General Gregg left us . . . and it is only necessary to say further in regard to this column that it was not molested on its march to Rappahannock Station, and that it crossed the river there in safety, accompanied by [Brigadier General David A.] Russell's brigade of infantry, which, as a precautionary measure to protect the lower fords, had hugged the river bank all day. . . . General Pleasonton at the same time began the withdrawal of the cavalry and infantry from Saint James Church, and . . . I was dispatched by him with orders to General Buford to give up his attack and retire to Beverly Ford. . . .

"I saw Buford's troops engaged on high ground at the extreme end of [a] valley in the edge of a wood, and I should say some two miles or more from the river. He was entirely isolated from the rest of the command with Pleasonton . . . but, paying no undue attention to that fact, was fighting straight on. As I rode rapidly up the valley, I met with a stream of wounded men flowing to the rear, and the rattle of carbines in

front was incessant. On reaching the plateau at the end of the valley . . .
I inquired for General Buford, but could not learn where he was. . . . It
was but a few yards . . . to the troops who were actually engaged, and as
I rode among them I found myself with . . . the 6th Pennsylvania Cavalry, and at that moment the adjutant, Lieutenant Rudolph Ellis, was
severely wounded. . . . I said a word to him, and was then immediately
confronted by Captain Wesley Merritt, commanding the 2nd Regulars,
who was dashing through the woods without a hat, having just lost it by
a saber cut." It wasn't until some moments later that Newhall's search
was rewarded: "I caught sight of a group of officers on a bare hill to the
left . . . and, galloping there, found General Buford with his staff. I
informed him of General Pleasonton's order, and, as he proceeded to
carry it into effect I remained with him long enough to see that he had
no difficulty in withdrawing, and that as his troops fell back they were
permitted to go in peace."

Newhall rejoined Pleasonton, and the general ordered a reserve
regiment, that of Captain Richard Lord, to take up a position on the
south side of the river to cover Buford's crossing. Newhall continues:
"Captain Lord deployed his whole regiment as mounted skirmishers on
a long line which had for its center the knoll where our artillery had
been posted in the morning. The sun had now set, but there was a
mellow light on the fields, and the figures of Lord's troopers stood boldly
out against the background of yellow sky above the horizon. Occasionally the dust would fly from the ground between the horses where a
bullet struck, and there was a scattering fire kept up by Lord's regiment,
but he did not lose a man. Meantime our guns were unlimbered on the
bluff on the north bank of the river . . . and at this commanding point a
large group of officers was gathered, including General Pleasonton and
all his staff, who watched with interest the closing scene of the long day's
action. . . .

"There could not be a prettier sight. . . . The river flowed beneath
us. As far as we could see to the right and left on the southern bank no
living object was visible. The plain and woods in front of us were growing misty, but the burnished and glowing horizon threw everything on
high ground into wonderful relief. Where the skirmishers of Lord's
undulating line rose to the crest of the knoll we could see even their
features when turned in profile. The commands were all by bugle, and
the notes came to us distinctly from the skirmish line until, no other
troops of ours remaining on that side, the rally was sounded, and then
the retreat, and the regiment trotted down to the ford and crossed it,

entirely unmolested by the enemy. . . . If there was a sense of victory remaining with Stuart's men, it was natural on their seeing our men withdraw to the fords and recross the river; but there was not the slightest sense of defeat on our side."

Southerner Henry McClellan concedes that "this battle . . . *made* the Federal cavalry. Up to that time confessedly inferior to the Southern horsemen, they gained on this day that confidence in themselves and in their commanders which enabled them to contest so fiercely . . . subsequent battlefields."

Casualties of Brandy Station in killed, wounded, and missing (with most of the missing in captivity) were: Federals, 866; Confederates, 523. Among the Confederate wounded was Rooney Lee, shot through the thigh late in the day. Robert E. came forward from Culpeper as his son was being carried from the field. The elder Lee wrote his wife: "He is young and healthy, and I trust will soon be up again. He seemed to be more concerned about his brave men and officers who had fallen in the battle than himself."

Jeb Stuart was the object of a good bit of censure in the wake of Brandy Station. "The battle," said the Richmond *Examiner,* "narrowly missed being a great disaster to our arms. Our men were completely surprised, and were only saved by their own indomitable gallantry and courage." An official in the Confederate Bureau of War wrote in his diary: "Stuart is so conceited that he got careless." A female resident of Culpeper, signing herself "a Southern Lady," sent a note to Jefferson Davis in which she accused Stuart of being more interested in conducting reviews to impress his lady friends than in doing his job. The woman went so far as to say that she feared for the Confederate cause if Stuart was kept in command.

3

Hooker Extends His Right

BRANDY STATION had little effect on Lee's campaign other than to delay Stuart's move northward. As for the intelligence acquired by Pleasonton, it did not, as he and his troopers liked to believe, banish all of Hooker's uncertainty about what was happening. The discovery of Stuart's intention to cross the Rappahannock was not proof positive that Lee was launching a major invasion. Not even the unmasking of the Confederate infantry units at Culpeper provided such proof. Hooker believed it possible that Lee's sole aim was to subject the North to a large-scale raid.

On June 10, the day after Brandy Station, the Union commander wired President Lincoln from Falmouth: "If it should be the [enemy's] intention to send a heavy column of infantry to accompany the cavalry on the proposed raid, he can leave nothing behind to interpose any serious obstacle to my rapid advance on Richmond. I am not satisfied of his intention in this respect, but from certain movements in their corps I cannot regard it as altogether improbable. If it should be found to be the case, will it not promote the true interest of the cause for me to march to Richmond at once? From there all the disposable part of this army can be thrown to any threatened point north of the Potomac at short notice. . . . If left to operate from my own judgment, with my present information, I do not hesitate to say that I should adopt this course as being the most speedy and certain mode of giving the rebellion a mortal blow."

Lincoln received the telegram at 5:10 P.M. At 6:40 he wired back: "I think Lee's army, and not Richmond, is your sure objective point. If he comes toward the Upper Potomac, follow on his flank and on his inside track, shortening your lines while he lengthens his. Fight him, too, when opportunity offers. If he stays where he is, fret him and fret him." On the following day Hooker received another wire from Washington, this one signed by General-in-Chief Henry Halleck: "The President has just referred to me your telegram and his reply of yesterday, with directions to say to you whether or not I agree with him. I do so fully." Assenting to Washington's view of the situation, Hooker improved his deployment against Lee's maneuvering by ordering one of his corps, the 3rd, up the Rappahannock to Beverly Ford.

In the words of Jesse Bowman Young, a boyish lieutenant with the 3rd Corps: "The Army of the Potomac had been warned . . . to be ready for any sort of work that might develop; but nobody thought there was any hurry in the case until one day [June 11] couriers were seen flying in all directions with orders to march in two hours with sparse baggage and plenty of ammunition. . . . The hurry and commotion, the stir and haste, the excitement and effervescence of the scattered camps of [the 3rd Corps] . . . that day may be fitly likened to the fermentation occasioned in a wasp's big nest when stirred up by a long pole. Wagons were driven hurriedly from the place where they had been parked and were loaded with desperate haste; tents were torn down in a jiffy; the stuff that had accumulated through the . . . stay in front of Fredericksburg was sifted out, some of it thrown away or burnt, and that which was valuable packed up for shipment to Washington; knapsacks were rolled up and thrown into a pile, ready to be slung on the multitudinous shoulders of the great army; staff officers and generals were to be seen galloping in all directions, arraying their troops in marching order. . . .

"Bugles were sounded, and . . . [the 3rd Corps] began its journey away from its quarters in front of Fredericksburg, the long trains of baggage and ammunition wagons—flanked, preceded, and followed by guards—taking the safest roads; the cavalry trotting in the distance ahead of the other troops . . . ; the artillery wheeling into line and lumbering along the dusty highways; the generals, with their brilliant array of staff officers, riding proudly at the head of their commands; and the long lines of blue-coated infantry, laden with well-filled haversacks, knapsacks, and cartridge boxes, and girded about with their blankets and carrying their muskets 'at will,' sallied forth, taking up the line of march and proceeding in utter uncertainty across the hot and dusty plains."

According to P. Regis de Trobriand, a French soldier of fortune serving the Union cause with the rank of colonel: "We passed through a country ruined by the war, devastated by the hand of man. . . . If we halted near any house . . . we found the dwelling abandoned and sacked. No doors, no windows, no furniture; the lawns cut to pieces by the wheels of the trains or of the artillery; the flower beds polluted by dirty refuse; remnants of the huts [i.e., the wooden frames] which had been used for tent supports. But everywhere eternal Nature, smiling in her new [late springtime] dress, sowed the ruins with flowers, always ready to repair evil in the inexhaustible fertility of her transformations."

Because they had made no long marches for some time, the troops were not in top condition, and by the second day they were tiring, a condition aggravated by the heat and a scarcity of good drinking water. Many of the men grew irritable and began criticizing their brigade and division commanders. In the words of Henry Blake, the captain from Massachusetts: "There is not more than one in ten officers of high rank that understands the proper mode of moving divisions; and the fatigue that so often results is caused not by merely traveling a large number of miles but by the omission to halt them at regular intervals. . . . Mounted upon their horses, unencumbered by rations or clothing, and usually carrying a small flask and a light sword, it was a pastime for the subordinate generals and their staffs to ride or race from town to town, and issue stringent orders to court-martial the weary men for what they termed straggling.

"The division marched from 5:20 A.M. to 9:20 P.M. upon one of the warmest days of the month, and was always . . . halted in the open fields, while [our] general and his staff enjoyed the comfort of the extensive forests in the vicinity." A rumor began circulating that the general (presumably Blake's brigade commander, Joseph B. Carr) was, as the result of a warped conception of discipline, overexposing the troops by design and was making jokes about their misery.

Blake had a further complaint about the marching practices of the Army of the Potomac's high brass. "The newspapers contained, at this time, accounts of the operations of General Grant . . . [who was besieging] Vicksburg, and described the scanty wardrobe with which he was furnished upon the campaign; and the contrast between this simplicity and the immense quantity of personal baggage which the general commanding [an Eastern] brigade carried in the wagons was . . . striking. . . . Whenever a halt was ordered at the end of a march, a score of servile pioneers pitched his capacious tent upon the most pleasant spot of ground, and placed in it a carpet, camp chairs, tables, and an iron bedstead, so that he was probably more comfortable than he would have been at home."

On the evening of the second day's march through the river country, the specific object of Blake's censure did not order his tent set up, for a Confederate mansion was handy. Some of the troops who had occasion to pass the place shouted such things as "Kick him out of the house!," "I hope the rebels will kill him!," and "Shoot the scoundrel!" Blake says that a party of men "seized the general's servant, who had walked a long distance to procure cool water, and spitefully confiscated the property."

That night Blake and his comrades encamped at Beverly Ford, where, three days earlier, Pleasonton and Buford had launched the Battle of Brandy Station. The south bank, it was noted, held Confederate pickets. Blake continues: "The presence of the enemy intimidated the general who had been so eager to place his troops in the open fields upon the march. The campfires were prohibited or kept low, and strong guards were posted to prevent [the men] from leaving the woods in which they were concealed. The river was only 100 feet in width at the ford. . . . Wounded horses were limping about on the ground in the vicinity; the carcasses of dead animals . . . were scattered in every direction; and I saw one floating in the stream that was fully equipped and still bore the rations, blankets, and overcoat of its absent rider."

It was the 3rd Corps' mission to perform picket duty in the Beverly Ford area, at the same time maintaining a readiness for further movement. The remainder of Hooker's forces were also poised for a change of position.

By this time the Northern states were busy preparing for the emergency that appeared to be developing. The governors of Maryland and Pennsylvania issued proclamations calling for the people to rally to the protection of their homes. Thousands of dwellers in urban areas such as Baltimore, Harrisburg, and Pittsburgh took up picks and shovels and began studding their environs with breastworks. Gangs of black laborers, with the hopes of their race hinging on the outcome of the war, could be heard singing the words to a popular abolition song: "John Brown's body lies a-moldering in the grave; his soul is marching on. . . ." The breastworks were intended for the use of the state militiamen, who became the object of urgent appeals to muster. Pennsylvania was divided into two defense departments, that of the Monongahela in the west and the Susquehanna in the east. Washington assigned Major General Darius N. Couch to head the Department of the Susquehanna, which included the Gettysburg area.

The residents of Maryland and Pennsylvania had been worrying about Lee's ability to invade their territory at will ever since Antietam.

38

Citizens of Pennsylvania digging entrenchments

There had been several false alarms, and these had occasioned many people to make temporary flights northward, chiefly with the thought of saving their horses, which they knew were coveted by the enemy. Now, with Lee's second invasion imminent, Pennsylvania residents experienced another false alarm. Among those it affected was William Hamilton ("Billy") Bayly, who, in June 1863 was a thirteen-year-old living on a farm three miles northwest of Gettysburg. Billy relates: "The rumors of the near approach of the enemy became so alarming and convincing that my father, with some of our neighbors, joined a procession of hundreds of skedaddlers en route for Harrisburg. After having worked on the farm all day, I rode one horse and led another through that night, reaching the State Capital, thirty-five miles distant, next morning. Once across the Susquehanna, we felt comparatively safe, and, having taken up our quarters with a Dauphin County farmer, our party of six men and two boys turned in and helped our farmer friend harvest his wheat crop. No enemy appearing, we returned home several days later and found our wheat cut and stacked by a party of skedaddlers from Maryland who had spent some days on our farm in our absence."

During this alarm, as during previous ones, many of Gettysburg's citizens remained in their homes or at least in the immediate area. Despite her moments of concern, a fifteen-year-old girl named Tillie Pierce found the period productive of episodes to smile at. "An amusing incident . . . was the manner in which some of our older men prepared to meet the foe. . . . One evening . . . a number of them . . . assembled to guard the town . . . against an attack from the enemy. They were 'armed to the teeth' with old, rusty guns and swords, pitchforks, shovels, and pick-axes. Their falling into line, the maneuvers, the commands given and not heeded, would have done a veteran's heart good. . . .

"On these occasions it was also amusing to behold the conduct of the colored people of the town [all of whom were free]. Gettysburg had a goodly number of them. They regarded the Rebels as having an especial hatred toward them, and believed that if they fell into their hands, annihilation was sure. These folks mostly lived in the southwestern part of the town, and their flight was invariably down Breckenridge Street and Baltimore Street and toward the woods on and around Culp's Hill."

The throng consisted of "men and women with bundles as large as old-fashioned feather ticks slung across their backs, almost bearing them to the ground; children also, carrying their bundles and striving in vain to keep up with their seniors. The greatest consternation was depicted on all their countenances as they hurried along, crowding and running against each other in their confusion, children stumbling, falling, and crying. Mothers, anxious for their offspring, would stop for a moment to hurry them up, saying, 'Fo' de Lod's sake, you chillen, cum right long quick! If dem Rebs dun kotch you, dey tear you all up!' and similar expressions. These terrible warnings were sure to have the desired effect; for, with their eyes open wider than ever, they were not long in hastening their steps."

4

The Battle of Winchester

BEFORE HE COULD CROSS the Potomac into Maryland, Lee had a loose end to tie up. There was a Union outpost at Winchester, in the Shenandoah Valley about twenty-five miles southwest of the river. This garrison, numbering some 9,000 men, covered not only Harpers Ferry but also the upstream crossings at Shepherdstown and Williamsport, which were best suited to Confederate use. Aside from their inimicalness to Lee's plans, the Yankees at Winchester were a particularly irritating thorn in Virginia's side, for they were commanded by an old-time United States Army regular, Major General Robert H. Milroy, who regarded all Confederates, military and civilian alike, as odious rebels, and conducted his occupation accordingly.

It was six months since Milroy had taken command at Winchester, and the Confederate citizens were still talking about the way he had settled in. As explained by one of Winchester's aristocrats, Mrs. Mary Tucker Magill: "He furnished his headquarters on Main Street by pressing furniture from the different residences in the town, giving a certificate that it should be paid for at the close of the war if the owners should be found to have sustained the character of 'loyal citizens' during the struggle. Of course, this was the most useless form, as they did not take the property of 'loyal citizens,' so-called [i.e., citizens whose views had remained Unionist].

"Presently Mrs. Milroy and her children were brought in to share the grandeur of the general. She was a woman not above but below the stamp of a servant. We amused ourselves very much with her general appearance and manners. When she arrived she was much disappointed

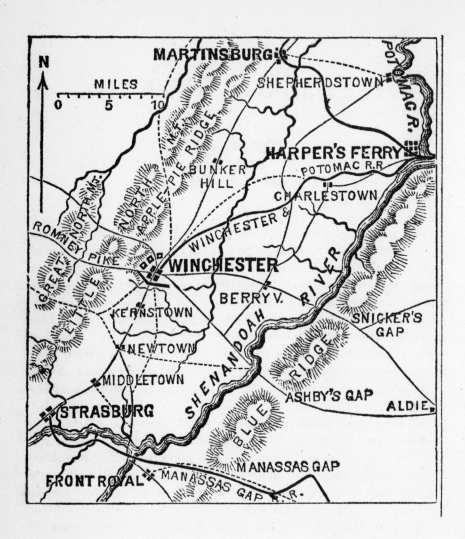

Winchester and vicinity

that her appearance created no . . . enthusiasm [among the soldiers of her husband's command]. Putting her head out of the carriage, she said, 'I'm the wife of Gener'l Milroy. Why don't you hurrar?' But they still refused to 'hurrar.'

"Mrs. Milroy was much dissatisfied with the quarters provided for her. With all the fine houses the 'Rebels' had, she did not see why she should be stuck down on Main Street in the dust. The result was the seizure of Mrs. Lloyd Logan's beautiful house, which was appropriated to the use of General Milroy and his staff as headquarters. . . . Mrs. Logan was an invalid, and had been for years. Her husband was away, and she had her three young daughters and two sons with her. General Milroy refused to allow her to take anything out of the house. . . . He placed a guard over the ladies while they packed up their personal clothing, and then exiled them. As the ladies went down the front steps . . . Mrs. Milroy and her brood stepped out of a fine carriage and took possession of the house. Of course the community was terribly excited at the outrage, for which there was not even the pretense of an excuse."

Lee had begun working on the problem of Milroy and his command some days before the Battle of Brandy Station. The Confederate general had selected Ewell's corps to march from Culpeper through the Blue Ridge Mountains and attack Winchester, but the attack could not be made until Milroy's position was scouted. A major of cavalry, venturesome Harry Gilmor, was given a few picked men and sent ahead through the Blue Ridge, his orders specifying that he undertake the needed reconnaissance after reporting to Brigadier General Albert G. Jenkins, a trooper who commanded one of the Valley outposts maintained in opposition to Milroy. As Gilmor tells it: "On my way down the Valley [i.e., northward; the Shenandoah River flows in a northerly direction], I met at Woodstock my old acquaintance, Miss Belle Boyd [the celebrated Southern spy], whom I had known since the autumn of '61. Miss Belle begged to accompany me on my expedition. I got off by telling her she must first have General Jenkins' permission."

Jenkins was at Strasburg, ten miles farther down the Valley. With night approaching, Gilmor and Boyd took rooms at a Woodstock hotel. Gilmor continues: "I rose before the sun, and was ready to start, when I discovered she had carried my saber and pistols to her room to prevent my slipping off without her, as she was shrewd enough to know I would do. Down came Miss Belle, dressed in her neat-fitting habit, with a pretty little belt round her waist, from which the butts of two small pistols were peeping, cased in patent leather holsters. She rode with me to the quar-

Robert H. Milroy

ters of General Jenkins, to whom I had to report before passing out through his lines. We found him sitting before his tent, and after dispatching my business Miss Belle presented her request. I fixed myself rather behind her, that I might give a signal to the general not to consent. The fact is, I did not care to be accompanied by a woman on so perilous an enterprise; for, though she was a splendid and reckless rider, of unflinching courage, and her whole soul bound up in the Southern cause, yet she was a little—mark you, only a *little*—headstrong and willful, and I thought it best, both for her sake and mine, that she should not go. . . . The general, of course, refused, which made her furious; but he was firm, and I rode off without her.

"I was gone three days, and returned without even having drawn my revolvers, though I had several chances; but I was on special business, and so let the various opportunities pass. The enemy's picket line being only a mile out of Winchester, I made easily the entire circuit of that town, as well as Martinsburg [a secondary outpost some twenty miles northeast of Winchester], in which I learned the exact position of every stationary force, large and small, in the Lower Valley, with an accurate account of their numbers. A courier was sent immediately to General Ewell with the information I had gained. He was then marching through Chester's Gap, near Front Royal. But this was kept so secret that even I would not have known it had I not been selected to do his scouting, and, of course, I did not breathe it to any of the men with me."

The secret was so well kept that not an inkling of it reached Union General Milroy. He states: "When I first occupied Winchester, the Valley of the Shenandoah from Staunton to Strasburg was occupied . . . with a [Confederate] force variously estimated at from 5,000 to 6,000 men and constituted principally of cavalry. [Brigadier General John D.] Imboden at the same time occupied the Cacapon Valley [in West Virginia] with a force composed of infantry, cavalry, and artillery estimated at 1,500 men. These were the only forces by which I was in danger of being assailed, unless by a force from Lee's army, which, it was supposed, would be prevented from hostile demonstrations in my direction by the Army of the Potomac. . . . By means of . . . cavalry expeditions and information furnished me by Union citizens I kept myself continually posted as to the rebel forces in the Valley. . . .

"On Friday, June 12, for the purpose of ascertaining whether there had been any accumulation of rebel forces in my front I sent out two strong reconnoitering parties, one on the Strasburg and the other on the Front Royal road. The one on the Strasburg road . . . was conducted with energy . . . and we took thirty-seven prisoners. . . . All belonged to the Maryland Battalion and 14th Virginia Cavalry, troops which had been in the Valley and on picket duty during the whole period of my occupancy of Winchester. Besides, separate examinations of the prisoners disclosed that there was no accumulation of forces there. . . . It was now known that no portion of Lee's army approached Winchester from that direction."

Milroy had ill luck with the Front Royal expedition, which was the critical one. "Its commanding officer reported that at Cedarville, a place about twelve miles from Winchester, he had encountered a large force of the enemy, composed of cavalry, infantry, and artillery. It did not appear, however, that he had placed himself in a position to ascertain the number or character of the force which he had encountered, or exercised the usual and necessary efforts to obtain that essential information. Officers of his command and reliable scouts who were present gave contradictory reports. This report was discredited by myself and by General [Washington L.] Elliott, my second in command. There was nothing in the report which indicated the presence of General Lee's army. It was supposed that the force on the Front Royal road could not be other than the enemy which we had faced during the occupancy of Winchester, or that the anticipated cavalry raid of General Stuart was in progress, against either or both of which combined I could have held my position. I deemed it impossible that Lee's army, with its immense artillery and baggage trains, could have escaped from the Army of the Potomac and crossed the Blue Ridge. . . . The movement [from Fredericksburg] must have occupied five or six days [the actual time was nine days, since Ewell's march was interrupted at Culpeper], and notice of its being in progress could have been conveyed to me from General Hooker's headquarters in five minutes, for telegraphic communication still existed."

Because of their uncertainty over the situation between Hooker and Lee, both General Halleck in Washington and Milroy's immediate superior, Major General Robert C. Schenck, headquartered in Baltimore, had been urging Milroy to abandon Winchester and fall back down the Valley to Harpers Ferry. Milroy had put them off with such statements as "I have the place well fortified and am well prepared to hold it . . . and I can and would hold it, if permitted to do so, against any force the rebels can afford to bring against me, and I exceedingly regret the prospect of having to give it up; and it will be cruel to abandon the loyal people that are in this county to the rebel fiends again." On the day that

Milroy made his reconnaissances toward Strasburg and Front Royal, Schenck notified him: "You will make all the required preparations for withdrawing, but hold your position in the meantime. Be ready for movement, but await further orders." Within a matter of hours, Schenck decided that Milroy had better retreat at once, but by the time the message was in the hands of Schenck's telegraph operator, the Confederates had cut Milroy's wires. With Ewell's troops gathering in heavy numbers before him, and with scant knowledge of what was happening, Milroy was left on his own.

Ewell spent Saturday, June 13, driving in Milroy's advanced troops, both cavalry and infantry, the latter most numerous at Berryville. By late afternoon the Winchester garrison was making its defense along a creek and a millrace just south of the town. Milroy says that "the enemy advanced his skirmishers, and brisk skirmishing ensued until dark. About 5 o'clock the enemy advanced and took possession of a picket post . . . from which they were dislodged. . . . In this affair . . . we captured a prisoner . . . whom I learned . . . belonged to . . . Ewell's corps. . . . This was the first intimation that I received that Lee's army had quietly retired before the lines of the Army of the Potomac. . . . The Blue Ridge screened the operations of Lee's army from me. I had always relied with implicit confidence upon receiving timely notice by telegraph of its advance in my direction.

"On Saturday, under cover of the night, I withdrew my forces on the Strasburg and Front Royal roads in front of Winchester to the southern suburbs of the town, under orders to retire to the forts [i.e., the sets of earthworks] north of the town at 2 o'clock in the morning. . . . At this time . . . I still hoped that there had been some corresponding action of the Army of the Potomac, and that if I could sustain myself for twenty-four hours I would be relieved."

By dawn Milroy had abandoned Winchester except for a skirmish line in its northern suburbs. The forts were manned as he had ordered. Ewell decided to work his forces around to the east and west of the town and into position to bring the forts under attack. Only one battalion was sent probing into Winchester. Major Harry Gilmor, who had done Ewell's original scouting, rode with this battalion and was one of the first men to enter the town. "While talking to some ladies, who were perfectly wild with joy and excitement, a mounted man [one of the enemy] came within a short distance of where I stood. I drew my revolver and rode toward him; but he fired upon me and ran, firing back all the time. My horse was very fleet, and I gave chase, but every cap of my pistol snapped. I ran him past nearly four squares, when I suddenly came to a cross street in which a regiment of infantry were in line of battle. I wheeled as quickly as possible, but, before getting behind the corner, a ball struck my horse in the muscle above the hock, and for a few jumps he went on three legs; then all was right, and he soon carried me out of danger. I found that the ball had passed through without doing much injury." Gilmor's comrades of the probing battalion became involved in some heavy skirmishing, and Ewell soon ordered the troops withdrawn from the town. The general had begun to fear that their presence would bring Federal fire upon the civilian populace.

Responsibility for the main attack on Milroy's forts had been assigned to the column working its way around the town on the west. These troops were led by Major General Jubal Anderson Early, a Virginian who was misshapenly arthritic, religious but profane, snappish with his orders, and impatient of failure, a commander who inspired little enthusiasm but had won a full share of trust. "Old Jube" himself tells of his march around Winchester: "I was conducted . . . by a very intelligent and patriotic citizen, Mr. James C. Baker, who had a son in the service and who had been made to feel the tyranny of Milroy. Mr. Baker thoroughly understood the object in view and fully appreciated the advantage of the position I was seeking to reach, and it was mainly owing to the intelligent and skilful manner in which he guided me that I was able to get there without attracting the slightest attention from the enemy. . . .

"On the route, we had not seen a solitary man from the enemy's force. . . . We had met two very ordinary looking men in the roads, and from prudential motives they were carried with us. . . . After that the only person we saw was a young girl of about thirteen years of age whom we met on horseback with her young brother behind her. She was carrying before her a large bundle of clothes tied up in a sheet, and when she unexpectedly came upon us she was at first very much frightened, but soon discovering that we were Confederates, she pulled off her bonnet, waved it over her head and 'hurrahed,' and then burst into tears. She told us that the enemy had been shelling the woods all around, firing occasionally into her father's house, and that she had been sent from home by her father and mother to get out of the way. She said that they had not been able to imagine what the shelling meant, as they did not know that any of 'our soldiers,' as she called us, were anywhere in the neighborhood. It was not necessary to use any precaution as to her, and she was permitted to pass on, feeling much happier for the encounter. . . .

"The position which I reached proved to be a long ridge . . . immediately confronting the fortified hill which I wished to carry. . . . I reached this position about four o'clock P.M."

According to one of Early's artillerymen, young Robert Stiles, a law student who had interrupted his schooling to enlist in the Richmond Howitzers: "The infantry now lay down to rest and recover breath, while the men of Hilary Jones' battalion of artillery shoved their guns forward by hand up to and just back of a rock fence. . . . They next removed a few of the stones in front of the muzzle of each gun, taking great care to remain concealed while doing this; and when everything was ready and everyone warned to do his part on the instant, the guns were discharged simultaneously upon the outwork and a rapid fire kept up upon it."

To help cover Early's attack, the troops Ewell had sent around Winchester on the east had been demonstrating against the forts and keeping their attention. Now the men in the forts, surprised by the new development, began pouring artillery and small arms fire in both directions, and the uproar became general. Ewell had established his headquarters on a hill among the eastern forces, and at this time cavalry trooper Harry Gilmor, who had been off on a scout, came riding in to make his report. "What a magnificent spectacle met my view! . . . From the general's quarters we could see everything going on except round about Early's force, now going up on the southwestern slope of the heights on which the enemy's works were built. . . . The firing was terrific, and yet all of us crowded on the heights to see Early's charge. We could hear his skirmishers keeping up a continual rapid fire, and occasionally a volley and a yell as he charged some advanced position; and we could tell . . . that he was getting the advantage. Every piece seemed to be turned on him; but, amid the thunders of thirty or forty guns, there broke on our expectant ears heavy volleys of musketry, and the terrible, long, shrill yell of the two brigades of Louisiana Tigers who were charging up those heights crested with rifle pits and redoubts.

"The enemy stood firm for a while, and old Ewell was jumping about upon his crutches, with the utmost difficulty keeping the perpendicular. At last the Federals began to give way, and pretty soon the Louisianians, with their battle flag, appeared on the crests charging the redoubts. The general, through his glass, thought he recognized old Jubal Early among the foremost mounted, and he became so much excited that, with moistened eyes, he said, 'Hurrah for the Louisiana boys! There's Early. I hope the old fellow won't be hurt.' Just then a spent ball struck General Ewell on the chest, almost knocking him down, and leaving a black mark. His medical director, Hunter McGuire, took away his crutches, telling him he 'had better let those sticks alone for the present.' He was soon on his feet again, or, rather, on the only one he had left. Early had taken two of the forts. . . . Ewell [at once] named the elevation on which they stood 'The Louisiana Heights' in honor of the two gallant brigades that had left so many of their dead and wounded on its side and crest."

The Federals still held their main forts, and, with the day fast waning, there was little the Confederates could do to press the advantage they had gained. In its final moments, the fighting was mostly a matter of artillery exchanges. Southerner Robert Stiles was an active participant. "Upon one of our shiftings of position . . . I was on foot, abreast of one of the guns of the Charlottesville Battery and following close after John Hunter, sergeant of that piece, who was riding his little chestnut mare, Madge, when a 30-pounder Parrott shell passed through her body, just back of the legs of the rider, exploding as it emerged and spattering me profusely with the blood of the poor animal. Little Madge . . . never knew what hit her, but sank gently down, while Hunter did not get even so much as a decent shaking up. . . . When his feet touched the ground— they were not far from it even while Madge stood up on all fours—he simply disengaged them from the stirrups, turned around, glanced a moment at the bloody horror, and said, 'Well, poor little Madge!' . . .

"During our next change of position, or it may have been during the same move, I witnessed a scene of horror and of agony so extreme that I would not describe it were it not that a knowledge of the widest swings of the pendulum of war through the entire orbit of human experiences and emotions is needed for adequate appreciation of the life of the soldier. The entire battalion, Hilary Jones', was moving in column, the Charlottesville Battery, in which I was serving, following immediately after [A. W.] Garber's. The farm road we were using led between two heavy old-fashioned gateposts. . . . One of Garber's men, belonging to his rear gun [and at this time on foot], attempted to run abreast of the piece between the gateposts. . . . There was not room enough for him to pass, and, the wheel crowding him against the post, the washer hook caught and tore open his abdomen, dragging the poor wretch along by his intestines, which were literally pulled from his body in a long, gory ribbon.

"At one of the last positions we took in the fight—it may have been the very last—there passed before me one of those scenes which give a flash-light revelation of the incomparable greatness of war and the sublime self-abnegation of the true soldier. The fire of the Federal guns was very deadly and demoralizing, and the captain of the battery next on our right, I think the Louisiana Guard Artillery, came up the hill between his battery and ours to steady his men. He was a fine horseman, finely mounted, and might well have served as a model for an equestrian statue as he rode out between the smoking muzzles, and, rising in his stirrups, cheered on his gunners. At that moment a shell tore away his bridle arm high up near the shoulder. Instantly he caught the reins with his right hand and swung his horse's head sharply to the left, thus concealing his wounded side from his men, saying as he did so, 'Keep it up, boys; I'll be back in a moment!' As he started down the hill I saw him reel in the saddle, and even before he reached the limbers [i.e., the detached foreparts of the gun carriages] the noble fellow fell from his horse—dead."

The field of action grew quiet as the day ended. It was a day that saw action also at Martinsburg, the secondary Union station northeast of Winchester. Here a brigade of Federals under Colonel Benjamin F. Smith was confronted by a strong detachment from Ewell's command, its cavalry component led by Albert Jenkins. At 1 P.M. Jenkins sent Smith the following message: "I herewith demand the surrender of Martinsburg. Should you refuse, you are respectfully requested to notify the inhabitants of the place to remove forthwith to a place of safety. Small arms only will be used for one hour upon the town after your reception of this note. After that I shall feel at liberty to shell the town, if I see proper. Should you refuse to give the necessary notification to the inhabitants, I shall be compelled to hold your command responsible."

Colonel Smith responded: "Martinsburg will not be surrendered. You may commence shelling as soon as you choose. I will, however, inform the women and children of your threat." Smith tells us that he did indeed spread the promised word, and that many inhabitants fled the town. "Jenkins did not open his musketry and artillery, as he threatened, but was held in check until near sunset, when . . . I was prepared to fall back." The garrison headed for Harpers Ferry, seriously pressed only at the outset, during which time several guns were lost and numerous men were taken prisoner.

As for the situation at Winchester that Sunday evening, Confederate General Jubal Early made this assessment: "It was very apparent that the enemy's position was now untenable, and that he must either submit to a surrender of his whole force or attempt to escape during the night."

Milroy explains the course he took: "About 9 o'clock in the evening I convened a council of war. . . . It was certain that Lee had eluded the Army of the Potomac. . . . Our position at Winchester, although affording facilities for defense which would enable an inferior to maintain itself against a superior number for a limited time, could not be successfully defended by the limited means at my command against such an army as surrounded me. Six principal roads . . . lead into the town. . . . Cavalry and artillery can approach the town and the forts from every direction. We had but one day's rations left, and our artillery ammunition was almost entirely exhausted. . . . Precedents which have occurred during this rebellion and in other countries would have justified a capitulation; but I thought, and my comrades in council thought, that we owed our lives to the Government rather than make such a degrading concession to rebels in arms against its authority.

"The propositions concluded upon in that council were that . . . it was impossible to hold the post against the overwhelming forces of the enemy, and that a further prolongation of the defense could only result in sacrificing the lives of our soldiers without any practical benefit to the country; that we owed it to the honor of the Federal arms to make an effort to force our way through the lines of the beleaguering foe; that the artillery and wagons should be abandoned, and the division, brigade, and regimental headquarters instructed to bring away all public horses, and that the brigades, in the order of their numbers, should march from the forts at 1 o'clock in the morning, carrying with them their arms and the usual supply of ammunition. . . .

"The forts were evacuated at the time designated, and immediately thereafter the cannon spiked and the ammunition which could not be carried by the soldiers thrown into the cisterns of the forts. The column proceeded through a ravine . . . [north] of Winchester about one mile until it struck the Martinsburg road. It then proceeded . . . to where a road leads . . . to Summit Station, about four and a half miles from Winchester, when I received a message from General Elliot [who was in the lead] that he was attacked by the enemy's skirmishers. I had heard the firing and was riding forward. The enemy was on elevated ground in a woods . . . and a field. . . . This occurred between 3 and 4 o'clock in the morning. . . . It soon became evident that the enemy was present in considerable force. . . . A retreat could not be effected excepting under cover of a heavy contest with him."

The confrontation in the darkness began with an episode of pure confusion, as Milroy's quartermaster, Captain M. L. de Motte, attests: "I had under my command about 800 horses. They were ridden by convalescents, detailed men, sutlers' clerks, and other unarmed *attachés*. . . . My party were in column of fours, and I attempted to withdraw them to the left side of the road, in the timber. This movement was about half completed when I presume the enemy saw it and thought we were cavalry, and turned their artillery upon us fiercely. The horses now became frantic, and their riders, having the ordinary wagon bridles, and generally being without saddles, could not control them. They consequently took toward the left, toward Berkeley Springs instead of toward Harpers Ferry, as they were ordered. I tried to rally them in a wheat field about one-quarter of a mile from the road, but it was impossible."

The Union infantry met the situation gamely but ineffectively. As narrated by Colonel John W. Schall, commander of the 87th Pennsylvania Volunteer Infantry: "I received orders . . . to form my regiment in line. General Milroy was close by. I immediately brought my men into line, and immediately afterward had orders, I think from General Milroy direct, to change from front to right. During this movement I noticed several regiments of the 1st Brigade to my left. I was ordered to advance in the direction I held after changing front, and I noticed a regiment on my left advancing at the same time. It was still quite dark, and I could just see them. . . . I had orders to advance in the direction of the woods, and had gone but a few steps when skirmishing commenced. I advanced within a short distance of the woods, and during this time the enemy opened upon us with artillery that was stationed only a short distance in our front. . . .

"While engaged with the enemy, another regiment of our brigade was brought in my rear, who also opened fire, right through us almost, which brought confusion in the ranks of my regiment, and it fell back. It was either the 18th Connecticut or the 5th Maryland Infantry; I think the former. General Milroy appeared in front of that regiment and ordered them to cease firing, telling them that they were firing on their own men. It was still dark when this occurred. We again formed, and advanced with other regiments to the woods, but soon fell back, under the heavy fire, to a ravine about 150 yards from the woods.

"I afterward received orders to advance into the woods with two regiments on my right. I think they were the 18th Connecticut and 123d Ohio. My regiment went about forty yards into the woods. My horse was killed. The regiment immediately halted and kept up a skirmishing fire for twenty or thirty minutes. I saw that I was being flanked on my left, and gave orders to fall back. This was done amid some confusion. The enemy followed us closely in large numbers to the edge of the woods. My command became scattered, some going to the right and some to the left."

Beginning to lose entire companies of his men as prisoners, Milroy tried to continue the fight. Then he learned of a threat from another quarter. "A signal gun fired at Winchester announced the approach of the enemy in my rear. . . . I . . . gave instructions that my unengaged forces and trains should retreat under cover of the contest, taking the Martinsburg Road for a short distance and then turning to the right. . . . These forces immediately marched, but, instead of taking the route indicated, took a road which leads to the left, through Bath in Morgan County. They were followed by considerable bodies of the 18th Connecticut and 87th Pennsylvania, and some stragglers from the 123d, 110th, and 122nd Ohio Volunteer infantry. . . . About the time that I had given the directions above indicated, my horse was shot under me. Some time intervened before I could be remounted. When remounted [with the fighting in its final moments], I went in the direction of the 110th and the 122nd Ohio, and met them falling back by the Martinsburg Road. The retreat was now in full progress—the two columns by different routes—and it was impossible to unite them. I proceeded with the 110th and 122nd Ohio Regiments and fragments of other regiments which followed after them. This portion of the command, by way of Smithfield, arrived at Harpers Ferry late in the afternoon of Monday [June 15]. I was not pursued. The column that proceeded in the direction of Bath crossed the Potomac at Hancock, and subsequently massed at Bloody Run."

In the three-day action, pressed at low cost by Ewell, Milroy lost nearly half his command, about 4,000 men, most of whom were captured. It was a disappointment to Ewell's troops that the Union general himself got away. According to Private John O. Casler: "Our corps was rather anxious to capture Milroy, as he had tyrannized over the citizens of Winchester, insulting ladies—so it was reported—and rendering himself obnoxious in different ways, more so than any Federal general had done during the war; and if he had been captured by some of our men he would have fared badly."

For not retreating from Winchester until disaster loomed, Milroy came under a good deal of censure in Northern quarters, and his conduct was later analyzed by a military court of inquiry. The verdict, endorsed by President Lincoln, was that the general deserved no particular blame, that he had probably acted as judiciously as the circumstances permitted. Milroy himself maintained, with considerable justification, that his resistance at Winchester had delayed Lee's invasion by three days, giving the North that much extra time to prepare for it.

5

Exodus from Falmouth

DURING THE SAME WEEKEND the Battle of Winchester was fought, General Hooker decided to move the entire Army of the Potomac from its position at Falmouth. Hooker was still uncertain of Lee's intentions, finding it hard to believe that the Confederate general planned to take his whole army any great distance from Richmond. It was clear, however, that large numbers of the enemy were now in the Shenandoah Valley, and Hooker was obliged to place his own forces in a better position to cover Washington. He issued orders for a move toward Virginia's Manassas-Fairfax area, west of Washington and south of Edward's Ferry on the Potomac, with the ferry available as a crossing if it became necessary for the army to continue into Maryland and Pennsylvania. The orders called for the troops in the vicinity of Beverly Ford, now substantially reinforced, to march northeastward by way of the Orange and Alexandria Railroad while those still at Falmouth headed directly northward.

Saturday, June 13, saw the Falmouth area seized by the same kind of busyness as that of June 11. "At length the trains were off and the whole army in motion," says Surgeon George T. Stevens of the 77th Regiment, New York Volunteers. "Our own corps . . . started at ten o'clock at night. The darkness was intense, and a thunder shower prevailed. Our route for a long time lay through a thick woods where the branches of the trees, meeting over our heads, shut out the little light that might have penetrated the thunder clouds, and the column was shut in perfect darkness. The road was terribly muddy, and the batteries [of artillery] which were trying to pass over the same route were frequently stuck in the mire. Our men stumbled over stones and fallen trees, often falling beneath the feet of the horses. Men fell over logs and stones, breaking their legs and arms. Thus we continued the hasty and difficult march, while the rain poured in torrents upon us.

"Later in the night the road became more open and the rain ceased. The darkness was not so black; still it was difficult to see the road. We were passing over corduroy. Some of the logs were a foot, and others a foot-and-a-half through. They were slippery from the rain, and the men, heavily laden with knapsacks, guns, and cartridges, tumbled headlong, many of them going off at the side and rolling far down the steep embankments. A laugh from the comrades of the luckless ones, while someone would call out, 'Have you a pass to go down there?' was the only notice taken of such accidents; and the dark column hurried on, until at three o'clock in the morning we halted at Potomac Creek, where we slept soundly upon the ground until morning.

"The following day was Sunday. Our corps did not march until evening. We lay resting from the fatigues of the night before and watching the immense army trains hurrying by, the horses and mules lashed to their full speed, or viewing the destruction of the great [army] hospitals which had been established here. There were here immense quantities of stores; bedding, glass and earthenware, instruments and medicines, with cooking and other utensils which could not, in the haste of breaking up, be transported; so they were thrown in great heaps and burned.

"All day long the trains crowded by, four and five wagons abreast, the drivers shouting and lashing their beasts to their greatest speed. No one who has not seen the train of an army in motion can form any just conception of its magnitude and of the difficulties attending its movements. . . . How little did the impatient people who clamored at all times, in winter as well as summer, for an immediate advance of the army, consider that this immense body must always advance with the army. . . . It is no small undertaking to move an army with such a train; yet there were many at home who thought the army could move from one place to another with the greatest ease. . . .

"Thus, through the day, we watched the hurrying trains as they swept by with immense clatter and tumult, and the files of troops, guards to the trains, pressing forward amid the clouds of dust and the rattle and noise of the wagons. As the sun sank in the west, we gathered about a green knoll in the shade of a pine grove, and sang old familiar hymns; then the chaplain made a prayer; thus was offered the evening sacrifice

Breaking up the camp at Falmouth

for the Sabbath. Few . . . [ever] offered more heartfelt thanksgiving or more earnest supplications for future protection than the band of veterans seated on that mossy bank, while about them was the confusion of a great army, pressing to meet its foe.

"At length, at nine o'clock at night we took the road, and, joining the mighty column, marched rapidly forward. The night was dark and the roads uneven, yet the men pressed forward with wonderful spirit. They had heard during the day that Lee with his army . . . moving with secrecy, had already eluded us and was rapidly making his way into Maryland, taking his route through the Shenandoah Valley. . . . The rebels were invading Northern soil . . . and the men knew no limit to their enthusiasm. 'We can whip them on our own soil,' said they. 'There is no man who cannot fight the better when it is for his own home.' Such expressions passed from lip to lip as the dark column pushed on during the whole night. . . .

"Morning dawned. The march was becoming tedious. The men were faint and wanted rest and coffee, but there was no halt. . . . At length, as the morning advanced, the heat of the sun was almost intolerable, and the dust suffocating. Not a leaf stirred on the trees. Vegetation drooped under the scorching rays, and the clouds of dust were so dense that one could not see half the length of a regiment. The men at length began to fall from exhaustion. One after another, with faces burning with a glow of crimson, and panting for breath, would turn to the surgeons of their regiments and receive passes to the ambulances and a draught from the surgeon's flask; but at length . . . the ambulances were crowded, and so many were falling on every side that it became useless to require or attempt to give passes, or even for the surgeons to attempt to relieve the sufferers.

"In every corner of the rail fences and under every tree and bush, groups of men with faces glowing with redness, some with streams of perspiration rolling down their cheeks and others with their red faces dry and feverish, strewed the wayside and lined the hedges. Here the color-bearer of a regiment, his color lying beside him, lay gasping for breath; there a colonel, his horse tied to the fence, strove to fan the air into a little life with his broad-brimmed hat. Under one little clump of cedars might be seen an exhausted group of line officers, captains and lieutenants, and under the next a number of enlisted men. . . . The spectacle along the roadside became appalling. Regiments became like companies, and companies lost their identity. Men were dying with sunstroke, and still the march was continued.

"This could not last much longer, for the brave men who still held out were fast losing strength, and soon there would be no troops able to move. At length, at nearly three o'clock, we came in sight of the little old depopulated town of Dumfries. Here, to the joy of all, we saw men filing into the fields for a halt. There was no cheer, no expression of gladness, for the tired men, with feet blistered and raw, worn out by seventeen hours' constant march, almost melted and smothered, cared little for demonstrations. Throwing themselves upon the ground, they rested for half an hour, and then, rousing long enough to cook their coffee, they refreshed themselves with their hardtack, pork, and coffee, and were ready to sleep. . . . All who were participants of that day's work remember it as the most trying march of the Army of the Potomac."

The column's rear guard, made up of units of the 2nd Corps, experienced an unusual disturbance that night. As explained by the corps' assistant adjutant general, Francis A. Walker: "About midnight the bivouac of the 2nd Division was rudely disturbed by hideous outcries, followed by the noise of men rushing hither and thither among frightened mules and horses. Headquarters turned out in dire alarm, and the soldiers, waked suddenly from the deep slumber that follows a painful march, seized their arms. The coolest believed that a band of guerillas hanging upon the flanks of the column had taken advantage of the darkness to dash among the sleeping troops. At last it turned out that all the fright sprang from a soldier being seized with a nightmare from which he waked screaming."

Returning to Stevens' narrative: "Very grateful to the weary army was sleep that night; but at two o'clock in the morning the shout passed along the line, 'Fall in! Fall in!' And so, without coffee, we rolled our blankets and fell into line. But, as often happens when the whole army is to move, some parts must wait long before the others are out of the way. So we of the 6th Corps waited until four o'clock, and got our coffee, finally, before the rest of the column had made way for us.

"It was another hot, dusty day, but not so intolerable as the day before; and about two or three o'clock we arrived at Occoquan Creek, crossing at Wolf Run Shoals. Here we had two or three hours' rest. The men had no sooner halted than they plunged into the stream, and the wide creek was soon alive with swarms of men splashing and diving in the cooling element. It was a novel sight, an army bathing. . . .

"Although we had already made a long march, at four o'clock we were again on the road, and after dark we reached Fairfax Station, six miles from Wolf Run Shoals. This was a more cheerful march than the others. The men, refreshed by their bath and strengthened by a good dinner and two hours' rest, now went shouting, singing, and laughing, as though marching was but play."

It was now Tuesday, June 16, and the western column had also reached the Manassas-Fairfax area, its struggle with Monday's heat quite as debilitating as that of the eastern column. General Hooker, headquartered at Fairfax, became involved in a somewhat frictional telegraphic correspondence with Lincoln and Halleck. Hooker fretted at not being allowed more freedom in dealing with Lee's movements, while Lincoln and Halleck considered their dominance over Hooker necessary because they mistrusted his leadership after his failure at Chancellorsville. The strategic discussions at this time were much concerned with Harpers Ferry, which was believed to be in danger of attack after Milroy's rout from Winchester. The worry was a needless one, for Lee planned to bypass this Potomac post. Hooker was still trying to make up his mind whether or not Lee was bent upon a full-scale invasion of the North. Convinced that Lee's army was stronger than his own, Hooker asked Washington for reinforcements, but few were forthcoming. Actually, Hooker continued to outnumber Lee by about 25,000 men.

Many Northern citizens, in the full belief that an invasion was imminent, were now in a state close to panic. Even the residents of cities as far from the Potomac as New York considered themselves threatened. The situation on June 16 at Harrisburg, Pennsylvania, located in one of the more vulnerable areas, is described by an unnamed observer: "The morning broke upon a populace all astir, who had been called out of bed by the beat of the alarming drum, the blast of the bugle, and the clanging of bells. The streets were lively with men who were either returning from a night's work on the fortifications or going over to relieve those who were toiling there. As the sun rose higher the excitement gathered head. All along the streets were omnibuses, wagons, and wheelbarrows taking in trunks and valuables and rushing them down to the depot to be shipped out of rebel range. The stores, the female seminaries, and almost every private residence were busy all of the forenoon in swelling the mountain of freight that lay at the depot. Every horse was impressed into service, and every porter groaned beneath his weight of responsibilities. The scene at noon at the depots was indescribable, if not disgraceful. A sweltering mass of humanity thronged the platform, all furious to escape from the doomed city.

"At the bridge and across the river [the Susquehanna, on the city's southwestern side] the scene was equally exciting. All through the day a steady stream of people on foot and in wagons, young and old, black and white, was pouring across it from the Cumberland Valley, bearing with them their household goods and all manner of goods and stock. Endless trains, laden with flour, grain, and merchandise, hourly emerged from the Valley and thundered across the bridge and through the city. Miles of retreating baggage wagons filled with calves and sheep tied together, and great old-fashioned furnace wagons loaded with tons of trunks and boxes defiled in continuous procession down the pike and across the river, raising a dust that marked the outline of the road as far as the eye could see."

These people, of course, had every reason to be alarmed. General Ewell, after his success at Winchester, had pushed his van across the Potomac and was in possession of Williamsport, Maryland; and Jenkins and his cavalry had ridden as far as Chambersburg, Pennsylvania, about twenty-five miles northwest of Gettysburg. But a full-scale invasion was not quite as close as the North believed. The center of the campaign's development remained in Virginia.

6

Another Test for the Cavalry

WHEREAS MID-JUNE found Hooker's army well in hand, that of Lee was stretched along an irregular north-south line extending for more than a hundred miles. Hooker's departure from Falmouth had freed A. P. Hill from Fredericksburg, and he was marching toward Culpeper. Longstreet was on the way from Culpeper to the eastern slopes of the Blue Ridge, his orders from Lee specifying that he deploy there in such a way as to cover the gaps offering access to the northern part of the Shenandoah Valley. The purpose was to prevent Hooker from sending troops into the Valley, should the Union general be entertaining such plans. Jeb Stuart had been assigned the job of screening Longstreet's march from Hooker's observation, and Stuart's troopers were moving to take up the necessary stations east of the Blue Ridge, a region veiled from Federal eyes by the Bull Run Mountains, which lay on a north-south course west of Fairfax.

As related by Stuart's aide, the big Prussian aristocrat Heros von Borcke: "The morning of the 16th found us betimes en route, and in high glee at the thought of once more invading Yankeedom. Having crossed the Hazel and Rappahannock rivers, we marched on in the same line we had followed in our retreat of November '62 [after the Battle of Antietam], and at noon halted for an hour to feed our horses at the little town of Orleans, where General Stuart and his staff made a point of visiting our old friend Mrs. M., by whom we were received with her usual kindness and hospitality. Our march thence lay through the rich and beautiful county of Fauquier, which as yet showed but little signs of suffering from the war, and at dark we reached the Piedmont Station of the Baltimore-Ohio Railway, where we bivouacked.

"Next morning, as soon as it was light, the famous guerilla chief Major [John S.] Mosby, who had selected this part of the country for the scene of his extraordinary achievements, made his appearance in camp, reporting that the enemy's cavalry, which till recently had fronted us near Culpeper, was rapidly following a line of march parallel to our own [on the right], although as yet only small detachments were occupying the neighboring county of Loudoun."

There were, however, many more Federal troopers on their way to this area. In order to learn more about Lee's movements, Hooker had decided to turn Alfred Pleasonton's forces leftward, toward the Bull Run Mountains, on a scout. As Stuart rode north on the western side of the mountains, Pleasonton's troopers, in two columns, approached the mountains from the east, starting through the very gaps that Stuart, whose forces were also divided, was positioning himself to cover. The result was two simultaneous engagements late in the day on the 17th, one at Aldie and the other at Middleburg, about five miles apart. The greater fight was that at Aldie, where Pleasonton himself, seconded by Gregg, led the advance. Stuart was not present here; he was at Middleburg. The Confederate forces at Aldie were those of Fitzhugh Lee's brigade. Lee, a nephew of Robert E., happened to be suffering from a debilitating bout with rheumatics, and Colonel Thomas T. Munford was in active command.

Riding at the head of Pleasonton's column was Judson Kilpatrick's brigade. In the words of Willard Glazier, a trooper with the 2nd New York (known as the "Harris Light"): "We marched in column of fours, and on that day my squadron was the advance guard. As I was at that time chief of the first platoon my place was at the head of the long column which wound down the road. As we came upon Aldie, the advance guard of the enemy . . . was unexpectedly encountered. But Kilpatrick proved himself equal to the occasion and met the surprise gallantly. Dashing to the front, he made a rapid survey of the situation; and then came the command, in his clear, ringing tones, 'Form platoons! Trot! March!' Down through the streets of the town we charged, and . . . over the low hill beyond. This fine position was gained so quickly and so successfully that [the enemy], taken by surprise, made no opposition to our brilliant advance; though immediately afterwards he rallied and fought desperately for two hours to gain the lost position, while the guns of his battery blazed destruction upon our lines. But [Captain Alanson M.] Randol's guns blazed in return, tearing open the Confederate ranks with their shot and shell. . . .

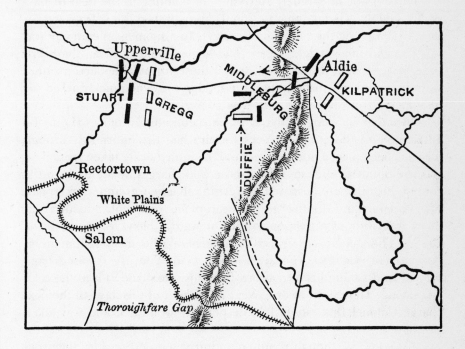

Cavalry fights at Aldie, Middleburg, and Upperville

"On the crest of the hill up which our platoons charged there was a field of haystacks, not yet garnered, enclosed in a barricade of rails. Behind these the enemy occupied a strong position, and their sharp-shooters had annoyed our lines to such an extent that they prevented our advance on the left. . . . Kilpatrick, ordering forward a battalion of the Harris Light and, giving the men a few words of encouragement, turned to [Captain Samuel] McIrvin and, pointing to the field of hay-stacks, said . . . 'Go take that position!' Away dashed this officer and his men [followed by the 6th Ohio Cavalry]. In a moment the enemy was reached and the struggle began. The horses could not leap the barri-cade, but the men dismounted, scaled those formidable barriers, and, with drawn sabers, rushed upon the hidden foe, who quickly asked for quarter.

"Another incident occurred worth mentioning. Colonel [Louis P.] Di Cesnola of the 4th New York Cavalry had that morning, through mistake, been placed under arrest and, his sword being taken from him, was without arms. But in one of those wild charges, made early in the contest, his regiment hesitated. Forgetting that he was under arrest and without command, he flew to the head of his regiment, reassured his men, and, without a weapon to give or ward a blow, led them to the charge. This gallant act was seen by his general who, meeting him on his return, said, 'Colonel, you are a brave man. You are released from arrest.' And, taking his own sword from his side, handed it to the colo-nel, saying, 'Here is my sword. Wear it in honor of this day.' In the next charge Colonel Di Cesnola fell, desperately wounded, and was taken prisoner. . . .

"The enemy, though repulsed and driven on every side, again ral-lied. . . . Massing a heavy force on our right, [Colonel Thomas L.] Rosser led them in a wild charge upon our lines. The 1st Massachusetts, on the extreme right, received the shock of this terrible onset, and, though compelled to fall back, they fought steadily and bravely until the rest of the right gave way. Then ensued a scene of confusion and flight that sickened the heart of their brave general. But Kilpatrick quickly rushed to the rescue and prevented the threatened disaster. Randol was or-dered to double-shot the guns of his battery; the center and left were told to hold their ground; and, placing himself at the head of the 1st Maine, he waited until the Confederate columns were within fifty yards of Randol's battery. 'Forward!' was the order that then rung along the lines, and with resistless fury they swept down on the advancing rebel ranks, causing them to reel and break."

The fight ended with the Confederates withdrawing from the field, but this wasn't because they were beaten. Orders for the retreat had come by way of a rider from Middleburg sent by Jeb Stuart, who wanted to gain firmer control of his forces after a jarring personal experience. He and his staff had entered Middleburg in company with only a handful of troops. Von Borcke tells what happened: "We were received in this pleasant little town with marked demonstrations of joy; and as my friends here had heard from Richmond the news of my death [a rumor dating back to the Battle of Chancellorsville] but not its contradiction, I underwent [an] ovation at my quasi-resurrection. While paying one of the many visits I had to make to give bodily assurance of my presence in the world of the living, and relating my adventures to a circle of pretty young ladies, the streets suddenly resounded with the cry of 'The Yankees are coming!' raised by a party of horsemen who galloped through the town in frantic excitement, having formed part of one of our pickets, on whom the enemy, not supposed to be so near, had rather suddenly fallen. I had just time to rush out of the house and mount my horse when the enemy's cavalry poured into the town from various directions. I soon joined General Stuart, however, and the remainder of his staff, who were riding off as fast as their steeds could carry them in the direction of our [nearest] troops, which we soon reached; and General Stuart gave orders that General Robertson should move his regiments at a trot upon Middleburg and drive the enemy from the town without delay.

"As I had a better knowledge of the country than Robertson I was ordered to accompany the general, who was an old friend and gladly consulted me as to the best mode of attack. It was already dark by the time we came up with our advanced pickets, about half a mile from Middleburg, and we found them, supported by their reserve under the command of Captain [W. B.] Wooldridge, of the 4th Virginia, engaged in a lively skirmish with the hostile sharpshooters. We were informed by this brave officer that the Federals held the town in considerable force [actually, the number of Pleasonton's troops in this column was only about 300, with Colonel Duffié commanding], and had erected a barricade at its entrance, which he begged as a favor to be allowed to storm. This was of course granted; and, with a cheer, forward went the gallant little band, driving the tirailleurs [i.e., the skirmishers] rapidly before them and taking the barricade after a short but sanguinary struggle. At the same moment, our sabers rattled from their scabbards, and the main body of the brigade dashed forward to the charge at a thundering gallop along the broad turnpike road and down the main street, while two of our squadrons went round outside the village to protect us from a flank attack.

"As I had felt rather ashamed at having been forced to run from the enemy under the very eyes of my fair friends, and was naturally anxious to afford them a spectacle of a totally different character, I assumed my place of honor, leading the charge with General Robertson, and to my intense satisfaction plunged into the enemy's ranks opposite the precise spot whence I had commenced my flight, and whence, regardless of danger, the ladies now looked on and watched the progress of the combat. It lasted but a few seconds, for the enemy, unable to withstand the shock of our charge, broke and fled in utter confusion—a part of the fugitives taking the straight road along the main street, and the other turning off by the shorter route out of the town to the right. Leaving General Robertson to pursue the former with one of his regiments, I took upon myself the responsibility of following the latter with several squadrons, anticipating that the Federal reserves were in this direction. My supposition proved only too correct, for they were soon at hand to rescue their comrades, and in a few minutes we were engaged in a severe conflict. Bullets whizzed from either side—men and horses fell dead and wounded amidst unavoidable confusion through the extreme darkness of the night, and for a time it seemed doubtful whether I should be able to hold my ground. . . .

"Fortunately General Robertson, hearing the firing, soon came up with his regiment, and, taking now the offensive, we charged the Federals with our united force in front, while the squadron we had sent round the village to the right took them in flank, the effect of which was to force our antagonists into a rapid retreat, in the course of which we took several officers and seventy-five privates prisoners.

"On our return to Middleburg the General and I remained another hour with our lady friends, who, with their accustomed devotedness, were busy nursing the wounded, large numbers of whom were collected in several of the residences."

Duffié's ill-used command made its bivouac alongside a road east of Middleburg, only to be aroused at 3:30 A.M. by the approach of another of Stuart's brigades, that of Colonel J. R. Chambliss, Jr. Duffié rushed to put his troopers on the road to meet the threat, hoping to be able to force his way back to Hooker's lines east of the Bull Run Mountains. The colonel relates: "An engagement commenced at once, the enemy opening on both flanks with heavy volleys, yelling to us to surrender. I at once ordered Captain [A. H.] Bixby, the officer commanding the advance, to charge any force in his front. . . . This order was executed most admirably. Captain Bixby's horse was shot and he himself wounded. My command was in a most hazardous position, the enemy being in front, rear, and on both flanks; and we were intermixed with them for more than an hour, until we struck the road leading to Hopewell Gap. . . . The brave officers and men . . . were fighting side by side with overwhelming numbers of the enemy with the most determined valor, preferring rather to die than to surrender. I returned [to Hooker's lines] . . . with the gallant debris of my much-loved regiment—four officers and twenty-seven men." Duffié counted his losses in the two fights—killed, wounded, and missing—at twenty officers and 248 men. Some of the missing, however, soon began filtering in.

News of the actions at Aldie and Middleburg told Hooker little, for there was no word of Longstreet's movement. Early in the morning on June 18 Hooker wired Halleck in Washington, saying that he had instructed Pleasonton to learn what was behind the Confederate cavalry, and that, as a precaution, a part of the Army of the Potomac was being sent northward to Leesburg, Virginia, to cover Edward's Ferry and the other Potomac crossings in the area, which might be needed. In his return wire, Halleck responded to a complaint Hooker had raised that Washington was not supplying him with enough intelligence on Lee's movements. Halleck stated: "I can get no information of the enemy other than that sent to you. Rumors from Pennsylvania are too confused and contradictory to be relied on. Officers and citizens are on a big stampede. They are asking me why does not General Hooker tell where Lee's army is? He is nearest to it. There are numerous suppositions and theories, but all is yet mere conjecture. I only hope for positive information from your front."

Union General Pleasonton was not seriously diminished by the loss of Duffié's column. But, pending the arrival of infantry supports from Hooker's army, he moved from Aldie only gingerly on the eighteenth, sending out scouting parties and taking up a position east of Middleburg. Stuart was glad for the respite, for not all of his troops were up from the Rappahannock. Moreover, Longstreet was not yet established in the Blue Ridge gaps. The morning of the nineteenth found Pleasonton still unready for an all-out effort, but he decided to make a push through Middleburg. Stuart had established his lines west of the town on a road leading toward the Blue Ridge by way of Upperville.

"The rising of the sun," says Heros von Borcke, "was . . . the signal for the recommencement of hostilities, and before we had had time to breakfast a rapid succession of cannon shots summoned us to the front. The enemy in strong force were advancing upon a patch of wood, about a mile [west of] Middleburg, which was held by our troops. . . . The dismounted sharpshooters on both sides were exchanging a lively fire and the shells from a number of hostile batteries were bursting with a sharp crack in the treetops. General Stuart took up his position on a hill, about half a mile to the rear, commanding a good view of the plain in front and over the fields to the right and left. Our chief of artillery being engaged in another direction, I received orders to place our batteries in position. . . .

"I then rode forward to the extreme front, and, carefully reconnoitring the position of the enemy, I found that their force was . . . superior to our own and that they were overlapping us on either wing. General Stuart gave me so little credit for the accuracy of my report that he was for some time convinced that he could hold his ground with ease . . . and I was again dispatched to the front to see if I had not overrated the forces of the enemy. What I saw only too thoroughly confirmed my first observations; and I reported to General Stuart that in my opinion he would be forced to retreat. . . . But again he refused credit to the result of my observations, and said laughingly, 'You're mistaken for once, Von. I shall be in Middleburg in less than an hour.' . . .

"Suddenly the firing increased in heaviness, and we saw our men hastening from the woods in considerable confusion, followed by a dark mass of Federals in close pursuit. 'Ride as quickly as you can and rally those men. I will follow you immediately with all the troops I can gather,' were Stuart's hasty instructions to me as he suddenly, though rather late, became convinced that I had all along been right. Just as I reached our breaking lines the 9th Virginia, which had been in reserve, dashed forward in a magnificent charge; the batteries I had previously posted opened a well-directed crossfire on the Federal horsemen; the flying regiments responded to my call and turned upon their pursuers, whom we drove rapidly back into the woods, killing and wounding a large number and taking many prisoners, until a severe fusillade from the enemy's sharpshooters posted on the outskirts of the wood protected their retreat.

"I had just succeeded in re-forming our own men, about 200 yards from the wood, when Stuart came up and, riding along the lines of his troops, who always felt relieved by his appearance in the moment of extreme danger, was received by them with enthusiastic cheers. He now ordered the regiments to withdraw by squadrons to a better position—a movement which was executed under cover of a spirited fire from our batteries.

"The general and his staff being the last to remain on the spot, we soon became a target for the Federal sharpshooters who, by the cheering, had become well aware that Stuart was in that small group of officers. Being dressed in the same fashion as the general—a short jacket and gray hat with waving ostrich plume, and mounted on my handsome new charger—I was mistaken for him, and my tall figure soon engaged their particular attention, for the bullets came humming round me like a swarm of bees. A ball had just stripped the gold lace from my trousers, and I was saying to the general, riding a few steps before me on my left—'General, those Yankees are giving it rather hotly to me on your account,'—when I suddenly felt a severe dull blow, as though somebody had struck me with his fist on my neck; fiery sparks glittered before my eyes, and a tremendous weight seemed to be dragging me from my horse.

"After a few moments of insensibility I opened my eyes again, to find myself lying on the ground, my charger [standing] beside me, and a number of officers and men pressing round and endeavoring to raise me. My left arm hung still and lifeless, and the blood was spouting from a large wound on the side of my neck and streaming from my mouth at every breath. Unable to speak, I motioned for my comrades to leave me and save themselves from the hail of bullets the enemy were concentrating on them, two of the soldiers about me having already fallen lifeless. At the same moment, I saw the Yankees charging towards us from the woods; and, certain that a few minutes more would leave me a prisoner in their hands, the hateful thought inspired me with the courage to summon all my strength and energy, and, managing to regain my legs with the assistance of Captain [William W.] Blackford and Lieutenant [F. S.] Robertson of our staff, I mounted my horse and rode off from the field, supported by these two officers. . . .

"After a painful ride of more than a mile, coming across an ambulance, my comrades placed me in it, gave orders to the driver to carry me further to the rear, and then galloped off in another direction in search of our surgeon, Dr. [Talcott] Eliason. Meanwhile, the Federals were rapidly advancing, and numbers of their shells burst so near the ambulance that the driver was seized with fright, and, believing that anyhow I was nearly dead, drove off at a gallop over the rocky road regardless of my agonized groans, every movement of the vehicle causing a fresh effusion of blood from my wound. At last I could stand it no longer, and, crawling up to him, I put my cocked pistol to his head and made him understand that I should blow out his brains if he continued his cowardly flight.

"This proved effectual, and, driving along at a moderate pace we were overtaken by Dr. Eliason, who at once examined my wound and found that the ball had entered the lower part of my neck, cut through a portion of the windpipe, and, taking a downward course, had lodged somewhere in my right lung, and that my left arm was entirely paralyzed. . . . A shadow passed over the doctor's face as he examined me, for he had a liking for me; and, reading in my eyes that I wished to have his undisguised opinion, he said, 'My dear fellow, your wound is mortal, and I can't expect you to live till the morning,' offering at the same time to execute my last wishes. This was sad enough intelligence for me; but the very positiveness of the opinion aroused within me the spirit of resistance, and I resolved to struggle against death with all the energy I possessed."

Von Borcke would make an excellent recovery, but he would see no further service on Civil War battlefields. As for Stuart that day, he gave up less than a mile of territory. His new position went untested by the Federals. It rained the next day, and the action was limited to skirmishing. Both sides made preparations for the looming showdown. Stuart's entire command was now with him, but he lacked infantry support. Pleasonton was bolstered by three brigades.

On this day General Hooker took the precautionary step of sending additional infantry in substantial numbers as far as the eastern base of the Bull Run Mountains. On their march, these troops (who would never be needed) saw something they would not forget. As recorded in a letter written by Captain Samuel Fiske of the 14th Connecticut Volunteers: "We passed . . . the field of the two Bull Run battles; and I was much shocked to find such great numbers of the bodies of Union soldiers lying still unburied. Their skeletons, with the tattered and decaying uniforms still hanging upon them, lie in many parts of the last year's battlefield, in long ranks, just as they fell; and in one place, under a tree, was a whole circle of the remains of wounded soldiers who had been evidently left to die under the shade to which they had crawled, some of them with bandages round their skeleton limbs, one with a battered canteen clasped in his skeleton hand, and some with evidence, as our boys fancied, of having starved to death. On one old broken cart lies what is left of eight Union soldiers, left to decay as they were laid to be borne off the field, and the vehicle struck, probably, by a cannonball. In many instances, the bodies which were partially or hastily buried are now much uncovered; and a grinning skull meets your gaze as you pass, or a fleshless arm stretches out its ghastly welcome.

"Still it is wonderful to notice how quickly and how kindly Nature covers up the traces of murderous conflict on her face. The scars are mostly healed, verdure reigns, and beauty smiles over the bloody field; and save in a lonely chimney here and there [the residue of a burnt house], and the ghastly sights I have above referred to—which result from human neglect and barbarity, and are not to be charged at all to Nature—, you would not suspect your feet were pressing the sod that one year and two years ago was reddened in human gore."

The narrative of the contest between Pleasonton and Stuart is taken up by Confederate gunner George Neese of Chew's Battery: "June 21. This Sabbath morning, instead of the peaceful tones of the church bells floating out on the quiet air, the deep harsh roar of booming cannon rolled over the hills and fields of Loudoun and proclaimed the opening of the butcher business for the day. The enemy advanced on us this morning from the direction of Middleburg with cavalry and artillery. We fell back . . . and moved in the direction of Upperville."

Union trooper Willard Glazier explains that "the country between Middleburg and Upperville is a succession of ridges and hollows, and our artillery was rushed forward and planted on one eminence after another as we advanced, from which positions we shelled the opposing guns of the enemy. Along this uneven ground, stone fences occurred with unpleasant frequency, the Confederates taking shelter behind them and firing to great advantage upon our advancing troops. But our brave boys of the saddle galloped forward, charging the Rebels behind their stone barricades and sending them flying before the Union sabers."

According to Southerner Neese, there was less flying than organized retreating. "The enemy drove us back slowly all day. Several times . . . I saw our shell plunge right in their advancing line, break their ranks, and check for a moment the oncoming host, but they quickly closed up and came at us again. They were certainly the bravest and boldest Yanks that ever fought us on any field. But I think that the cause of their prowess was more in their belief in strength of numbers than in their efficacy of cool courage, as they had . . . more men engaged than we had."

Developments at Upperville are described by Jeb Stuart: "I was anxious on account of the women and children to avoid a conflict in the

Union troops at Upperville

village, but the enemy, true to those reckless and inhuman instincts, sought to take advantage of this disinclination on our part by attacking furiously our rear guard. In an instant the same men who had with so much coolness retired before the enemy wheeled about and with admirable spirit drove back the enemy, killing, wounding, and capturing a large number. In this, General Hampton's brigade participated largely and in a brilliant manner."

The retreat was soon resumed. Again in the words of Southern artilleryman Neese: "During the last part of the cavalry fight the Yankee infantry flanked round on our right and attempted to cut us off from Ashby's Gap in the Blue Ridge. But we caught the gentlemen at their sly little game, put our guns in position and gave them a few drastic and effective doses of shell, which . . . wound up the flanking business."

"The last charge of the day," says Stuart's aide, Henry McClellan, "was made by Colonel P. G. Evans' regiment of North Carolina Cavalry, of Robertson's brigade. . . . Placing himself at the head of his column of fours . . . and pointing with his drawn saber toward the enemy, [Evans] cried, as with the voice of a trumpet, 'Now, men, I want you to understand that I am going through!' He kept his word, but fell mortally wounded in the midst of the enemy, whose ranks he had penetrated too far for the recovery of his body.

"A feeble attempt to follow this regiment as it returned from the charge was checked by Hampton's brigade, and darkness closed down upon the scenes of this hard-fought day. Had a longer term of daylight permitted any further advance by the enemy they would have come into collision with Longstreet's infantry, which had come down from the gap to Stuart's aid."

Pleasonton had now pressed his mission as far as he dared. The several days of fighting had cost him about 800 men in killed, wounded, and missing. Stuart's loss was about 500. During the early hours of June 22, Pleasonton fell back to Aldie in the Bull Run Mountains. He had learned that the Loudoun Valley was free of Confederate infantry, but Stuart had kept him from learning much else. In a prompt report to Hooker, however, Pleasonton included some intelligence, procured from Confederate deserters, indicating—and correctly—that not only Longstreet but also A. P. Hill and Robert E. Lee himself were now in the Shenandoah Valley, following in Ewell's wake. Hill had come up on the western side of the Blue Ridge. Unfortunately for Hooker's purposes, information given by deserters was always considered suspect. What Hooker had wanted most of all was for Pleasonton's reconnaissance to include a penetration of the Shenandoah Valley that gained some positive intelligence. Pleasonton's report closed with this frustrating scrap: "General Buford operated independently yesterday. . . . He sent a party to the top of the Blue Ridge that saw a rebel infantry camp about two miles long on the Shenandoah [River], just below Ashby's Gap. The atmosphere was so hazy they could not make out anything more beyond."

7

Gettysburg and Jubal Early

On June 23 Hooker made a flying visit to Washington to consult with Lincoln, Secretary of War Edwin M. Stanton, and General Halleck. It was reported that Hooker, who sometimes drank to excess, was drunk when he left the capital. On the twenty-fourth, back in camp, the harried commander wired Halleck, saying that his limited knowledge of the situation, coupled with a lack of definite orders from the War Department, had him in a quandary. "Outside of the Army of the Potomac, I don't know whether I am standing on my head or feet." He said that there was still no certain indication that Lee intended a major invasion of the North. "Ewell, I conclude, is over the river and is now up the country, I suppose for purposes of plunder.... If the enemy should conclude not to throw any additional force over the river, I desire to make Washington secure, and, with all the force I can muster, strike for his line of retreat in the direction of Richmond."

It so happened that even while Hooker's message was in transit, A. P. Hill and Longstreet were hurrying toward the mouth of the Shenandoah Valley in order to follow Ewell into Maryland and Pennsylvania.

The columns reached the Potomac on the twenty-fifth. According to an unnamed artilleryman in Longstreet's corps: "We crossed ... at Williamsport. The river is 150 yards wide here but not more than two and a half feet deep. The day was cool and rainy, but the boys waded in cheerfully, and the air was rent with shouts of laughter as now and then some clumsy fellow stumbled and went under, head and ears."

Another artilleryman, a junior officer from Louisiana named William Miller Owen, says that the entire membership of many units "de-nuded themselves of their nether garments and shoes, making a bundle of them and carrying them and their cartridge boxes upon their shoulders. A number of carriages containing ladies, mostly young and guile-less, crossed the ford, coming from Maryland, as our men were crossing to the other side. The sight of thousands of 'Confeds' in the water . . . *sans culotte* must have been astounding and novel in the extreme, and something the young ladies would not soon forget."

Halting on the Maryland bank, the chilled men were allowed to build fires. W. C. Ward, a private with the 4th Alabama Regiment, re-lates that, with "the rain still falling, the commissary department, with whisky . . . undertook to wet the inside of the tired, hungry, and wet soldiers by distributing about one-half gill to each man. It was good whisky, [and] we had not had any for many months. Knowing how good such a stimulant was at the end of a hard day's march, this private soldier attempted to do a prudent thing. Instead of pouring his whisky into his stomach, he turned it into his canteen. The march was resumed; and after moving rapidly northward for about one hour the division was halted to rest. All lay down on the roadside, wet though it was; and when we arose again to resume the march the canteen in which the whisky had been so carefully poured had been reversed and all that soldier's good spirits lost."

The narrative is taken up by Colonel William C. Oates, commander of the 15th Alabama: "We marched into Pennsylvania that afternoon and went into camp before night [south of] Greencastle. I, with Adju-tant Waddell, rode out into the country and found some of the soldiers committing depredations upon the Dutch farmers, which I promptly rebuked, and ordered the men to camps wherever we found them. This was done in obedience to General Lee's order forbidding interference with private property because it was wrong and should never be done, even in an enemy's country, except when absolutely necessary. But, as far as I saw, these depredations extended only to taking something to eat and burning fence rails for fuel. Some men would do this when they had plenty of rations in camp. At one house we found some of our regiment milking the cows and catching the milk in canteens, which seemed to be very expert work of that kind. The people, as far as I could learn, seemed a good deal alarmed but behaved well. Waddell and myself took supper that night with some very loyal people to the Union. . . .

"There were two young ladies in the family, and they, in common with the men of the household, conversed very freely after I assured

Southern soldiers at a ford

them of their perfect right to speak their real sentiments. One of the ladies said she wished that the two armies would hang the two presidents, Jeff Davis and Lincoln, and stop the war. These people, although educated in books of some kind, and apparently well informed on nearly everything else, were remarkably ignorant of the causes of the war and the real character of the [Confederate] Government. They looked upon the war as a personal contention between two ambitious men for the supremacy, and they were particularly spiteful toward Davis because they seemed to think that he wanted to dissolve the Union merely to be President of the Southern Confederacy."

Private Ward explains how the march was resumed the next morning: "We were a merry lot. Entering the one long street of Greencastle, we found the people not at all afraid of us, as might have been expected. John Young, a private of Company I, of Huntsville, Alabama, a man so bow-legged that he took in all sides of the street . . . went up to an old gentleman standing in the presence of some ladies . . . and lifted from the gentleman's head a beautiful new felt hat, at the same time carelessly dropping [to the ground] his own well-worn Confederate wool covering. The old gentleman seemed dazed. Rubbing his hands through his thin hair, he . . . was overheard to say, 'I really believe that soldier has taken my hat.'

"While going through Greencastle, the fife and drum of the 48th Alabama Regiment played 'The Bonnie Blue Flag.' The doors of the houses were all closed, but there was evidence of life in the upper stories. . . . We never halted. Marching through fields, over newly planted corn and waving wheat, through orchards and currant bushes, we reached Chambersburg about noon. It was a beautiful town. Everything was fresh, indicating prosperity, and no signs of war. The stores were all closed, and the men, bareheaded, were standing in front. To our laughing inquiry, 'Where are your hats?' they replied, laughing, 'We have had some experience.' There was nothing to indicate from the deportment of the citizens that their country was being invaded by a hostile army.

"Passing out of Chambersburg by the northeast pike, as we went through a gateway under a hill crowned with a beautiful residence, we observed many ladies, well dressed, bearing on their bosoms the Union flag. . . . We took all of this in great good humor, neither giving nor taking offense. . . . One of the young ladies, bolder than all the others, made a somewhat conspicuous and aggressive display of her flag and herself, accompanied by remarks. A bold Texan . . . said to the brave young woman, 'Madam, you are doing a very dangerous thing. . . . We

Invaders marching into Pennsylvania

rebels never see that flag flying over breastworks without charging them.' The young woman made no reply, but her companions had a good laugh at her expense. The Texan shouldered his Springfield and went on his way as if regretting there were no orders to charge."

The troops of Longstreet and Hill interrupted their march, pending further orders from Lee, just north of Chambersburg. Ewell's column, winding along a few miles ahead and charged with the vital mission of requisitioning supplies, had instructions to proceed to Harrisburg. Jubal Early's division, however, was sent on a southeasterly detour toward Gettysburg. Not for the first time since he had entered Pennsylvania, Early noted something curious. "As we moved through the country, a number of people made mysterious signs to us. . . . Some enterprising Yankees had passed along a short time before, initiating the people into certain signs—for a consideration—which they were told would prevent the 'rebels' from molesting them or their property. . . . These things were all new to us, and the purchasers of the mysteries had been badly *sold*. The . . . signs . . . were supposed by the Confederates to be made by Knights of the Golden Circle, a secret organization said to sympathize with the South, but of which our soldiers knew nothing."

Early's column was accompanied by elements of Jenkins' cavalry, and trooper James H. Hodam relates: "The country through which we passed toward Gettysburg [on June 26] seemed to abound chiefly in Dutch women who could not speak English, sweet cherries, and apple-butter. As we marched along, the women and children would stand at the front gate with large loaves of bread and a crock of apple-butter, and effectually prevent an entrance of the premises by the gray invaders. As I said before, the women could not talk much with us, but they knew how to provide 'cut and smear,' as the boys called it, in abundance.

"The cherry crop was immense through this part of the state, and the great trees often overhung the highway laden with ripened fruit. The infantry would break off great branches and devour the cherries as they marched along. Regiments thus equipped reminded me of the scene in Macbeth where 'Birnam's wood do come to Dunsinane.'

"Near Gettysburg we captured the camp and equipage of a force of Pennsylvania militia, and after an exciting chase of several miles our regiment succeeded in picking up over 300 [actually, less than 200] of the 'band-box boys,' as we called them. But few shots were fired on either side, but the yelling on our side would have done credit to a band of Comanche Indians. The main body of the fleeing enemy kept together in the highway, but many, as they became exhausted, sought refuge in the fields, orchards, and farm buildings by the way, and many laughable incidents occurred as we gathered them in. Six were found hid among the branches of a large apple tree. One portly lieutenant, in attempting to crawl under a corncrib, had stuck fast by the head and shoulders, leaving the rest of his person exposed. Comrades Charlie Hyson and Morgan Feather had hard work to drag him out by the heels. But the most fun came when we dragged from a family bake-oven a regimental officer who, in his gold-laced uniform, was covered with soot and ashes. He was a sight to behold.

"While returning from escorting a lot of prisoners to the rear, I met a large party of prisoners hurrying by, while a short distance behind them a little drummer boy was trying to keep up. He was bareheaded, wet, and muddy, but still retained his drum. 'Hello, my little Yank, where are you going?' I said. 'Oh, I am a prisoner and am going to Richmond,' he replied. 'Look here,' I said, 'you are too little to be a prisoner, so pitch the drum into that fence corner, throw off your coat, get behind those bushes, and go home as fast as you can.' 'Mister, don't you want me for a prisoner?' 'No.' 'Can I go where I please?' 'Yes.' 'Then you bet I am going home to mother!' Saying this as he threw his drum one way and his coat another, he disappeared behind a fence and some bushes, and I sincerely hope he reached home and mother."

Some of the stampeding militiamen rode into Gettysburg crying, "The rebels are coming! The rebels are coming!" One of the first citizens to be caught up in the commotion was fifteen-year-old Tillie Pierce. "We were having our regular literary exercises on Friday afternoon at our Seminary when the cry reached our ears. Rushing to the door and standing on the front portico, we beheld in the direction of the Theological Seminary a dark, dense mass moving toward town. Our teacher, Mrs. Eyster, at once said, 'Children, run home as quickly as you can.' It did not require repeating. I am satisfied some of the girls did not reach their homes before the rebels were in the streets. As for myself, I had scarcely reached the front door when, on looking up the street, I saw some of the men on horseback. I scrambled in, slammed shut the door, and, hastening to the sitting room, peeped out between the shutters. What a horrible sight! There they were . . . riding wildly pell-mell down the hill toward our home, shouting, yelling most unearthily, cursing, brandishing their revolvers and firing right and left. I was fully persuaded that the rebels had actually come at last. What they would do with us was a fearful question to my young mind."

As explained by another resident, Michael Jacobs, professor of

Gettysburg Theological Seminary

mathematics and chemistry at Pennsylvania College: "This advance party was soon followed by 5,000 infantry, being General [John B.] Gordon's brigade of Early's division of Ewell's corps. Most of the men were exceedingly dirty, some ragged, some without shoes, and some surmounted by the skeleton of what was once an entire hat, affording unmistakable evidence that they stood in great need of having their scanty wardrobe replenished; and hence the eagerness with which they inquired after shoe, hat, and clothing stores, and their disappointment when they were informed that goods of that description were not to be had in town. . . . Being wet from the rain that had fallen during most of the day, and considerably heated by a long march . . . the air was filled with the filthy exhalations from their bodies. . . . It was difficult for us to recognize, in the great body of them, the character previously heralded in our community by a lady sympathizer of 'chivalrous Southerners, all from the first families of the South.' But we do not intend to reproach them for not presenting a better appearance. They doubtless did the best they could, and had come a long journey for the express purpose of supplying their pressing wants.

"General Early, who accompanied this brigade . . . demanded of the authorities of our borough 1,200 pounds of sugar, 600 pounds of coffee, 60 barrels of flour, 1,000 pounds of salt, 7,000 pounds of bacon, 10 barrels of whisky, 10 barrels of onions, 1,000 pairs of shoes, and 500 hats, amounting in value to $6,000; or, in lieu thereof, $5,000 cash. To this demand Messrs. D. Kendlehart and A. D. Buehler, as representatives of the town council, replied in substance that it was impossible to comply with their demands; that the goods were not in town or within reach; that the borough had no funds and the council had no authority to borrow, either in the name of the borough or county; and that, as we were at the mercy of the general and his men, they could search and take from citizens and the empty stores whatsoever they might be able to find. No attempt was made to enforce the requisition, and but few of the houses . . . were robbed."

Returning to Tillie Pierce: "Just previous to the raid, the citizens had sent their horses out the Baltimore Pike as far as the cemetery. There they were to be kept until those having the care of them were signaled that the enemy was about, when they were to hasten as fast as possible in the direction of Baltimore. Along with this party, Father sent our own horse, in charge of the hired boy we then had living with us. I was very much attached to the animal, for she was gentle and very pretty. I had often ridden her.

Pennsylvania College

"The [Confederate] cavalry . . . came so suddenly that no signal was given. They overtook the boys with the horses, captured and brought them all back to town. As they were passing our house my mother beckoned to the raiders, and some of them rode over to where she was standing and asked what was the matter. Mother said to them, 'You don't want the boy!' . . . One of the men replied, 'No, we don't want the boy. You can have him. We are only after the horses.' . . .

"After we saw that the boy was safe, Mother and I began to plead for the horse. As I stood there begging and weeping . . . one impudent and coarse Confederate said to me, 'Sissy, what are you crying about? Go in the house and mind your business.' I felt so indignant at his treatment I only wished I could have had some manner of revenge on the fellow.

"They left . . . without giving us any satisfaction. About one half hour after this, some of these same raiders came back, and, stopping at the kitchen door, asked Mother for something to eat. She replied, 'Yes, you ought to come back and ask for something to eat after taking a person's horse.' She nevertheless gave them some food. . . . Their manner of eating was shocking in the extreme. As I stood in the doorway and saw them laughing and joking at their deeds of the day, they threw the apple-butter in all directions while spreading their bread. I was heartily glad when they left, for they were a rude set."

An unnamed housewife who lived at the northeastern edge of town tells of watching the Confederates pass on their way toward a set of fields they intended to use as a temporary campground. "I was on the porch. . . . To be candid, they had my sympathy. I was reminded of Falstaff's recruits—ragged and with a look of hunger in their eyes—telling plainly of suffering and privations endured beyond description. As they marched by, some of them would talk to the children. One of them said to my son, 'Bub, would you like to shoot a rebel?' . . . I had a visit from two of these soldiers, asking me to sell them bread and butter. . . . I did not sell, but gave one a loaf of bread . . . the other, part of my very small quantity of butter. . . . They crossed the street, sitting on a porch to eat. . . . The lady of the house heard one say, 'I think the people of this place are very kind, considering we came here to kill off their husbands and sons.'

"In the evening a cavalryman rode up to the house and called to me. He said he wanted his horse shod. . . . There was a blacksmith shop to rear of our home. I told him there was no blacksmith here, and I knew nothing of his whereabouts. 'Well,' he said, 'if I could get in the shop and get shoes, I would shoe the horse myself.' I said to him, 'Do as you please; I am not concerned in the shop or its owner.' In a few minutes

I saw he had forced a window, and my son, a boy of four years, was holding the window up with the soldier's carbine, evidently feeling very important. I went out and objected. The soldier answered, 'No danger. I've got the shoes and am sorry the blacksmith is not here; I would like to pay him for them.' I said, 'Leave the money with me, if you are anxious about it. I know where he lives, and will send it to him.' He got out his pocketbook, searched it, and there was nothing to be found. He laughingly said, 'I brought the wrong pocketbook.' . . .

"He [asked], 'Why are you women so afraid of the rebels?' 'Why,' I said, 'that is news to me; I did not know we were.' He added: 'General Lee ordered us to treat the women with respect; not like your men treated our women in Winchester.' I said, 'Your women spat upon our men . . . and when women resorted to such insults they deserved all they got.' I asked him, 'Where are you going?' 'Oh,' he said, 'to Bunker's Hill, and we will not leave one stone on another there.' [This was a boast alluding to the statement of prominent Georgian Robert Toombs that he would call the roll of his slaves at the foot of the Bunker Hill Monument.] I answered, 'Before many days you will wish you were across the Potomac.' 'Well, it might be,' he replied, and, lifting his hat, said, 'Good-bye.' "

Professor Jacobs explains that before nightfall "the rebels burned the railroad bridge and a few cars, took from the few articles that our merchants had not sent away such as suited them, and divested the taverns and liquor stores of their liquors. Besides this, they did not do much damage in the town. In the country, however, they treated the farmers less gently. They there reenacted their old farce of professing to pay for what they took by offering freely their worthless Confederate scrip, which they said would, in a few days, be better than our own currency. In the town they obtained but little booty because all the valuables of the bank, and nearly all those of the merchants, had been previously sent for safety to Philadelphia. This proved a great disappointment to them, and they . . . consequently hurried forward, that night and the next morning, towards Hanover and York."

John B. Gordon

8

Meade Replaces Hooker

UNTIL THIS TIME Lee's campaign had gone well. His bold invasion had placed the North in a state of alarm and confusion, and he was finding the supplies he needed to augment those he had brought from Virginia. His plan from the start had been to combine an offensive strategy with defensive tactics. If a major confrontation developed, which he knew was likely, he expected to enjoy the advantage of choosing the battle-field, and he meant this to be a spot where he could set up a strong defense and await attack. In order for his scheme to succeed he had to keep abreast of the enemy's whereabouts, and he intended to rely on Jeb Stuart to provide this information.

In the aftermath of the cavalry fighting in the Loudoun Valley, Stuart was located in the Confederate army's right-rear. His new mission called for him to proceed to Pennsylvania and take up a position on the right of Lee's advance, keeping alert for Federal countermeasures. Stuart was given a choice between two routes northward: he could follow the Confederate army through the Shenandoah and Cumberland valleys and work his way around it, or he could make a southerly arc to the east, coming up between Hooker and Washington, doing what damage he could to Federal communications along the way, and, after crossing the Potomac, swinging westward in front of Hooker to Lee's right flank.

Eager to refurbish a reputation dimmed by the surprise at Brandy Station and the Loudoun Valley retreat, Stuart chose the more spectac-ular course. He believed that Hooker's forces occupied a relatively tight area east of the Bull Run Mountains and that they were stationary. Unfortunately, the Federals were a good deal spread out; and, worse yet, as Stuart expanded his swing to make up for this, Hooker, finally aware of Lee's purpose, began sending his troops toward the Potomac before marching them northward on what Lincoln called Lee's "inside track." Stuart plunged ahead, unaware that he would be forced into making his way northward on a course parallel to that of the Federals, cut off from Lee during the climactic days of the invasion's development. At least for the time being, Stuart had swashbuckled himself right out of the campaign. The mistake was a serious one, quite as much Lee's fault as Stuart's. Lee should have kept a tighter rein on his able but sometimes impulsive cavalry chief.

It took Hooker three days—June 25, 26, and 27—to move his army across the pontoon bridges emplaced at Edward's Ferry. As explained by Captain Henry Blake: "The Potomac, that separated Virginia from this section of Maryland, was the boundary between institutions as conflicting as slavery and freedom. . . . The soldiers had witnessed for two years, in [Virginia], barren lands, a treacherous and benighted race, children in rags and filth, miserable roads, the rude cabins of the poor whites and African bondmen, and empty churches . . . the bells . . . cast into cannon. . . . The scenes were changed so suddenly that it seemed like a delightful vision to behold the schoolhouses, the noble faces of the people, the splendid streets of a civilized age, the cultivated farms and orchards, the cottages ornamented with flowers, and, above all, the smiles and words of welcome from loyal men and women who publicly displayed the American flag, gave refreshing water to the soldiers while they were marching, and refused in many places to accept any compensation for food."

Brigade commander Regis de Trobriand says that the troops passed through the villages in "columns of companies, music at the head, and flags flying." The arrival at Frederick, designated as the army's point of assembly, "was almost triumphal. All the houses were draped; all the women were at the windows, waving their handkerchiefs; all the men were at their doors, waving their hats. In the middle of the principal street a pretty child, ten or twelve years of age, left a group collected on the sill of a house of modest appearance. Her mother had just given her a large bouquet, pointing me out with her hand. The little girl came bravely forward in front of the horses, holding towards me her little arms full of flowers. I leaned from my saddle to receive the fragrant present, and she said, with a rosy smile, 'Good luck to you, General!' I thanked her to the best of my ability. I would have liked to have embraced the little messenger with her happy wishes, but the march could not halt for so small an affair. When she rejoined her family, running along, I turned to kiss my hand to her in adieu. She nodded her head, and, blushing, hid it in her mother's bosom. 'Well!' said I, riding on, 'that little girl ought to bring me good fortune.'

"These encouragements cheered our hearts. They were as the voice of our country, of our common mother calling on us to defend her. Here we were amongst our own people. In talking of the Confederates, the inhabitants said 'the enemy' or 'the rebels.' It was not as in Virginia, where they said 'our men,' 'our army,' thus identifying themselves with our adversaries. So that, on crossing the Potomac, the army appeared to be morally transformed. A generous indignation caused all patriotic chords to vibrate. What! Had the troopers of Jenkins penetrated into Pennsylvania . . . and levied contributions on the country, picking up all the horses and all the cattle that they could find! And the cowardly farmers, the timorous militia, instead of defending themselves, could do no better than run away like a flock of sheep before a band of wolves. Ours the duty to do justice to these hordes of gray-jackets. Ours the task to drive them back into their land of slaves. . . . Such were the feelings of the army. We were no longer the defeated of yesterday; we felt ourselves predestined conquerors of the morrow."

This sentiment was not shared by General Hooker. During the three days occupied by the move across the Potomac to Frederick, he became increasingly nervous about Lee's "superior numbers." Someone reported to Lincoln a rumor that the general had slipped in and out of Washington during the night of the twenty-fifth, probably for the purpose of drinking at his favorite haunts. On the twenty-sixth Lincoln queried Hooker by telegram: had he really paid a secret visit to the capital? The general responded: "My compliments to the President, and inform him that I had not that honor. . . . Was it from the newspapers that you received a report, or an idea, that I was in Washington last night?" Lincoln closed the discussion with: "It did not come from the newspapers, nor did I believe it, but I wished to be entirely sure it was a falsehood."

The mistrust between Hooker and Washington came to a head on June 27. Hooker requested permission of Halleck to add the Harpers Ferry garrison to the Army of the Potomac, since this 10,000-man force was serving no useful purpose where it was. Upon receiving a negative reply, Hooker wired back: "My original instructions require me to cover Harpers Ferry and Washington. I have now imposed upon me, in addition, an enemy in my front of more than my number. I beg to be understood, respectfully but firmly, that I am unable to comply with this condition with the means at my disposal, and earnestly request that I may at once be relieved from the position I occupy."

That evening, at an emergency meeting, the President and Secretary Stanton decided to give command of the Army of the Potomac to Major General George G. Meade, one of Hooker's senior corps commanders. Meade was a Pennsylvanian, and the earthy Lincoln is supposed to have said that he would doubtless "fight well on his own dunghill." The general was forty-seven years old, about six feet tall, adorned with a grizzled beard and possessed of a Roman nose that was often obscured by a low-drawn hat brim. Altogether lacking in dash and glamour, Meade had a nervous temperament and was prone to fits of ill humor. He was known to his subordinate officers as "the old snapping turtle." Meade had proved his dependability as a commander during several previous campaigns, and he did not share the fear of Lee's talents that made many other Federal officers unsure of themselves.

After the emergency meeting, it was only a matter of hours until a special courier, bearing orders written by Halleck, reached Meade's tent near Frederick. The general was found asleep on his cot, partly clothed. He was shaken awake, and the courier announced, with a sly smile, that the general had been relieved of the command of his corps. A modest man, Meade replied that he wasn't surprised, that he had been expecting something like this. When the courier explained his real mission, Meade began to protest; but, told that he had no choice in the matter, he accepted the orders, which said, in part: "Considering the circumstances, no one ever received a more important command; and I cannot doubt that you will fully justify the confidence which the Government has reposed in you. You will not be hampered by any minute instructions from these headquarters. Your army is free to act as you may deem proper under the circumstances as they arise. You will, however, keep in view the important fact that the Army of the Potomac is the covering army for Washington as well as the army of operation against the invading forces of the rebels. You will, therefore, maneuver and fight in such a manner as to cover the capital and also Baltimore, as far as circumstances will admit. Should General Lee move upon either of these places, it is expected that you will either anticipate him or arrive with him so as to give him battle. All forces within the sphere of your operations will be held subject to your orders. Harpers Ferry and its garrison are under your direct orders." It was obvious that Meade was to have a freedom of decision not accorded to Hooker.

George G. Meade

By 7 A.M. on June 28 Meade had dispatched his reply to Halleck: "The order placing me in command of this army is received. As a soldier, I obey it, and to the utmost of my ability will execute it. Totally unexpected as it has been, and in ignorance of the exact condition of the troops and position of the enemy, I can only now say that it appears to me I must move toward the Susquehanna, keeping Washington and Baltimore well covered, and if the enemy is checked [by the militia] in his attempt to cross the Susquehanna, or if he turns toward Baltimore, to give him battle."

Among the news correspondents with the Army of the Potomac on June 28, which was a Sunday, was Charles Carleton Coffin of the Boston *Journal,* who relates: "It was a dismal day at Frederick when the news was promulgated that General Hooker was relieved of the command. Notwithstanding the result at Chancellorsville, the soldiers had a good degree of confidence in him. General Meade was unknown except to his own corps. . . . Meade cared but little for the pomp and parade of war. His own soldiers respected him because he was always prepared to endure hardships. . . . He was plain of speech, and familiar in conversation. . . . I saw him soon after he was informed that the army was under his command. There was no elation, but on the contrary he seemed weighed down with a sense of the responsibility resting on him. It was in the hotel at Frederick. He stood silent and thoughtful by himself. Few of all the noisy crowd around knew of the change that had taken place. The correspondents of the press knew it . . . before the corps commanders were informed of the fact. . . .

"General Hooker bade farewell to the principal officers of the army [in] the afternoon. . . . They were drawn up in line. He shook hands with each officer, laboring in vain to stifle his emotion. The tears rolled down his cheeks. The officers were deeply affected. He said that he had hoped to lead them to victory, but the power above him had ordered otherwise. He spoke in high terms of General Meade. . . .

"All Sunday the army was passing through Frederick. It was a strange sight. The churches were open, and some of the officers and soldiers attended service. . . . The stores also were open, and the town was cleaned of goods—boots, shoes, needles, pins, tobacco, pipes, paper, pencils, and other trifles which add to a soldier's comfort.

"Cavalry, infantry, and artillery were pouring through the town, the bands playing, and the soldiers singing their liveliest songs. The 1st Corps moved up the Emmitsburg Road and formed the left of the line; the 11th Corps marched up a parallel road a little farther east. . . . The

3rd and 12th Corps moved on parallel roads leading to Taneytown; the 2nd and 5th moved still farther east ... while the 6th, with Gregg's division of cavalry, [was ordered toward] Westminster, forming the right of the line. The lines of march were like the sticks of a fan, Frederick being the point of divergence."

9

Early at York and Wrightsville

DEPRIVED OF Jeb Stuart's eyes, Lee was not immediately aware of the threat emanating from Frederick. In fact, through most of the weekend of June 27–28 the general believed that all of the Federals were still south of the Potomac, and that it was safe for him to proceed with his original plans, which called for Longstreet and Hill to tarry at Chambersburg while Ewell continued toward the Susquehanna. Ewell personally took a column toward Carlisle, while Jubal Early's division remained on its course from Gettysburg to York. Early's expedition was the more eventful.

As narrated by brigade commander John Gordon: "The Valley of Pennsylvania, through which my command marched from Gettysburg . . . awakened the most conflicting emotions. It was delightful to look upon such a scene of universal thrift and plenty. Its broad grain fields, clad in golden garb, were waving their welcome to the reapers and binders. Some fields were already dotted over with harvested shocks. The huge barns on the highest grounds meant to my sore-footed marchers a mount, a ride, and a rest on broad-backed horses. On every side, as far as our alert vision could reach, all aspects and conditions conspired to make this fertile and carefully tilled region a panorama both interesting and enchanting. It was a type of the fair and fertile Valley of Virginia at its best, before it became the highway of armies and the ravages of war had left it wasted and bare. This melancholy contrast between these charming districts, so similar in other respects, brought to our Southern sensibilities a touch of sadness. In both these lovely valleys were the big red barns. . . . In both were the old-fashioned brick or stone mansions. . . . In both were the broad green meadows with luxuriant grasses and crystal springs.

"One of these springs impressed itself on my memory by its great beauty and the unique uses to which its owner had put it. He was a staid and laborious farmer of German descent. With an eye to utility, as well as to the health and convenience of his household, he had built his dining-room immediately over this fountain gushing from a cleft in an underlying rock. My camp for the night was nearby, and I accepted his invitation to breakfast with him. As I entered the quaint room, one half floored with smooth limestone, and the other half covered with limpid water bubbling clear and pure from the bosom of Mother Earth, my amazement at the singular design was perhaps less pronounced than the sensation of rest which it produced. For many days we had been marching on the dusty turnpikes under a broiling sun, and it is easier to imagine than to describe the feeling of relief and repose which came over me as we sat in that cool room, with a hot breakfast served from one side, while from the other the frugal housewife dipped cold milk and cream from immense jars standing neck-deep in water.

"We entered the city of York on Sunday morning. [This was June 28, the day of Meade's promotion at Frederick.] A committee composed of the mayor and prominent citizens met my command on the main pike before we reached the corporate limits, their object being to make a peaceable surrender and ask for protection to life and property. They returned, I think, with a feeling of assured safety.

"The church bells were ringing, and the streets were filled with well-dressed people. The appearance of these church-going men, women, and children in their Sunday attire strangely contrasted with that of my marching soldiers. Begrimed as we were from head to foot with the impalpable gray powder which rose in dense columns from the macadamized pikes and settled in sheets on men, horses, and wagons, it is no wonder that many of York's inhabitants were terror-stricken as they looked upon us. We had been compelled on these forced marches to leave baggage wagons behind us, and there was no possibility of a change of clothing, and no time for brushing uniforms or washing the disfiguring dust from faces, hair, or beard. All these were the same hideous hue. The grotesque aspect of my troops was accentuated here and there, too, by barefooted men mounted double upon huge horses with shaggy manes and long fetlocks.

"Confederate pride, to say nothing of Southern gallantry, was subjected to the sorest trial by the consternation produced among the ladies of York. In my eagerness to relieve the citizens from all apprehension, I lost sight of the fact that this turnpike powder was no respecter of persons, but that it enveloped all alike—officers as well as privates. . . . Halting on the main street, where the sidewalks were densely packed, I rode a few rods in advance of my troops in order to speak to the people from my horse. As I checked him and turned my full dust-begrimed face upon a bevy of young ladies very near me, a cry of alarm came from their midst. But after a few words of assurance from me, quiet and apparent confidence were restored. I assured these ladies that the troops behind me, though ill-clad and travel-stained, were good men and brave; that beneath their rough exteriors were hearts as loyal to women as ever beat in the breasts of honorable men; that their own experience and the experience of their mothers, wives, and sisters at home had taught them how painful must be the sight of a hostile army in their town; that under the orders of the Confederate commander-in-chief both private property and noncombatants were safe; that the spirit of vengeance and of rapine had no place in the bosoms of these dust-covered but knightly men; and I closed by pledging to York the head of any soldier under my command who destroyed private property, disturbed the repose of a single home, or insulted a woman."

It was about this time that Jubal Early himself rode into York. Less chivalrous than Gordon, and having orders from Ewell to requisition supplies, the commander was quick to inform the town that its safety had a price. According to a Northern civilian named J. H. Douglas, who was not a native of York but was a visitor there on that feverish day: "General Early made a levy upon the citizens, promising, in the event of its being complied with promptly, to spare all private property in the city; otherwise he would allow his men to take such things as they needed, and would not be responsible for the conduct of his men while they remained in the city. The beef, flour, and other articles, and $28,000 in money were speedily collected and handed over to the rebels. The general expressed himself satisfied with what he had received, and scrupulously kept his word in regard to the safety of private property."

John Gordon had orders to march his brigade entirely through York. "As we moved along the street . . . a little girl, probably twelve years of age, ran up to my horse and handed me a large bouquet of flowers, in the center of which was a note, in delicate handwriting, purporting to give the numbers and describe the position of the Union [militia] forces of Wrightsville, toward which I was advancing. I carefully read and reread this strange note. It bore no signature, and contained no assurance of sympathy for the Southern cause; but it was so terse and explicit in its terms as to compel my confidence.

"[That afternoon] we were in front of Wrightsville, and from the high ridge on which this note suggested that I halt and examine the position of the Union troops I eagerly scanned the prospect with my field-glasses in order to verify the truth of the mysterious communication or detect its misrepresentations. There, in full view before us, was the town, just as described, nestling on the banks of the Susquehanna. There was a blue line of soldiers guarding the approach, drawn up, as indicated, along an intervening ridge and across the pike. There was the long bridge spanning the Susquehanna and connecting the town with Columbia on the other bank. . . . There was a deep gorge or ravine running off to the right and extending around the left flank of the Federal line and to the river below the bridge. Not an inaccurate detail in that note could be discovered."

Most of the militiamen facing Gordon were levies raised in the counties of Schuylkill, Northampton, and Berks; and they had been mustered into the service at Harrisburg only nine days earlier. They had lost one youth who probably would have made an excellent soldier. As explained by a writer for the *Miners' Journal* of Pottsville, Schuylkill County: "A young Irishman, who had joined one of the companies from Ashland, was seized by his father at [the train station] and dragged from the cars, when he was also seized by his mother. He rescued himself and they seized him again, when he struck his father a blow and attempted to get off again; but, while struggling, the cars departed." The few experienced soldiers at Wrightsville were convalescents of earlier battles, some wearing bandages over unhealed wounds, and more than one suffering the additional handicap of an arm in a sling.

The officer in charge of defending the bridge was Colonel Jacob B. Frick, who relates: "The main body of the enemy . . . composed of cavalry, artillery, and infantry, took up their position about 6 o'clock P.M. on the turnpike in our immediate front and within three-quarters of a mile of our rifle pits. A force of cavalry and infantry moved down the railroad on our left and attacked our skirmishers, who, after replying to their fire for a short time, retired to the main body, which kept up a steady fire and held the enemy in check until they received orders to retire to the bridge. The rebels succeeded in getting a battery in position on the elevated ground on our right, and a section in our immediate front. These guns were used most vigorously against those of my command occupying the rifle pits. In the meantime, they sent a column of infantry, under cover of a high hill on our right, within a few hundred yards of the river.

"None but their skirmishers approached within range of the guns of the men occupying the rifle pits, and these [Confederates] being in a grain field, and obscured from our view except when they would rise to fire, it was difficult to do them much harm or dislodge them. They depended exclusively upon their artillery to drive us from our position here. Having no artillery ourselves on that side of the river with which to reply, and after retaining our position for about 1¼ hours, and discovering that our remaining longer would enable the enemy to reach the river on both of my flanks, which I was unable to prevent because of the small number of men under my command, and thus get possession of the bridge, cut off our retreat and secure a crossing of the Susquehanna, which I was instructed to prevent, I retired in good order and crossed the bridge. . . .

"[Even] before the enemy had left York for the river here, I made, as I supposed, every necessary arrangement to blow up one span. . . . When they got within sight, the gentlemen charged with the execution of that work repaired promptly to the bridge and commenced sawing off the arches and heavy timbers, preparatory to blowing it up with powder, which they had arranged for that purpose. After an abundance of time was allowed, and after, I supposed, every man of my command was over the river, and when the enemy had entered [Wrightsville] with his artillery and reached the barricade at the bridge head, I gave the order to light the fuse. The explosion took place, but our object in blowing up the bridge failed. It was then that I felt it to be my duty, in order to prevent the enemy from crossing the river . . . to order the bridge to be set on fire."

The sight of the flames was a frustration to the victorious John Gordon, who had planned to cross the bridge and press toward Lancaster. "With great energy my men labored to save the bridge. I called on the citizens of Wrightsville for buckets and pails, but none were to be found. There was, however, no lack of buckets and pails a little later, when the town was on fire. The bridge might burn, for that incommoded, at the time, only the impatient Confederates, and these Pennsylvanians were not in sympathy with my expedition, nor anxious to facilitate the movement of such unwelcome visitors. But when the burning bridge fired the lumber yards on the river's banks, and the burning lumber fired the town, buckets and tubs and pails and pans innumerable came from their hiding places, until it seemed that, had the whole of Lee's army been present, I could have armed them with these implements to fight the rapidly spreading flames. My men labored as earnestly and bravely to save the town as they did to save the bridge. In the absence of fire engines or other appliances, the only chance to arrest the progress of the flames was to form my men around the burning district, with the flank resting on the river's edge, and pass rapidly from hand to hand the pails of water. Thus, and thus only, was the advancing, raging fire met, and at a late hour of the night checked and conquered.

"There was one point especially at which my soldiers combated the fire's progress with immense energy, and with great difficulty saved an attractive home from burning. It chanced to be the home of one of the most superb women it was my fortune to meet during the four years of war. She was Mrs. L. L. Rewalt. . . . She had witnessed the furious combat with the flames around her home, and was unwilling that those men should depart without receiving some token of appreciation from her. She was not wealthy, and could not entertain my whole command, but she was blessed with an abundance of those far nobler riches of brain and heart which are the essential glories of exalted womanhood. Accompanied by an attendant, and at a late hour of the night, she sought me, in the confusion which followed the destructive fire, to express her gratitude to the soldiers of my command and to inquire how long we would remain in Wrightsville. On learning that the village would be relieved of our presence at an early hour the following morning, she insisted that I should bring with me to breakfast at her house as many as could find places in her dining room. She would take no excuse, not even the nervous condition in which the excitement of the previous hours had left her.

"At a bountifully supplied table in the early morning sat this modest, cultured woman, surrounded by soldiers in their worn, gray uniforms. The welcome she gave us was so gracious, she was so self-possessed, so calm and kind, that I found myself in an inquiring state of mind as to whether her sympathies were with the Northern or Southern side in the pending war. Cautiously, but with sufficient clearness to indicate to her my object, I ventured some remarks which she could not well ignore and which she instantly saw were intended to evoke some declaration on the subject. She was too brave to evade it, too self-poised to be confused by it, and too firmly fixed in her convictions to hesitate as to the answer.

"With no one present except Confederate soldiers who were her guests, she replied, without a quiver in her voice, but with womanly

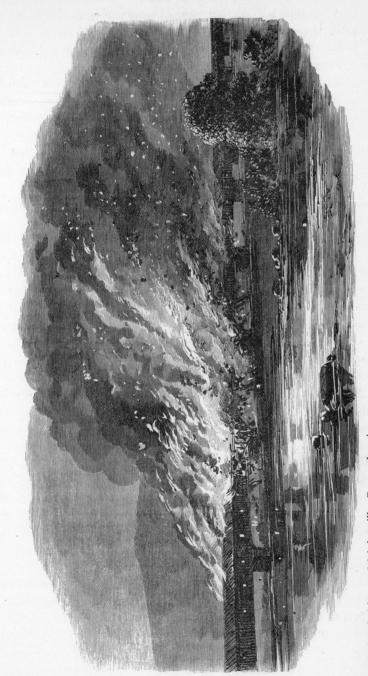

Blazing bridge at Wrightsville, Pennsylvania

gentleness, 'General Gordon, I fully comprehend you, and it is due to myself that I candidly tell you that I am a Union woman. I cannot afford to be misunderstood, nor to have you misinterpret this simple courtesy. You and your soldiers last night saved my home from burning, and I was unwilling that you should go away without receiving some token of my appreciation. I must tell you, however, that, with my assent and approval, my husband is a soldier in the Union army, and my constant prayer to Heaven is that our cause may triumph and the Union be saved.'

"No Confederate left that room without a feeling of profound respect, of unqualified admiration, for that brave and worthy woman."

An unhappy postscript to the foregoing story is that the Northern press, far from crediting John Gordon and his men with checking the Wrightsville fire, reported that they had set it.

As for the wing of the march that Ewell was leading, it had reached Carlisle on Saturday and had occupied itself with making requisitions. Numbers of the men were left in a state of idleness. "As we lay in camp . . . and I saw we were not going to march," says Private John Casler, "I told Charlie Cross of the 10th Louisiana, a messmate of mine, that we would go out to some farmhouse and get a good dinner and some cherries. We went about one mile, when we came to a large farmhouse. A picket was posted there [as protection for the country people], and they would not let us go any farther. We then went into the house and found the family were Dutch; an old man, his wife and daughter. We asked if we could have some cherries. He said that we could have all we wanted, except from two trees that stood near the house; that he wanted them for their own use.

"When we examined the other trees we found very few cherries, as the soldiers had stripped them. We then got up in the trees the old man had reserved and ate what we wanted and broke off several limbs, and went to the house and sat down on the porch where the old folks were, and asked them if they would not have some cherries, but they declined. We then asked them if we could get dinner. They said no, the soldiers had eaten all they had.

"While sitting there conversing with the old people, we heard a terrible racket around in the back yard, and did not know what to make of it. The old woman jumped up and ran around the house, and soon came back with both hands up. By the expression on her face we knew something terrible had happened. She kept on talking Dutch all the time. So we all ran around to see what was the cause. We found one of the horses had fallen into the cistern, and there lay doubled up, all in a mass, at the bottom.

"The old man then explained that he had run all his horses off to the mountains when he heard the Rebels were coming, except this one, which was an old family mare that they prized very highly for the good service she had done them, and as she was getting old he thought the Rebels would not take her. He had turned her loose in the yard so he could watch her, but as there had been no horse in the yard for years, and the old cistern was not used anymore and had no water in it, it was only covered with some loose planks. The old mare had stepped on them, when they broke and precipitated her to the bottom.

"The cistern was very wide, and about twelve feet deep. We felt sorry for the old folks, as they appeared so distressed about the fate of the old mare. They would doubtless rather have lost their best horse than to lose her. Cross, who had been an old sailor, soon climbed down the wall to see what could be done. He found her doubled up considerably, but still alive, and asked the old man if he had any stout rope. He replied that he had a block and tackle out at the barn. We told him to go and get it, and to tell two of the soldiers at the picket post to come and help. He went to the barn and got the rope. He also found some other soldiers there, stealing eggs, and got them to come along.

"We then got ropes around the old mare, and fastened one end around a tree nearby, and commenced hauling away, and as we would raise her we would dig down the bank and fill up under her, and in this way finally got her out. . . . We rubbed and worked with her some time, until she stood up and commenced eating grass.

"The old folks were very much rejoiced. When we all went around to the porch, the old man took me to one side and told me and Cross to remain awhile and they would have something to eat. The pickets went back to their posts and the others went off, and then we were invited in to dinner. We sat down to the best meal we had had in many a day.

"We parted good friends, leaving the impression that the Rebels were not such a detestable set as he had been led to believe."

10

To the Center of the Web

When the sun went down on Sunday, June 28, General Lee, then headquartered at Chambersburg with Longstreet and Hill, was still unaware that the Federals were hard upon his inside track. The troops with Lee had done little that day except to lie in camp. Lieutenant William Owen of the Washington Artillery, Longstreet's corps, found himself bored. "In the evening, rode over to General Lee's headquarters on the Gettysburg Road. The general has little of the pomp and circumstance of war about his person. A Confederate flag marks the whereabouts of his headquarters, which are here in a little enclosure of some couple of acres of timber. There are about half a dozen tents and as many baggage wagons and ambulances. The horses and mules for these, besides those of a small—very small—escort, are tied up to trees or grazing about the place. The general has a private carriage, or ambulance as it is called, of his own; but he never uses it. It formerly belonged to the Federal General [John] Pope. [Lee] was evidently annoyed at the absence of Stuart and the cavalry, and asked several officers, myself among the number, if we knew anything of the whereabouts of Stuart. The eyes and ears of the army are evidently missing and are greatly needed by the commander."

This had been a busy day for the sidetracked Stuart. He had crossed the Potomac under a bright moon the previous night and at dawn started for Rockville, which was guarded by only a handful of Federals from the Washington defenses. "It was not long," relates staff officer John Esten Cooke, "before we came on the blue people. 'Bang! Bang! Bang!' indicated that the advance guard was charging a picket. The shots ended. We pushed on, passing some dead or wounded forms bleeding by the grassy roadside; and the town of Rockville came in sight. The present writer pushed on after the advance guard . . . and, riding *solus* along a handsome street, came suddenly upon a spectacle which was truly pleasing. This was a seminary for young ladies . . . and doors and windows were full and running over with the fairest specimens of the gentler sex that eye ever beheld.

"It was Sunday, and the beautiful girls in their fresh gaily colored dresses, low necks, bare arms, and wildernesses of braids and curls, were 'off duty' for the moment, and burning with enthusiasm to welcome the Southerner; for Rockville, in radical parlance, was a 'vile secesh hole.' Every eye flashed, every voice exclaimed, every rosy lip laughed, every fair hand waved a handkerchief or a sheet of music—smuggled—with crossed Confederate flags upon the cover. . . .

"As the present historian drew near, riding . . . ahead of his commander, a beautiful girl of about sixteen rushed forth from the portico, pirouetting and clapping her hands in an ecstasy at the sight of the gray uniform, exclaiming, 'Oh! Here is one of General Stuart's aides!' and finished by pulling some hair from the mane of my calm and philosophic old war-horse, on the expressly stated ground that he was a 'Secession horse!' Then General Stuart approached with his column—gay, laughing, his blue eyes, under the black feather, full of the joy of the soldier; and a wild welcome greeted him. . . .

"Stuart did not tarry. In war there is little time for gallant words, and news had just reached us from the front which moved the column on like the sound of a bugle. This news was that while we approached Rockville from the south a mighty train of nearly two hundred wagons— new, fresh-painted, drawn each by six sleek mules, as became the 'Reserve Forage Train' of the Department at Washington—had . . . approached from the east, intent on collecting forage. The rumor of the dread vicinity of the graybacks had come to them, however, blown on the wind; the column of wagons had instantly counter-marched in the opposite direction; they were now thundering at full gallop back toward Washington, pursued by the advance guard.

"Stuart's face flushed at the thought of capturing this splendid prize; and, shouting to a squadron to follow him . . . he went at a swift gallop on the track of the fleeing wagons. Soon we came up with them; and then commenced an indescribably grotesque scene. The immense train was seen covering the road for miles. Every team in full gallop, every wagon whirling onward, rebounding from rocks and darting into the air—one crashing against another 'with the noise of thunder'—here one overturned and lying with wheels upward, the mules struggling and kicking in the harness; then one toppling over a steep bank and falling with a loud crash; others burning, others still dashing for shelter to the woods—the drivers cursing, yelling, lashing, blaspheming, howling amid the bang of carbines, the clatter of hoofs, and cries of 'Halt! Halt! Halt!'

"Stuart burst into laughter, and, turning round, exclaimed, 'Did you ever see anything like that in all your life!' And I certainly never had. The grotesque ruled; the mules seemed wilder than the drivers. They had been cut by the score from the overturned wagons, and now ran in every direction, kicking up at every step, sending their shrill cries upon the air, and presenting a spectacle so ludicrous that a huge burst of 'Olympian laughter' echoed from end to end of the turnpike.

"Soon [the wagons] were all stopped, captured, and driven to the rear by the aforesaid cursing drivers, now sullen, or laughing like the captors. All but those overturned. These were set on fire, and soon there rose for miles along the road the red glare of flames and the dense smoke of the burning vehicles. They had been pursued within sight of Washington, and I saw, I believe, the dome of the capitol. That spectacle was exciting—and General Stuart thought of pushing on to make a demonstration against the defenses. This, however, was given up; and between the flames of the burning wagons we pushed back to Rockville, through which the long line of captured vehicles . . . had already defiled amid the shouts of the inhabitants. Those thus 'saved' were about one hundred in number."

This frolicsome cavalry feat, although impressive in itself, did nothing to enhance Stuart's value to Lee's campaign. On the contrary, as the troopers continued northward, the captured wagons retarded their pace. Fortunately for Lee, it was during the very night of this event-filled Sunday, June 28, that he received information about the Federals from an unexpected source. James Longstreet explains: "While at Culpeper [in early June] I sent a trusty scout . . . with instructions to go into the Federal lines, discover [Hooker's] policy, and bring me all the information he could possibly pick up. When this scout asked me very significantly where he should report, I replied, 'Find me wherever I am when you have the desired information.' I did this because I feared to trust him with a knowledge of our future movements. I supplied him with all the gold he needed, and instructed him to spare neither pains nor money to obtain full and accurate information. . . .

"At about ten o'clock [P.M. on June 28], Colonel [G. M.] Sorrel, my chief of staff, was waked by an orderly who reported that a suspicious person had just been arrested by the provost marshal. Upon investigation, Sorrel discovered that the suspicious person was the scout . . . that I had sent out at Culpeper. He was dirt-stained, travel-worn, and very much broken down. After questioning him sufficiently to find that he brought very important information, Colonel Sorrel brought him to my headquarters and awoke me. He gave the information that the enemy had crossed the Potomac . . . and . . . was at Frederick City, on our right. I felt that this information was exceedingly important and might involve a change in the direction of our march. General Lee had already issued orders that we were to advance toward Harrisburg. I at once sent the scout to General Lee's headquarters."

Soon convinced of the scout's reliability, Lee realized that his army, spread over a northerly arc extending for more than seventy miles, was in mortal danger. He must concentrate, and quickly. It was at this moment that Gettysburg assumed military importance, for it was the midpoint of a spiderweb of roads and a convenient place to assemble. Chambersburg, which lay west of South Mountain (an extension of the Blue Ridge), was, as mentioned earlier, about twenty-five miles northwest of the town. Carlisle was a like distance to the north, Wrightsville some forty miles to the northeast. Lee had Hill and Longstreet in hand in the Chambersburg area, but a party of horsemen had to be sent galloping through the night toward Ewell; his two columns must fall back at once.

A good summary of the Confederate point of view at this time is provided by a junior officer in Hill's corps, J.F.J. Caldwell of the 1st Regiment South Carolina Volunteers. "So far . . . the campaign had been one of maneuvers. . . . The army was rather scattered, but our experience of war taught us that a great blow was to be stricken by Federal or Confederate before the revolution of many suns. . . . [Our own] numbers were not so imposing, for the effective force of infantry did not exceed 60,000 men. But we were veterans—thoroughly experienced in all that relates to the march or the battlefield, sufficiently drilled to perform any maneuver at all likely to be demanded, sufficiently disciplined to obey orders promptly and with energy, yet preserving enough of the proud individuality of Southern men to feel the cause our own, and therefore to be willing to encounter the greatest amount of personal danger and moral responsibility. The world probably never saw all the advantages of the volunteer and the regular systems so admirably combined.

"In addition to this, we were in excellent health, and more properly equipped than at any period prior. . . . It is undoubtedly the moral force which enables a man to engage or to endure peril, but it is equally true that the physical condition has an incalculable influence on the spiritual system.

"A last and vastly important element in the army was the confidence of the troops in the valor of their comrades and the skill of their officers. The victories of 1862 and the great Battle of Chancellorsville this year had led us to believe scarcely anything impossible to Lee's army; and the management of our generals, which had wrung even from the North the highest encomiums, gave us assurance that every particle of our strength and courage would be most judiciously and powerfully applied. Lee, in himself, was a tower of strength. . . . He had ruined every Northern general sent against him, not merely with the South and with Europe, but in the eyes of their own people. . . . He now appeared to be invincible, immovable."

As for the attitude of Meade's troops at this critical time, perhaps no one entertained a more objective view of the situation than Captain Samuel Fiske, who, at the close of a long day in the saddle, took the time to expound in a letter: "Our marches . . . have been through the most lovely country, across the State of Maryland to the east of Frederick City. . . . It is a cruel thing to roll the terrible wave of war over such a scene of peace, plenty, and fruitfulness; but it may be that here on our own soil, and in these [latest] sacrifices and efforts, the great struggle for the salvation of our country and our Union may successfully terminate. Poor old Virginia is so bare and desolate as to be only fit for a battleground; but it seems that we must take our turn too, in the Northern States, of invasion, and learn something of the practical meaning of war in our own peaceful communities.

"I sincerely hope that the scare up in Pennsylvania isn't going to drive all the people's wits away and prevent them from making a brave defense of homes, altars, and hearths. When I read in a paper today of the chief burgess of York pushing out eight or ten miles into the country to find somebody to surrender the city to, I own to have entertained some doubts as to the worthiness and valor of that representative of the dignity of the city. It would be well for the citizens of Pennsylvania to remember that Lee's soldiers are only men, after all, and that their number is not absolutely limitless. . . .

"It is the very best time in the world now for everybody to keep cool and use a little common sense. . . . The simple truth is that the enemy cannot . . . carry into Pennsylvania anything like the number of forces we can bring to meet him; and it is only the circumstance of our being frightened to death at the audacity of his movement that can save him from repenting most ruefully . . . his crossing the Potomac. . . .

"We of the unfortunate 'Grand Army,' to be sure, haven't much reason to make large promises; but we are going to put ourselves again in the way of the Butternuts, and have great hopes of retrieving, on our own ground, our ill fortune in the last two engagements, and, by another and still more successful Antietam conflict, deserve well of our country.

"Our troops are making tremendous marches . . . and, if the enemy is anywhere, we shall be likely to find him and feel of him pretty soon. For sixteen days we have been on the move, and endure the fatigues of the march well. There is much less straggling and much less pillaging than in any march of the troops that I have yet accompanied. Our men are now veterans, and acquainted with the ways and resources of campaigning. There are very few sick among us. The efficient strength, in proportion to our numbers, is vastly greater than when we were green volunteers. So the Potomac Army, reduced greatly in numbers as it has been by the expiration of the term of service of so many regiments, is still a very numerous and formidable army."

General Meade spent the morning of Monday, June 29, expediting the movement of his various columns, arranging for the abandonment of Harpers Ferry and the employment of its garrison in the campaign, and consulting with his cavalry chief. Pleasonton relates: "General Meade . . . in strong terms deprecated the change in commanders with a battle so near at hand, acknowledged his ignorance with regard to the army in general, and said he would be obliged to depend a great deal upon me to assist him. Our relations were of the most cordial and friendly character. . . . While the general and myself were in conversation in reference to the campaign a . . . dispatch was brought him stating that Stuart, with his cavalry, were making a raid near Washington City [actually at Sykesville, Maryland, some thirty miles north of the capital], and had cut the wires, so that we had no telegraphic communication. I laughed at this news and said Stuart has served us better than he is aware of; we shall now have no instructions from the [War Department] until we have a battle.

"General Meade, however, took the matter very seriously; thought I should take all the cavalry and capture Stuart; that the Government would expect him to do so. I assured him that Lee was of more importance to us than Stuart; the latter was in a false position and useless to Lee, and that it was a maxim in war never to interfere with the enemy when he was making a false move. That Stuart could only rejoin Lee by [turning back and] recrossing the Potomac, which would occupy so much time as to prevent his being in the next battle; or he must pass round to the north of our army, in which event I should have the cavalry so placed that he would not be able to escape us. General Meade then decided to leave the affair with me."

Meade was hoping to establish his battle front along the line of Pipe Creek, Maryland, a few miles south of the Pennsylvania border, a position from which he could cover both Washington and Baltimore. At the same time, however, the general—drawn by the same spiderweb of roads as Lee—sent about a third of his army pushing toward Gettysburg, his purpose to ascertain the enemy's whereabouts and establish contact. The massive probe was led by John Buford's division of cavalry, which soon left the infantry miles behind.

During the afternoon of the twenty-ninth, while Buford was moving toward Gettysburg from the south, Ewell's columns were turning back from the Susquehanna. In John Gordon's words: "When . . . my command—which penetrated farther, I believe, than any other Confederate infantry into the heart of Pennsylvania—was recalled . . . I expressed to my staff the opinion that if the battle should be fought at Gettysburg, the army which held the heights would probably be the victor. The insignificant encounter I had had [with the Pennsylvania militiamen] on those hills impressed their commanding importance upon me as nothing else could have done."

A sidelight of the opening hours of Ewell's march is given by Private John Casler: "We met [some of] the paroled prisoners that Early had captured. . . . General [Edward] Johnson made them pull off their shoes and give them to his men who were barefooted. Some of our men thought it was cruel, but Johnson said they were going home and could get other shoes quicker than he could, as he had work for his men to do."

On that same day, Confederate General A. P. Hill began approaching Gettysburg from the west. Hill's leading division, that of Major General Henry Heth, drew up at Cashtown, only eight miles away. The next morning Heth, unaware that Buford was in the vicinity, ordered Brigadier General James J. Pettigrew to take his troops into Gettysburg and make a search for supplies, shoes in particular.

By this time the oft-alarmed citizens had been seized by the feeling that events of the utmost gravity were about to break upon them. As recalled by Henry E. Jacobs (son of Professor Michael Jacobs), then an eighteen-year-old student: "Our garret window afforded a clear view of the Chambersburg Road leading up to the Blue Ridge, eight miles away. I went up to the garret, taking with me the small telescope which was used in the astronomical department of the college, a powerful glass. I could see on the top of the hill west of the town a considerable force of Confederates who had come down from the mountains. On the summit stood a group of officers, sweeping the horizon with their fieldglasses. Back of them, but largely hidden by the shoulder of the hill, my glass enabled me to distinguish men both of infantry and artillery commands. Suddenly the officers on the crest of the hill turned and rode back, and almost on the heels of the retreat a roar of shouting arose from the streets below me. I hurried downstairs and saw General John Buford's cavalry division . . . riding into Gettysburg from the Taneytown Road, on the south. . . . His arrival had ended the facile control of the territory by the Confederates."

Tillie Pierce says that Buford's troopers "passed northwardly along Washington Street, turned toward the west on reaching Chambersburg Street, and passed out in the direction of the Theological Seminary. It was to me a novel and grand sight. I had never seen so many soldiers at one time. . . . I then knew we had protection, and I felt they were our dearest friends. . . . A crowd of 'us girls' were standing on the corner of Washington and High Streets as these soldiers passed by. Desiring to encourage them, who, as we were told, would before long be in battle, my sister started to sing the old war song 'Our Union Forever.' As some of us did not know the whole of the piece we kept repeating the chorus. Thus we sought to cheer our brave men; and we felt amply repaid when we saw that our efforts were appreciated. Their countenances brightened, and we received their thanks and cheers."

Simultaneously with Buford's entry into Gettysburg, something of comparable note was occurring a dozen miles to the east. Union cavalry leader Judson Kilpatrick, now a division commander (seconded by two newly appointed brigadiers: tall, spare Elon J. Farnsworth and a weak-browed but fiercely aggressive twenty-three-year-old named George Armstrong Custer), was in that eastern region helping to cover the right flank of Meade's advance.

As reported by E. A. Paul, a newsman who rode with the flanking troopers: "At about midday, General Kilpatrick, with his command, was passing through Hanover . . . and when the rear of General Farnsworth's brigade had arrived at the easterly end of the place . . . General Stuart made a simultaneous attack upon his rear and right flank. The attack was entirely a surprise, as no enemy had been reported in the vicinity;

George A. Custer

and under any ordinary general, or less brave troops, so sudden and impetuous was the first charge [that] the whole command would have been thrown into the wildest confusion. . . . The force was in the hands of a master. Speedily making his dispositions, [Farnsworth] hurled upon the insolent and advancing enemy the 5th New York Cavalry. . . .

"For some time the contest hung in the balance, but General Custer's brigade [joined in, and] after a severe struggle . . . the enemy was forced to retire. . . . The women in Hanover . . . cared for the wounded—even taking them from the streets while bullets were flying around promiscuously. . . . A little boy named Smith, twelve years of age . . . bugler in the 1st Maine Cavalry, was active in the fight, and had a horse killed under him."

Satisfied with his victory, Kilpatrick broke off contact; and Stuart, unaware of what was happening at Gettysburg, so close to his left flank, resumed his journey northward. His original orders called for him to locate and join Ewell and Early, and he had heard during his march that these two commanders had pressed to the Susquehanna—and he had not heard that they had turned back. And so, while everyone else in both armies was gravitating toward Gettysburg, Stuart left that area and headed toward the Susquehanna.

Returning to the day's affairs at Gettysburg and to narrator Henry Jacobs: "That Tuesday afternoon I took the telescope to the Lutheran Theological Seminary on Seminary Hill, west of the town, and went up to the observatory, where the whole horizon could be brought into view. I began a careful examination of the mountains to the west, where the Blue Ridge describes a semicircle. Wherever the mountainsides held clearings, smoke curled upward. About the fires I could see men walking, attending to camp chores, cooking—all the activities of an army held in leash. They showed as clearly as though they were not more than a couple of hundred yards away. And below me, within easy eyeshot, were both of Buford's Federal brigades. The tide of war was, for the hour, halted under my very eyes."

A similar experience is described by Lydia Catherine Ziegler, who was then a young girl living in the seminary, where her father held the post of steward: "That night . . . I stood in the Seminary cupola and saw, as in panoramic view, the campfires of the enemy all along the Blue Mountainside, only eight miles distant, while below us we beheld our little town . . . surrounded by . . . [the] campfires of the Union [cavalry]. As we stood on that height and watched the soldiers on the eve of battle, our hearts were made heavy. Many of the soldiers were engaged in letter writing, perhaps writing the last loving missives their hands would ever pen to dear ones at home. In the near distance we could see a large circle of men engaged in prayer, and, as the breezes came our way, we could hear the petitions which ascended to the Father in Heaven for His protecting care on the morrow. However, many of the boys seemed to be utterly oblivious to the dangers threatening them, and were singing with hearty good will 'The Star Spangled Banner' and many of the other patriotic songs which we loved to hear."

John Buford had established his main lines just west of the town. His pickets and those of Hill's advance were four miles apart on the Chambersburg Turnpike. Buford also stationed pickets to the north and northeast of Gettysburg to watch for the arrival of Ewell's columns. As for the Union infantry, two corps were en route to the scene. The 1st, that of Major General John F. Reynolds, was about five miles to the southwest, while the 11th, under Major General Oliver O. Howard, was an additional five in the same direction. General Meade, now headquartered at Taneytown, Maryland, had placed Reynolds in top command of the probe.

That night John Buford, whose strength did not exceed 5,000 men, remarked to one of his brigade commanders: "The enemy will attack us in the morning, and we shall have to fight like devils to maintain ourselves until the arrival of the infantry."

11

Collision at Willoughby Run

THE FIGHT FORESEEN by Buford was not of Lee's choosing. As explained by Henry Heth, commander of A. P. Hill's advance division: "It was a great misfortune to us . . . not to have the benefit of the cavalry service. . . . I attach no blame to Stuart, for he went with the full consent of Lee—it was one of the fates of war. If Lee had had his cavalry with him, he would have known the movements of his adversary, and if he had been compelled to meet him at Gettysburg he could have concentrated his army there two days before and held the choice of positions. As it was, we stumbled in there. . . . Lee wanted to fight the battle at Cashtown, with the mountain at his back, so his flanks would be well protected. There he could have whipped any army in the world. But . . . as yet he knew nothing of the movements of the enemy [from Frederick], but he well knew that great efforts were being made to bring on a battle, and that it must take place soon. . . .

"So far as the Battle of Gettysburg is concerned, that battle was fought by my going there after shoes for my division. On the 30th of June . . . Pettigrew . . . [had] returned without securing any shoes. When he made his report to me . . . I said to him there was no considerable force there. Just then Hill came up and I said to Pettigrew . . . repeat to the general what you said to me. After it was stated again by Pettigrew, Hill and myself both said there were no troops there of any moment. I turned to Hill and said, 'I will take my division and go down there and get the shoes myself,' which was assented to by him."

Says South Carolinian J.F.J. Caldwell, who was in Hill's corps: "Soon after daylight on Wednesday, July 1, we were roused by an order to fall in. We rolled up our blankets and flies in haste—knapsacks had been pretty generally dispensed with before this—and formed. The march was begun at once, down the turnpike towards Gettysburg."

In the threatened town, according to Tillie Pierce, most citizens arose early. "It was impossible to [remain] drowsy with the events of the previous day uppermost in our minds. We were prompt enough at breakfast that morning." Lydia Ziegler adds that "the sun shone in all its splendor. . . . All nature seemed to be offering praise to God for His manifold blessings. . . . But a spirit of unrest seemed to prevail everywhere." Many people, however, turned to their normal weekday activities. Eighteen-year-old Anna Garlach picked a panful of green beans from her family's backyard garden and sat in the early sunlight stringing them for her mother, who planned to cook them with a piece of ham. Other women busied themselves with the baking of bread. Professor Jacobs went off to Pennsylvania College to begin teaching his usual eight o'clock class. As for those citizens who were too fearful or too stimulated to deal in normalcy, numbers gathered in the streets and exchanged animated speculations. Some tried to secure a better knowledge of the situation by talking with Union troopers not yet in forward positions.

More than a few people strayed from home to make a personal investigation of developments. This element included both thirteen-year-old Billy Bayly and his mother, Mrs. Joseph Bayly, who, it will be recalled, lived three miles northwest of town. The two were drawn in different directions. Mrs. Bayly begins the story: "I . . . went to a point on the farm from which the mountains [to the west] for many miles are visible, and which also overlooks the valley in which the town lies. I found several of the neighbors, who were as anxious as I to see what was going on, at a blacksmith shop near this point. Everything, however, was quiet and not a soldier in sight. In fact, the stillness was oppressive, and this at a time of day when ordinarily the sounds from the farmyards are the loudest.

"My husband had gone early in the morning to a neighbor's on business. My oldest boy [Billy] had gone to town with some of the neighboring boys. . . . I was thinking of going back to the house when Uncle Robert said to me, 'Suppose we walk out the road a little ways and see if we can find out what is going on.' I said, 'All right,' and we started out the ridge road towards the Chambersburg pike. After walking about a mile we came to a number of mounted pickets standing by the roadside. They seemed to be worn out and their horses looked tired and dusty. . . . One of them told us that they were anticipating an attack at any time."

It was now nearly 9 A.M. Billy Bayly was no longer in Gettysburg but had wandered out into the area in which his mother walked. Neither, however, was aware of the other's presence. Billy and two chums had found a raspberry patch. "In the absorbing interest of filling our stomachs . . . [we] forgot all about war and rumors of war for the time being, until startled by the discharge of a cannon [a Union weapon firing on an advance party of Confederates], the sharp impact of which made us jump. . . . This was . . . followed by a . . . succession of discharges [as an artillery duel resulted], and we three boys broke for the open and back to the blacksmith's shop. But to me as a boy it was glorious! Here were my aspirations for months being gratified. . . .

"Realizing that the cannon balls were not coming in our direction, and that to run down the hill to my home would simply mean getting under cover where I could not see the battle . . . we perched ourselves on the topmost rail of the road fence and drank in the melody of the battle [as yet confined to cannon exchanges and low-key musketry between the advancing Confederate skirmishers and the retiring Union pickets]. But our gallery seats, although good for the whole show, began to have features of discomfort when we noticed up the road, coming over the nearest hill, great masses of [Confederate] troops and clouds of dust; how the first wave swelled into successive waves, gray masses with the glint of steel as the sun struck the gun barrels, filling the highway, spreading out into the fields, and still coming on and on, wave after wave, billow after billow. We waited not until we could 'see the whites of their eyes' but until there were but a few hundred yards between us and the advancing column, and then we departed for home."

Billy's mother and "Uncle Robert," farther forward than Billy and his chums when the shooting began, had run into trouble. The Union pickets had deserted them to gallop rearward, and their own retreat was soon cut off by a band of Confederate horsemen. "My companion," says Mrs. Bayly, "was halted and put under arrest. He said to me, 'You hurry home as fast as possible. I am old, and they won't keep me long.' The cavalrymen parted, and I passed on between them. Occasionally someone would say, 'Madam, where are the Yankees?' or 'How many Yankees are there out there?' To which I replied as I hurried along, 'Go on, and you will soon find out; I did not stop to count them.' An officer said to me, 'Madam, you are in a very dangerous position,' a statement which I did not dispute. . . . At [the blacksmith's shop] I left the public road, taking a shortcut across the fields. . . . I was halted and told that I was a prisoner before I got home, but it was only a few minutes until my guard

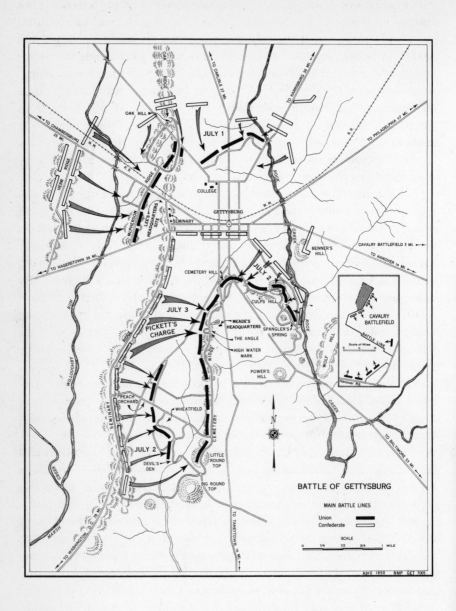

Battle of Gettysburg

was ordered to release me and I hurried home, where I found everything in confusion."

Billy was devoutly thankful for his mother's safe return, for the battle had now been joined. "The soldiers whom I had seen marching down the road went into action immediately south of us, between our home and the town." The opposing lines faced each other across Willoughby Run, a modest north-south waterway about a mile west of the populous area. Buford's outnumbered troopers met the attack staunchly, at first even aggressively.

No one was in a better position to observe the battle's opening moments than teen-aged Amelia E. Harmon. "We were living . . . in the big colonial mansion known as 'The Old McLean Place,' situated on the highest point of the bluff overlooking Willoughby Run [just west of the stream]. We had decided to remain in the house . . . although most of our neighbors had abandoned their homes, for ours was of the old-fashioned fortress type with eighteen-inch walls and heavy wooden shutters. My aunt and I . . . were quite alone, our farmer having gone away with the horses in the hope of hiding them in the fastness of the hills."

Startled by the cannon fire, the two females "rushed to the window, to behold hundreds of galloping horses coming up the road [from Willoughby Run, which they had crossed from the Union side], through the field, and even past our very door . . . their excited riders shouting and yelling to each other and pushing westward in hot haste, past the house and barn, seeking the shelter of a strip of woods on the ridge beyond. But the ridge was alive with enemy! A few warning shots from its cover sent them flying back to the shelter behind the barn, outbuildings, trees, and even the pump, seeking to hold the enemy in check. . . .

"We were in the very center of the first shock of battle between Hill's troops and the advance line of Buford's cavalry. Horses and men were falling under our eyes by shots from an unseen foe, and the confusion became greater every moment. Filled with alarm and terror, we locked all the doors and rushed to the second floor—and threw open the shutters of the west window. One glance only, and a half-spent minie ball from the woods crashed into the shutter, close to my aunt's ear, leaving but the thickness of paper between her and death. This one glance showed us that a large timothy field between the barn and the woods concealed hundreds of gray crouching figures stealthily advancing under its cover, and picking off every cavalryman who appeared for an instant in sight.

"An officer's horse just under the window was shot, and the officer

Buford's cavalry at Willoughby Run

fell to the ground. 'Look!' we shrieked at him, 'the field is full of rebels.' 'Leave the window,' he shouted in return, 'or you will be killed!' We needed no second warning, and rushed to the cupola. Here the whole landscape for miles around unrolled like a panorama below us. What a spectacle! It seemed as though the fields and woods had been sown with dragon's teeth, for everywhere had sprung up armed men where about an hour ago only grass and flowers grew."

In Gettysburg at this time, according to a schoolteacher and housewife named Sarah ("Sallie") Broadhead, who lived in a brick house just west of the center of town: "People were running here and there, screaming that the town would be shelled. No one knew where to go or what to do. My husband advised remaining where we were, but all said we ought not to remain in our exposed position, and that it would be better to go to some part of the town farther away from the scene of the conflict." The first reaction of the military occupants of Gettysburg was to order the people to stay off the streets. Numbers of residents took refuge in their cellars. A contrasting situation was experienced by youthful and vibrant Anna Mary Young, who lived in the northern outskirts, where, at least temporarily, people felt somewhat less threatened. "You could see the housetops covered with ladies, as well as gentlemen, watching the battle. Our family repaired to the attic, and from the windows we could see the movements of our troops."

For the first hour the cavalry forces were Gettysburg's only defenders. John Buford had set himself to a task of greater consequence than he knew. Of course, he must have been at least partially aware of the military importance of the three miles of rises extending southward from the town: Cemetery Hill, Cemetery Ridge, and the two Round Tops. There was Culp's Hill, too, just east of Cemetery Hill. (The configuration of the chain of elevations resembles a fish hook, with the eye at Big Round Top and the barb at Culp's Hill.) It would be well if Lee was kept from seizing this commanding ground. Buford's men, most of whom were fighting in the manner of infantry, were making their stand, pending Reynolds' arrival, at Seminary Ridge, a lesser prominence passing just west of the town on a southerly course roughly a mile from the line of Cemetery Ridge, with a belt of farmlands intervening. The ground in its entirety formed an excellent arena for hosting a major battle, and, whether he knew it or not, Buford was fighting to save the advantage of position for Meade.

The trooper had stationed a signal crew in the cupola of the seminary, which was just behind his lines, their purpose not only to monitor the battle but also to maintain a search southward for the appearance of Reynolds and the 1st Corps. Sometime before 10 A.M. the lookouts perceived a billow of dust on the road from Taneytown, and soon they could distinguish the flag of the 1st Corps rippling in the morning breeze. Buford, summoned to the cupola to observe the grand sight himself, had barely finished climbing the stairs when Reynolds, who had galloped a mile in advance of his column, drew up below and called out, "What's the matter, John?" Buford responded, "The devil's to pay!" Hurrying back down the steps for a conference, the trooper was asked whether he thought he could hold until the infantry began arriving, and he said he thought he could. Fortunately for Buford, Heth was not yet pushing at his full capacity.

The head of Reynolds' hastening column did not enter the town but cut leftward across the fields toward the seminary. Lydia Ziegler and her father were standing in the doorway of their living quarters in the building, the girl watching with wide eyes. "I asked father how the soldiers would cross the high fence surrounding our garden. I did not have to wait long until my curiosity was satisfied, for . . . the fence fell as if it were made of paper as the men pressed against it with crowbars and picks. I always had a desire to see something of a battle, so here was my opportunity. I quietly slipped from the house to the edge of the woods back of the Seminary, and was enjoying the awe-inspiring scene when a bullet flew so near my head that I could hear the whizzing sound it made. That, and a call from a signal officer on the cupola, sent me speeding to the house. There I found that all the family had repaired to the cellar for safety, and well they did, for in a very short time two shells struck the building."

Reynolds' entire force at this time consisted of a single division, that of the aging but vigorous James S. Wadsworth. The division held only two brigades, but one was the "Iron Brigade," famous for its stoutness under fire. Wadsworth's fresh regiments—if they could be called fresh after their forced march under a waxing sun—were thrown across the mile-wide front occupied by Buford's men, and the troopers were permitted to fall back. Reynolds sent word to Meade at Taneytown that Buford had found a place suitable for a definitive battle, and that sharp fighting had already begun. Word was also sent to the rest of the 1st Corps and the other troops of Reynolds' left-wing command to hurry forward. The general assumed that Meade would direct the right wing to Gettysburg and would come there himself. At about 10:15 Reynolds turned his full attention to the action. Fighting on the Union side were

Abner Doubleday

the Iron Brigade and that of Lysander Cutler, while Confederate General Heth, whose division held four brigades, had committed only those of Joseph R. Davis and James J. Archer. In front of the Union left was a patch of woods, part of a farm owned by a man named McPherson, and the woods had become a point of contention.

The moment is depicted by Union General Abner Doubleday, who had begun the war as one of the defenders of Fort Sumter and was now Reynolds' second-in-command: "Both parties were now trying to obtain possession of the woods. Archer's rebel brigade, preceded by a skirmish line, was crossing Willoughby Run to enter them on one side as the Iron Brigade went in on the other. General Reynolds was on horseback in the edge of the woods, surrounded by his staff. He felt some anxiety as to the result, and turned his head frequently to see if our troops would be up in time. While looking back in this way, a rebel sharpshooter shot him through the back of the head, the bullet coming out near the eye. He fell dead in an instant without a word.

"I felt the great loss the country had sustained in his death, and lamented him as almost a lifelong companion, for we were at West Point together, and had served in the same regiment—the old 3rd Artillery— upon first entering service. . . . When quite young we had fought in the same battles in Mexico. I had little time, however, to indulge in these recollections. The situation was very peculiar. The rebel left under Davis had driven in Cutler's brigade, and our left [the Iron Brigade] had charged into the woods . . . swept suddenly and unexpectedly around the right flank of Archer's brigade and captured a large part of it, including Archer himself. The fact is, the enemy were careless and underrated us, thinking . . . that they had only militia to contend with. The Iron Brigade had a different headgear from the rest of the army and were recognized at once by their old antagonists. Some of the latter were heard to exclaim, 'There are those damned black-hatted fellows again! 'Taint no militia. It's the Army of the Potomac.' Having captured Archer and his men, many of the Iron Brigade kept on beyond Willoughby Run and formed on the heights on the opposite side."

As for General Archer, he was mightily chagrined. According to one of Doubleday's aides, Captain Eminel P. Halstead: "A guard brought him back to General Doubleday, who, in a very cordial manner—they having been cadets at West Point together—said, 'Good morning, Archer! How are you? I am glad to see you!' General Archer replied, 'Well, I am not glad to see you, by a damned sight!' "

"The command," Doubleday explains, "now devolved upon me, with

Death of Reynolds as Battle of Gettysburg begins

its great responsibilities. The disaster on the right required immediate attention, for the enemy, with loud yells, were pursuing Cutler's brigade toward the town." One regiment of this brigade, the 147th New York, was engulfed by the savage tide and was badly cut up—207 killed and wounded out of a total of 380—before it managed to extricate itself. Also finding itself in serious trouble was Captain James A. Hall's 2nd Maine Artillery, which had been posted in a forward position. Hall relates: "The right section of the battery . . . was charged upon . . . and four of the horses from one of the guns shot. The men of the section dragged this gun off by hand. As the last piece of the battery was coming away, all its horses were shot, and I was about to return for it myself when General Wadsworth gave me a peremptory order to lose no time but get my battery in position near the town on the heights to cover the retiring of the troops."

In their eagerness to forge ahead, the Confederates exposed their right flank to the reserves on the Union left. The reserve numbers were small, but Doubleday ordered them to hazard an attack. Lieutenant Colonel Rufus R. Dawes led them on, and their approach in itself was enough to bring the pursuit up short. Dawes recounts: "The rebel line swayed and bent, and the men suddenly stopped firing and ran into the railroad cut which is parallel to the Cashtown Turnpike. I now ordered the men to climb over the turnpike fences and advance upon them. I was not aware of the existence of a railroad cut, and mistook the maneuver of the enemy for a retreat, but was soon undeceived by the heavy fire which they began at once to pour upon us from their cover in the cut. Captain John Ticknor, a dashing soldier, one of our finest officers, fell dead while climbing the second fence, and others were struck, but the line pushed on.

"When over the fences and in the field, and subjected to an infernal fire, I saw the 95th New York Regiment coming gallantly into line upon our left. I did not then know or care where they came from, but was rejoiced to see them. Farther to the left was the 14th Brooklyn Regiment, but we were ignorant of the fact. The 95th New York had about 100 men in action. Major Edward Pye appeared to be in command. Running hastily to the major, I said, 'We must charge,' and asked him if they were with us. The gallant major replied, 'Charge it is,' and they were with us to the end. 'Forward, charge!' was the order given by both the major and myself.

"We were now receiving a fearfully destructive fire from the hidden enemy. Men who had been shot were leaving the ranks in crowds. Any

Hall's 2nd Maine Artillery

Union dead on field west of town

correct picture of this charge would represent a V-shaped crowd of men with the colors at the advance point, moving firmly and hurriedly forward, while the whole field behind is streaming with men who had been shot and who are struggling to the rear or sinking in death upon the ground. The only commands I gave as we advanced were 'Align on the colors! Close up on that color! Close up on that color!' The regiment was being broken up so that this order alone could hold the body together. Meanwhile the colors were down upon the ground several times, but were raised at once by the heroes of the color guard. Not one of the guard escaped, every man being killed or wounded.

"Four hundred and twenty men started as a regiment from the turnpike fence, of whom 240 reached the railroad cut. . . . Every officer proved himself brave, true, and heroic in encouraging the men to breast this deadly storm, but the real impetus was the eager, determined valor of the men who carried muskets in the ranks.

"The rebel colors could be seen waving defiantly just above the edge of the railroad cut. A heroic ambition to capture it took possession of several of our men. Corporal Eggleston of Company H, a mere boy, sprang forward to seize it, and was shot dead the moment his hand touched the colors. Private Anderson, of his company, furious at the killing of his brave young comrade, recked little for the rebel colors but he swung aloft his musket and with a terrific blow split the skull of the rebel who had shot young Eggleston. . . . Lieutenant [W. M.] Remington was severely wounded in the shoulder while reaching for the colors. Into this deadly melee rushed Corporal Francis A. Waller, who seized and held the rebel battle flag. . . .

"[Another] incident is so touching in its character that it should be preserved. Corporal James Kelly, of Company B, turned from the ranks and stepped beside me as we both moved hurriedly forward on the charge. He pulled open his woolen shirt, and a mark where the deadly minnie ball had entered his breast was visible. He said, 'Colonel, won't you please write to my folks that I died a soldier?'

"My first notice that we were immediately upon the enemy was a general cry from our men of, 'Throw down your muskets! Down with your muskets!' Running quickly forward through the line of men, I found myself face to face with at least a thousand rebels, whom I looked down upon in the railroad cut, which was here about four feet deep. Adjutant [Edward P.] Brooks, equal to the emergency, had quickly placed men across the cut in position to fire through it. . . .

"I shouted, 'Where is the colonel of this regiment?' An officer in gray with stars on his collar, who stood among the men in the cut, said, 'Who are you?' I said, 'I am commander of this regiment. Surrender, or I will fire on you.' The officer replied not a word, but promptly handed me his sword; and all his men who still held them threw down their muskets. The coolness, self-possession, and discipline which held back our men from pouring in a volley saved a hundred lives. . . .

"The fighting around the rebel colors had not entirely ceased when this surrender was demanded. I took the sword. It would have been the handsome thing to say, 'Keep your sword, sir,' but I was new to such occasions, and when six other officers came up and handed me their swords I took them also, and held the awkward bundle in my arms until relieved by Adjutant Brooks.

"I directed the officer in command, who proved to be Major John A. Blair of the 2nd Mississippi Regiment, to have his men fall in without arms. He gave the command, and his men, to the number of seven officers and 225 enlisted men, obeyed. To our major, John F. Hauser, I assigned the duty of marching this body to the provost guard. Major Hauser, a thorough soldier, had been educated at a military school at Thun, Switzerland, and he had served with Garibaldi. His shout of 'Forwarts! Forwarts!' [had been heard by all] as we charged. . . .

"Corporal Waller now brought me the captured battle flag. It was the flag of the 2nd Mississippi Volunteers, one of the oldest and most distinguished regiments in the Confederate army. It belonged to the brigade commanded by the nephew of Jefferson Davis. It is a rule in battle never to allow sound men to leave the ranks. Sergeant William Evans, a brave and true man, had been severely wounded in the thighs. He had to use two muskets as crutches. To him I intrusted the keeping of the battle flag. Wrapping the flag around his body, he started for Gettysburg. . . . Adjutant Brooks buckled on one of the captured swords, but the other six were given to a wounded man to be delivered to our chief surgeon. . . .

"There was now a lull in the battle. Our comrades of the Iron Brigade, who had . . . routed Archer's brigade, capturing its commander and many of its men . . . [had] changed front to move to the relief of Cutler; but the charge upon the railroad cut, and its success, prevented that necessity. By this charge upon the cut . . . Davis' brigade was captured or scattered. Wadsworth's division had bravely opened the battle. They had fairly defeated, upon an open field, a superior force of the veterans of the army of General Lee. It was a short, sharp, and desperate fight, but the honors were with the boys in blue. . . . Defeat was never more swiftly turned into victory. . . . The 95th New York took prisoners, as did also the 14th Brooklyn. All the troops in the railroad cut threw down their muskets, and the men either surrendered themselves or ran away out of the other end of the cut. . . . At least one thousand muskets lay in the bottom of it."

It was about 11 A.M. when the lull in the action began and the sounds of battle were replaced by those of military music drifting faintly from Gettysburg's town square, where several regimental bands had assembled. The thunderous hour of heavy fighting had in no way diminished the concern of the town's citizens. Sallie Broadhead had gone against her husband's wishes that she remain with him in their home west of the square. "I took my child and went to the house of a friend up town. As we passed up the street we met wounded men coming in from the field. When we saw them we, for the first time, began . . . anxiously to ask, Will our army be whipped? Some said there was no danger of that yet, and pointed to Confederate prisoners who began to be sent through our streets. . . . Such a dirty, filthy set no one ever saw. . . . Some were barefooted, and a few wounded. Though enemies, I pitied them."

The greater number of the town's citizens remained in their homes for the purpose of protecting their property, relying on their cellars to keep them from harm. Many of these people had begun to receive unexpected visitors. In the words of a housewife named Jennie Mc-Creary: "Before we fully realized there was a battle, wounded men were brought into our houses and laid side by side in our halls and first-story rooms. . . . In many cases carpets were so saturated with blood as to be unfit for further use. Walls were bloodstained, as well as books that were used for pillows. The first public building that was opened for hospital purposes was the Lutheran Church on Chambersburg Street, generally known as the College Church. Forty men were laid in the lecture room and 100 in the church proper, beds being improvised by laying boards on top of the pews. Here they were laid, their army blankets, when they had them, between their racked bodies and the boards, and sometimes knapsacks for pillows. . . . Into all the hospitals our women went freely and gladly to help in the care of the wounded, showing kindness alike to all, seeming to forget that any were enemies. . . . One of my neighbors, who is ordinarily a very retiring woman, was perhaps the first to enter a hospital. Seeing the first wounded men carried into the church, she gathered up old linen and such things as she thought would be needed, and went straightway to their relief."

While Union General Doubleday and Confederate General Heth

Confederate prisoners marching under guard

reorganized their frayed lines, fresh regiments could be seen hurrying to the field on both sides. Heth was soon solidly supported by William D. Pender's division. The remaining division of A. P. Hill's corps, however, was still west of Cashtown. Behind this division (that of Richard H. Anderson) marched Longstreet's corps—minus George E. Pickett's division, left at Chambersburg as the army's rear guard. Ewell's columns from the Susquehanna were closing in north of Gettysburg, their participation imminent and no one in their way but elements of Buford's cavalry. Doubleday was joined by the remainder of the 1st Corps, the divisions of John C. Robinson and Thomas A. Rowley. At this time Oliver Howard, commander of the 11th Corps, was personally nearing the field, but his divisions were still some miles to the south. None of the other Union corps was close enough to figure in the first day's fight.

One of the members of Rowley's division was Thomas Chamberlain, a major with the 150th Pennsylvania Infantry, who tells how his regiment, with the men perspiring "in cascades," covered the final mile of its approach: "Below the town the column was diverted from the highway through the fields and urged into a 'double-quick,' which presently brought the mass of our regiment to the neighborhood of the seminary, but left two or three scores of our men stranded along the line of march, to be gathered up and reported for duty a little later by Captain Dougal, himself a sufferer from the excessive heat and overexertion.

"Generals Doubleday and Rowley, with portions of their staffs, met us in the open field some distance west of the seminary, where we were halted and the former addressed us briefly, urging the importance of a victory and reminding us that we were Pennsylvanians and might safely be entrusted with the defense of our own soil. Shells were whizzing overhead at the time from rebel batteries beyond the ridge to the west, and the instructions to our brigade and regimental leaders were necessarily brief. 'Forward!' cried Colonel [Langhorne] Wister, when a dozen voices exclaimed, 'Colonel, we're not loaded yet!' A burst of merriment followed in spite of the fact that we had just learned, with unfeigned sorrow, of the death of General Reynolds, whom all idolized, and who perhaps better than any other officer in the entire army met the limitless requirements of the ideal soldier.

"The loading was ordered, followed by the unslinging of knapsacks, and with full battalion front we moved rapidly westward to the brow of the hill overlooking Willoughby Run. On our immediate left lay the Iron Brigade, occupying the woods, while the 149th and 143rd Pennsylvania on our right extended beyond the McPherson farm buildings to the

Lutheran Church on Chambersburg Street

Chambersburg road or pike. The time of reaching our position was about 11:30 o'clock. . . . Evidences of hard fighting . . . by Wadsworth's division were to be seen in every direction, but, except [for] a fitful cannonading from rebel batteries on the next parallel ridge, looking west, and on the prolongation of our line northwardly, there was, at this hour, comparative quiet."

Major Chamberlain goes on to explain that he happened to be occupying a spot in which he gained first-hand knowledge of how Gettysburg civilian John Burns became a part of the battle. "While we were watching and waiting, our attention was called to a man of rather bony frame . . . who approached from the direction of the town moving with a deliberate step and carrying in his right hand an Enfield rifle at a 'trail.' At any time his figure would have been noticeable, but it was doubly so at such a moment, from his age—which evidently neared three-score and ten—and from the somewhat startling peculiarity of his dress. The latter consisted of dark trousers and waistcoat, a blue 'swallow-tail' coat with burnished brass buttons such as used to be affected by well-to-do gentlemen of the old school about forty years ago, and a high black silk hat, from which most of the original gloss had long departed—of a shape to be found only in the fashion plates of a remote past. The stiff 'stock' which usually formed a part of such a costume was wanting—presumably on account of the heat—and no neck-cloth of any kind relieved the bluish tint of his clean-shaven face and chin.

"As his course brought him opposite the rear of the left wing, he first [came to me] and asked, 'Can I fight with your regiment?' [I] answered affirmatively, but, seeing Colonel Wister approaching, said, 'Here is our colonel; speak to him.' 'Well, old man, what do you want?' bluntly demanded the colonel. 'I want a chance to fight with your regiment.' 'You do? Can you shoot?' 'Oh, yes,' and a smile crept over the old man's face which seemed to say, 'If you knew that you had before you a soldier of the War of 1812 who fought at Lundy's Lane you would not ask such a question.' 'I see you have a gun, but where is your ammunition?' Slapping his hand upon his bulging trousers' pockets, he replied, 'I have it here.' 'Certainly you can fight with us,' said the colonel, 'and I wish there were many more like you.' He advised him, however, to go into the woods to the line of the Iron Brigade, where he would be more sheltered from both sun and bullets, with an equal chance of doing effective work. With apparent reluctance, as if he preferred the open field, he moved towards the woods."

One of the soldiers in the Iron Brigade who noted Burns' approach

George E. Pickett

was Sergeant George Eustice. "We boys began to poke fun at him . . . as we thought no civilian in his senses would show himself in such a place. Finding that he had really come to fight, I wanted to put a cartridge box on him. . . . Slapping his pantaloons pocket, he replied, 'I can get my hands in here quicker than in a box. I'm not used to them new-fangled things.' In answer to the question what possessed him to come out there at such a time, he replied that the rebels had either driven away or milked his cows, and that he was going to be even with them.

"About this time the enemy began to advance. Bullets were flying thicker and faster, and we hugged the ground about as close as we could. Burns got behind a tree and surprised us all. . . . He was as calm and collected as any veteran on the ground. We soon had orders to get up and move about a hundred yards to the right, when we were engaged in one of the most stubborn contests I ever experienced. . . . I never saw John Burns after our movement to the right . . . and only know that he was true-blue and grit to the backbone, and fought until he was three times wounded." (Burns survived and became a national hero.)

12

A Losing Game for the Union

AT THE TIME the action was resumed, Lee was at Cashtown moving eastward with Richard Anderson's division of Hill's corps. Anderson relates: "About twelve o'clock I received a message notifying me that General Lee desired to see me. I found General Lee intently listening to the fire of the guns, and very much disturbed and depressed. At length he said, more to himself than to me, 'I cannot think what has become of Stuart. I ought to have heard from him long before now. He may have met with disaster, but I hope not. [Still unaware of what was happening at Gettysburg, Stuart was then on his way to Carlisle.] In the absence of reports from him, I am in ignorance as to what we have in front of us here. It may be the whole Federal army, or it may be only a detachment. If it is the whole Federal force, we must fight a battle here. . . .' "

Even as Lee spoke, the conflict was verging on a new dimension, for the first units of Ewell's corps, those from Carlisle, were forming north of Gettysburg, at a right angle to Hill's left flank. At the same time, the Federals of Oliver Howard's corps were nearing the town's southern environs. Howard and his second-in-command, Major General Carl Schurz, having ridden well ahead of the corps, had reached the crest of Cemetery Hill. Schurz recounts: "From where we stood we observed the thin lines of [Union] troops and here and there puffy clouds of white smoke on and around Seminary Ridge, and heard the crackle of the musketry and the booming of the cannon. . . . The affair appeared [small] to me, as seen from a distance in the large frame of the surrounding open country. . . . We received a report from General Wadsworth [still in the fore of Doubleday's lines] . . . that he thought that the enemy was making a movement toward his right. From our point of observation we could perceive but little of the strength of the enemy, and Wadsworth's dispatch did not relieve our uncertainty.

"If the enemy before us was only in small force, then we had to push on as far as might seem prudent. But if the enemy was bringing on the whole or a large part of his army, which his movement toward General Wadsworth's right might be held to indicate, then we had to look for a strong position in which to establish and maintain ourselves until rein-forced or ordered back. Such a position was easily found at the first glance. It was Cemetery Hill on which we then stood. . . . Accordingly, General Howard ordered me to take the 1st and 3rd divisions of the 11th Corps through the town, and to place them on the right of the 1st Corps, while he, General Howard, would hold back the 2nd division . . . and the reserve artillery on Cemetery Hill and the eminence east of it [Culp's Hill] as a reserve.

"About half past twelve the head of the column of the 11th Corps arrived. . . . The men, who had marched several miles at a rapid pace, were streaming with perspiration and panting for breath. But they hur-ried through the town as best they could."

They did well indeed, according to H. E. Jacobs, the professor's son: "Past our house [they] came, running at the double-quick. . . . They kept the pace without breaking ranks. . . . They flowed through and out into the battlefield beyond, a human tide, at millrace speed. . . . A roar of cheers began. It rolled forward, faster than the running of the men . . . like some high surge sweeping across the surface of a flowing sea. . . . The running force . . . [was] a splendid vision of high courage and eager hope."

"But," says General Schurz, "the deployment could not be made as originally designed, by simply prolonging the 1st Corps' line; for . . . a strong Confederate force . . . [was] on the right flank of the 1st Corps, so that, to confront it, the 11th had to deploy, under fire, at an angle with the 1st. General [Alexander] Schimmelfennig . . . commanding . . . the 3rd [division], connected with the 1st Corps on his left as well as he could under the circumstances, and General Francis Barlow, commanding our 1st Division . . . deployed on his right. General Barlow [new to the task of division commander] was still a young man, but with his beardless, smooth face looked even younger than he was. His men at first gazed at him, wondering how such a boy could be put at the head of regiments of men. But they soon discovered him to be . . . one of the coolest and bravest in action.

Francis C. Barlow

"I had hardly deployed my two divisions, about 6,000 men, on the north side of Gettysburg when the action very perceptibly changed its character. . . . The enemy began to show greater strength and tenacity. He planted two batteries on a hillside, one above the other, opposite my left, enfilading part of the 1st Corps. Captain [Hubert] Dilger, whose battery was attached to my 3rd Division, answered promptly, dismounted four of the enemy's guns, as we observed through our field-glasses, and drove away two rebel regiments supporting them. In the meantime the infantry firing on my left and on the right of the 1st Corps grew much in volume."

These moments brought a rude shock to Gettysburg's northerly residents, who had felt relatively secure at the battle's beginning. In Anna Mary Young's words: "It was not until I saw the fences on our own premises torn down, and cannon placed all around us, one battery just in our back yard, that I began to realize our danger. Then we shut up the house and went into the cellar, taking with us provisions to give our men, and rags for the wounded. Though the shells fell thick around us, shattering trees, knocking bricks out of the house, etc., Cousin Jennie stood on the cellar steps cutting bread, spreading it with apple-butter, and giving it to our poor men, who had been marched double-quick for miles without any breakfast. The poor fellows were *so* grateful, and would say, 'Courage ladies; we'll drive the rebs!' "

The action in Union General Doubleday's lines west of town at this time included an incident involving the Old McLean Place, abode of Amelia Harmon and her aunt. The estate had come to mark the southern end of the battlefield, which made it tactically important. After the withdrawal of John Buford's troopers at about 10 A.M., the grounds had fallen under control of the Confederates, but these men had not molested the house, in which Amelia and her aunt continued to occupy the cupola. Now a party of Federals rushed forward and drove the Confederates away, at the same time deciding that the house would make an excellent fortress. Amelia tells what happened next: "A sudden, violent commotion and uproar below made us fly in quick haste to the lower floor. There was a tumultuous pounding with fists and guns on the kitchen door, and loud yells of 'Open, or we'll break down the door,' which they [began] to do. We drew the bolt, and in poured a stream of maddened, powder-blackened bluecoats who ordered us to the cellar while they dispersed to the various west windows throughout the house. From our cellar prison we could hear the tumult above, the constant crack of rifles, the hurried orders, and, outside, the mingled roar of heavy musketry, galloping horses, yelling troops, and the occasional boom of cannon. . . . The suspense and agony of uncertainty were awful! We could hear the beating of our hearts above all the wild confusion."

For some time the Union troops thinly angled about Gettysburg not only held their own but matched their attackers blow for blow. At the northern end of Doubleday's lines, a Confederate brigade came to disaster much in the manner of that of James Archer in the morning. Pushing forward to support an imperiled artillery battery, three regiments of Alfred Iverson's brigade of North Carolinians were suddenly flanked and brought under a brutal enfilade. The survivors surrendered. An appalled Iverson was watching from a distance. "When I saw white handkerchiefs raised . . . I characterized the surrender as disgraceful; but when I found afterward that 500 of my men were left lying dead or wounded on a line as straight as a dress parade, I exonerated, with one or two disgraceful individual exceptions, the survivors, and claim for the brigade that they nobly fought and died without a man running to the rear. . . . I endeavored, during the confusion among the enemy incident to the charge and capture of my men, to make a charge with my remaining regiment and the 3rd Alabama [sent to the brigade's support], but in the noise and excitement I presume my voice could not be heard. The fighting here ceased on my part."

On the western battlefield, according to the Union's Major Chamberlain, conditions underwent a change at about 2:30 P.M. "The rebel batteries began to increase the rapidity of their fire. A glance to the west showed the troops of Heth's and Pender's divisions in motion, descending rapidly towards Willoughby Run—regiment upon regiment *en echelon*—followed by supporting columns extending . . . as far as the eye could reach. Their advance was magnificent, and as mere spectators or military critics we might have enjoyed and applauded it, but it boded evil to our scanty force. . . . The enemy drew nearer and nearer, firing rapidly as he came, but was met by a resistance which time and again staggered him, though it could not shake him off."

It was during this fighting that the party of Federals who had been using the McLean Place as a fortress found it necessary to retreat. The moment was a calamitous one for Amelia Harmon and her aunt, who had remained in the mansion's cellar. Amelia relates: "A swish like the mowing of grass on the front lawn, then a dense shadow darkened the low, grated cellar windows. It is the sound and shadow of hundreds of marching feet. We can see them to the knees only, but the uniforms are the Confederate gray! Now we understand the scurrying of feet over-head. Our soldiers . . . have been driven back . . . have left the house, and have left us to our fate.

"We rushed up the cellar steps to the kitchen. The barn was in flames and cast a lurid glare through the window. The house was filled with rebels and they were deliberately firing it. They had taken down a file of newspapers for kindling, piled on books, rags, and furniture, applied matches to ignite the pile, and already a tiny flame was curling upward. We both jumped on the fire in hopes of extinguishing it, and pleaded with them in pity to spare our home. But there was no pity in those determined faces. . . .

"We fled from our burning house, only to encounter worse horrors. The first rebel line of battle had passed our house and were now en-gaged in a hot skirmish in the gorge of Willoughby Run. The second line was being advanced just abreast the barn, and at that moment was being hotly attacked by the Union troops with shot and shell! We were between the lines! To go toward town would be to walk into the jaws of death. Only one way was open—through the ranks of the whole Confederate army to safety in its rear!

"Bullets whistled past our ears, shells burst and scattered their deadly contents around us. On we hurried—wounded men falling all around us, the line moving forward as they fired, it seemed, with deadly preci-sion, past what seemed miles of artillery with horses galloping like mad toward the town. We were objects of wonder and amazement, that was certain, but few took time to listen to our story, and none believed it. All kept hurrying us to the rear. 'Go on! Go on!' they shouted. 'Out of reach of grape and canister!'

"At last, after we had walked perhaps two miles, we came upon a group of officers and newspapermen in conference under a tree. We told them our story. The officers looked incredulous, the newspaper-men attentive. One of these, the Confederate correspondent of the *London Times*, seemed greatly interested in our tale, and was, I believe, the only one who credited it fully. He courteously offered to conduct us to a place of safety still further to the rear. Dismounting, he walked with us, showing great sympathy, and assuring us that the ruffians who fired our house would meet condign punishment at the hand of General Lee. Also that we would be fully reimbursed . . . for our property—in Confederate money, of course. He placed us in an empty cottage, and went directly to General Lee's headquarters, then quite close by. He returned shortly saying he had seen Lee in person, told him our story, and he had promised to station a guard around the house while the battle lasted, and send us rations."

The promise was kept. "We were doubtless the only persons on the Union side who were fed from General Lee's commissary during the Battle of Gettysburg. And so far as I know our house was the only one actually set on fire deliberately by the enemy."

The roaring flames and rolling smoke rising from the McLean Place were a part of the turbulence that marked the final moments of the Federal defense. It was about 3 P.M. when the Confederates in the north were reinforced by Jubal Early's division, which had arrived from the Susquehanna. The regiments formed on Ewell's left, which was, of course, the Federal right. Union General Carl Schurz found this new turn of events alarming. "I went up to the roof of a house behind my skirmish-line to get a better view of the situation, and observed that my right and center were not only confronted by largely superior numbers, but also that my right was becoming seriously overlapped. I had ordered General Barlow to refuse his right wing, that is, to place his right brigade, Colonel [Leopold von] Gilsa's, a little in the right rear of his other brigade, in order to use it against a possible flanking movement by the enemy.

"But I now noticed that Barlow, be it that he had misunderstood my order or that he was carried away by the ardor of the conflict, had advanced his whole line and lost connection with my 3rd division on his left, and, in addition to this, he had, instead of refusing, pushed forward his right brigade so that it formed a projecting angle with the rest of the line. At the same time I saw the enemy emerging from the belt of woods on my right with one battery after another and one column of infantry after another, threatening to envelop my right flank and to cut me off from the town and the position on Cemetery Hill behind.

"I immediately gave orders to the 3rd division to reestablish its contact with the 1st, although this made still thinner a line already too thin, and hurried one staff officer after another to General Howard [on Cemetery Hill] with the urgent request for one of his two reserve brigades to protect my right against the impending flank attack by the enemy. Our situation became critical.

"As far as we could judge from the reports of prisoners and from what we observed in our front, the enemy was rapidly advancing the whole force of at least two of his army corps, A. P. Hill's and Ewell's, against us—that is to say, 40,000 men, of whom at least 30,000 were then before us. We had 17,000, counting in the two brigades held in reserve

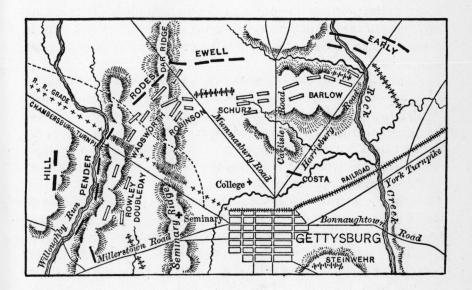

First day at Gettysburg, about 3 P.M.

by General Howard, and not deducting the losses already suffered by the 1st Corps. Less than 14,000 men we had at that moment in the open field, without the slightest advantage of position. We could hardly hope to hold out long against such a superiority of numbers, and there was imminent danger that, if we held out too long, the enemy would succeed in turning our right flank and in getting possession of the town of Gettysburg, through which our retreat to the defensive position on Cemetery Hill would probably have to be effected.

"For this reason I was so anxious to have one of the reserve brigades posted at the [northeast] entrance of the town, to oppose the flanking movement of the enemy which I saw going on. But before that brigade came, the enemy advanced to the attack along the whole line with great impetuosity."

It was John Gordon's brigade of Early's division that occupied the advantageous forward position on the Confederate left. Gordon relates: "With a ringing yell, my command rushed upon the line posted to protect the Union right. Here occurred a hand-to-hand struggle. That protecting Union line once broken left my command not only on the right flank but obliquely in rear of it. Any troops that were ever marshalled would, under like conditions, have been as surely and swiftly shattered. There was no alternative for Howard's men except to break and fly or to throw down their arms and surrender. Under the concentrated fire from front and flank, the marvel is that any escaped.

"In the midst of the wild disorder in his ranks, and through a storm of bullets, a Union officer was seeking to rally his men for a final stand. He, too, went down, pierced by a Minié ball. Riding forward with my rapidly advancing lines, I discovered that brave officer lying upon his back with the July sun pouring its rays into his pale face. He was surrounded by the Union dead, and his own life seemed to be rapidly ebbing out. Quickly dismounting and lifting his head, I gave him water from my canteen, asking his name and the character of his wounds. He was Major General Francis C. Barlow, of New York, and of Howard's corps. The ball had entered his body in front and passed out near the spinal cord, paralyzing him in legs and arms. Neither of us had the remotest thought that he could possibly survive many hours. I summoned several soldiers who were looking after the wounded and directed them to place him upon a litter and carry him to the shade in the rear."

(Unknown to Gordon, Barlow not only survived but regained the use of his limbs. A year later, Barlow learned that a Confederate General

J. B. Gordon had been killed in a battle near Richmond. This was actually a kinsman of the Gordon of Gettysburg, but Barlow naturally assumed it was the same man. A dozen years after the war, Barlow and Gordon met in Washington, D.C., and Gordon inquired, "Are you related to the Barlow who was killed at Gettysburg?" Barlow answered, "I am the man, sir. Are you related to the Gordon who killed me?" Said Gordon: "I am the man, sir!" A warm friendship resulted.

Among those Federals rendered true fatalities by Gordon's charge was a young officer in Barlow's artillery, Lieutenant Bayard Wilkeson, whose father, noted war correspondent Samuel Wilkeson, was on his way to Gettysburg to cover the action.)

With the collapse of the Union right, the entire northern line began giving way, its vulnerability increased by the weakness of its junction with Doubleday's northern extremity. Shortly Doubleday himself was beginning to reel, his right wing assailed from the north and his left subjected to heavy pressure from the west. A. P. Hill had ordered Pender's division to pass through that of Heth, now badly bloodied and drained of vigor. Southerner J.F.J. Caldwell describes the advance of Colonel Abner Perrin's brigade of South Carolinians, which made up Pender's center: "Passing an open meadow and a small stream of water [Willoughby Run], we mounted the smooth hill beyond. Here we found and marched over Pettigrew's brigade of North Carolinians. . . . The field was thick with wounded hurrying to the rear, and the ground was gray with dead and disabled. There was a general cheer for South Carolina as we moved past them. . . . The artillery of the enemy now opened upon us with fatal accuracy. They had a perfectly clear, unobstructed fire upon us."

Especially active at this time were the six guns of Battery B, 4th United States Artillery, commanded by Lieutenant James Stewart. The 'Old Man,' as he was characterized by his youthful cannoneers, was in personal charge of half the battery, while his second-in-command, Lieutenant James Davison, was directing the other half. One of the privates under Davison was Augustus Buell, who recounts: "We were formed . . . 'straddle' of the railroad cut, the Old Man with the three guns forming the right half-battery on the north side, and Davison with the three guns of the left half on the south side. Stewart's three guns were somewhat in advance of ours, forming a slight *echelon* in half-battery, while our three guns were in open order, bringing the left gun close to the Cashtown Road. We were formed in a small field . . . and our guns raked the road to the top of the low crest forming the east bank of Willoughby Creek. . . . Hall's and [Gilbert H.] Reynolds' batteries, which had held the crest in our front all morning, had retired either into the streets of Gettysburg town or to the grove near the Seminary, and all the infantry of the 1st Corps that had been fighting in our front had fallen back, except the invincible remnants of the 6th Wisconsin and 11th Pennsylvania, which were at that moment filing across the railroad cut close in our rear to support us in our final stuggle.

"Directly in our front—that is to say, on both sides of the pike—the rebel infantry, whose left lapped the north side of the pike quite up to the line of the railroad grading, had been forced to halt and lie down by the tornado of canister that we had given them from the moment they came in sight over the bank of the creek. But the regiments in the field to their right—south side of the pike—kept on, and kept swinging their right flanks forward as if to take us in reverse or cut us off from the rest of our troops near the Seminary. At this moment Davison, bleeding from two desperate wounds and so weak that one of the men had to hold him on his feet, one ankle being totally shattered by a bullet, ordered us to form . . . so as to bring the half-battery on a line with the Cashtown Pike, muzzles facing south, his object being to rake the front of the rebel line closing in on us from that side. Of the four men left at our gun when this order was given, two had bloody heads, but they were still 'standing by,' and Orderly Sergeant [John] Mitchell jumped on our off wheel to help us. 'This is tough work, boys,' he shouted as we wheeled the gun around, 'but we are good for it.' And Pat Wallace, tugging at the near wheel, shouted back, 'If we ain't, where'll you find them that is?'

"Well, this change of front gave us a clean rake along the rebel line for a whole brigade length, but it exposed our right flank to the raking volleys of their infantry near the pike, who at that moment began to get up again and come on. Then for seven or eight minutes ensued probably the most desperate fight ever waged between artillery and infantry at close range without a particle of cover on either side. They gave us volley after volley in front and flank, and we gave them double canister as fast as we could load. The 6th Wisconsin and 11th Pennsylvania men crawled up over the bank of the cut or behind the rail fence in rear of Stewart's caissons and joined their musketry to our canister, while from the north side of the cut flashed the chain-lightning of the Old Man's half-battery in one solid streak!

"At this time our left half-battery, taking their first line *en echarpe*, swept it so clean with double canister that the rebels sagged away from the road to get cover from the fences and trees that lined it. . . . Pender's division . . . suffered terribly . . . losing several hundred men . . . within a few minutes. Of course, no one claims that all this execution was done by our battery, because there was a section of Reynolds' 1st New York on the rising ground to our left-rear, toward the Seminary, playing on them with everything it could muster, and [Greenleaf T.] Stevens' old 5th Maine was blazing from the brow of the ridge, while the 6th Wisconsin's musketry and that of the 11th Pennsylvania was humming in our ears from the railroad cut behind us, and there was a straggling infantry fire from detachments all along the ridge. But, allowing for all these facts, it is true that Battery B was in the wide open jaws of the battle there."

Despite apprehensions for his personal safety, Buell found himself thrilled by "the picture of 'Old Griff' Wallace, his tough Irish face set in hard lines with the unflinching resolution that filled his soul while he sponged and loaded under that murderous musketry with the precision of barrack drill; of the burly Corporal, bareheaded, his hair matted with blood from a scalp wound, and wiping the crimson fluid out of his eyes to sight the gun; of the steady Orderly Sergeant . . . moving calmly from gun to gun, now and then changing men about as one after another was hit and fell, stooping over a wounded man to help him, or aiding another to stagger to the rear; of the dauntless Davison, [held erect] among the guns, cheering the men, praising this one and that one, and ever anon profanely exhorting us to 'Feed it to 'em, God damn 'em; feed it to 'em!' The very guns became things of life—not implements, but comrades. Every man was doing the work of two or three. . . .

"Up and down the line, men reeling and falling; splinters flying from wheels and axles where bullets hit; in rear, horses tearing and plunging, mad with wounds or terror; drivers yelling, shells bursting, shot shrieking overhead, howling about our ears, or throwing up great clouds of dust where they struck; the musketry crashing on three sides of us; bullets hissing, humming, and whistling everywhere; cannon roaring, all crash on crash and peal on peal; smoke, dust, splinters, blood, wreck and carnage indescribable; but the brass guns of Old [Battery] B still bellowed, and not a man or boy flinched or faltered! Every man's shirt soaked with sweat, and many of them sopped with blood from wounds not severe enough to make such bulldogs 'let go'—bareheaded, sleeves rolled up, faces blackened. . . . Out in front of us an undulating field, filled almost as far as the eye could reach with a long, low gray line creeping toward us, fairly fringed with flame. . . . The same sun that a day before had been shining to cure the wheat-sheaves of the harvest of peace now glared to pierce the gray pall of battle's powder smoke or to bloat the corpses of battle's victims. . . .

"When this desperate work began . . . I was wearing my jacket, and had the two top buttons buttoned. About our third load a bullet from the enemy behind the fence on our flank tore through the breast of the jacket, making the cloth fly and carrying away the second button from the top. It hurt like a sharp blow of a whip; but, running my finger along the track of the bullet, I saw that the skin was not broken. . . . My breast had a red welt across it."

Southerner J.F.J. Caldwell admits that the last-ditch fire laid down by Doubleday's artillery and infantry caused the Confederate lines to waver. "On the instant, Colonel Perrin spurred his horse . . . to the front [and] led the charge. Filled with admiration for such courage as defied the whole fire of the enemy—naturally drawn to his horse, his uniform, and his flashing sword—the brigade followed with a shout that was itself half a victory. The Federal infantry [and artillery] opened on us a repetition of the fire that had already slaughtered a brigade. This was particularly heavy on the two right regiments, for at that point the enemy were protected by a stone fence. Still there was no giving back on our part. The line passed on, many of the men throwing away their knapsacks and blankets to keep up. Struggling and panting, but cheering and closing up, they went through the shell, through the Minie balls, heeding neither the dead who sank down by their sides, nor the fire from the front which killed them, until they threw themselves desperately on the line of Federals. . . . The enemy, however, did not fly readily. They fought obstinately everywhere, and particularly opposite our right. In fact, it was not possible to dislodge them from that point until, having broken the portion of their line opposed to our left, we threw an enfilade fire along the wall. They then gave back at all points."

Returning to Union cannoneer Augustus Buell: "As Davison had now succumbed to his wounds, Orderly Sergeant Mitchell took command and gave the order to limber to the rear, the 6th Wisconsin and 11th Pennsylvania having begun to fall back down the railroad track toward the town, turning about and firing at will as they retreated. At the same time, Stewart began to limber up his half-battery on the north side of the cut. . . . The rebels could have captured or destroyed our left half-battery, and perhaps Stewart's, too, if they had made a sharp rush on both sides of the pike as we were limbering up, because, as our last gun . . . moved off, their leading men south of the pike were within fifty yards of us! But they contented themselves with file-firing, and did not come on with the cold steel. However, as soon as they saw the limbers coming up, the rebels redoubled their fire both in front and on our left flank, their object apparently being to cripple our teams so we would have to abandon the guns. They hit several horses, three or four of the drivers, and two or three more of the remaining cannoneers while we were limbering up.

"During all this wreck and carnage Sergeant Mitchell was perfectly cool, and all the men, following his example, were steady. The driver of our swing team being hit as they wheeled the limber to 'hook on,' Mitchell ordered me to mount his team. Just then the off-leader was shot and went down all in a heap. But Mitchell and [Edgar A.] Thorpe had him cut out of the traces sooner than it can be told, and off we went down the pike toward the town, the nearest houses of which were about a third of a mile off. By the time we had got into the town the other half-battery had come up, and the 6th Wisconsin, which had formed across the street, opened to let us pass. Adjutant Brooks of the 6th, having a musket in his hand, was loading and firing with the troops; in fact, most of the officers were doing the same thing. Colonel Rufus Dawes was in command at this point, and he had, besides his own regiment—or the remnant of it—a miscellaneous lot from several other commands whom he had rallied in the edge of the town.

"As the battery entered the town Colonel Lucius Fairchild of the 2nd Wisconsin was sitting on the porch of a house close to the road. He had been wounded in the battle of the forenoon, and his left arm had just been amputated. But he waved his remaining hand to us and called out, 'Stick to 'em, boys! Stay with 'em! You'll fetch 'em, finally!' . . . His ringing words of cheer under such circumstances did us much good. . . .

"I was astonished at the caution of the enemy at this time. He seemed to be utterly paralyzed at the punishment he had received from the 1st Corps, and was literally 'feeling every inch of his way' in his advance on our front. Riding the swing team on our gun, I kept looking over my shoulder to see him come on, and wondered why he was so cautious, knowing as I did that none of our troops were left in the position that we had just abandoned.

"Captain Jim Hall of the 2nd Maine had a section of his battery formed at the first cross-street we came to . . . and we heard him open on the advancing enemy as soon as the 6th Wisconsin cleared his front. This retreat into the town . . . was perfectly cool and orderly. There was not a sign of confusion, much less panic, in the 1st Corps. The troops of the 11th Corps were swarming into the town from the north at the same time."

13

The Retreat to Cemetery Hill

UNION GENERAL CARL SCHURZ and his two 11th Corps divisions, reinforced by the brigade so urgently requested from Oliver Howard, had made a valiant try at re-forming near the northern edge of town. Schurz says that "regiment stood against regiment in the open fields, near enough almost to see the white in one another's eyes, firing literally in one another's faces. The slaughter on both sides was awful." Anna Mary Young's house lay very close to this action. "The firing of the musketry," she affirms, "was more rapid than the ticking of a watch, and it seemed that for every gun fired there was a shriek. . . . All I could do was sit in the cellar corner and cry."

It was only a matter of minutes until Jubal Early's attack built to hurricane force. Among the Confederate reserves awaiting the outcome behind the lines was the regiment of Albert Jenkins' cavalry that included Private James Hodam (the trooper who had freed the Union drummer boy during Early's June 26 raid on Gettysburg). "Soon the 'rebel yell' could be distinguished in the mighty roar, and conveyed to us the gratifying intelligence that our boys were getting the best of the fight; and a signal officer of a station nearby soon verified the fact that the enemy was retreating from every position. Then the welcome order came for us to quickly advance to the front . . . and we spurred our horses along the road for Gettysburg. Through the timber, across a small stream—and the battlefield was before us in all its horrors and excitement.

"In our front were open fields and orchards, and a little further on, the town. Many pieces of artillery [had] occupied the high ground to our right, but their thunder was silenced now, while the heaps of dead and dying . . . told how the boys in blue had bravely stood by their guns. A little beyond, to judge from the windrows of the dead, a Union regiment had been blotted out. Along the road the blue and gray veterans lay thickly. . . . Dashing forward, we came up with our infantry, driving Howard's corps through the town. Confusion seemed to reign in the Federal ranks."

Another Confederate cavalryman, Major Harry Gilmor (whose active role in the campaign dated back to the Battle of Winchester), says that "we dashed among them, and had no difficulty in stopping just as many as we pleased. But few shots were fired at us, and those by Feds too much fluttered to take aim. Near the edge of the town was a regiment, apparently in a very disorganized condition but still holding on to their colors. In we dashed among them, slashing right and left. Most of them gave up, or, rather, threw down their arms and continued on. A small squad of ten or more rallied round their colors. We dashed at them. Two fired upon us, but so wildly that neither horse nor man was struck. They presented their bayonets, but, after knocking these aside and cutting down two or three of them, the rest surrendered."

Southerner Robert Stiles, the gunner in Hilary Jones' battery of the Richmond Howitzers, adds: "My gun had come again into battery in the outskirts of the town. No enemy was in sight in our front, but in anticipation of a sudden rush I had the piece loaded and several rounds of canister taken from the ammunition chest and put down hard by the gaping muzzle, ready to sweep the street in case they should turn upon us. At this moment little George Greer, a chubby boy of sixteen, rode on by further into the town. George was General Early's clerk and a favorite with Old Jube. . . . I shouted a caution to him as he passed, but on he went, disappearing in the smoke and dust ahead. In a few moments a cloud of blue coats appeared in the street in front of us, coming on, too, at a run. I was about to order the detachment to open fire when beyond and back of the men in blue I noticed little Greer, leaning forward over the neck of his horse, towering above the Federals, who were on foot; and with violent gesticulations and in tones not the gentlest, ordering the 'blue devils' to 'double quick to the rear of that piece,' which they did in the shortest time imaginable. There must have been over fifty of them.

"I am aware this statement sounds incredible, but the men had thrown away their arms and were cowering . . . in the streets and alleys."

Stiles goes on to depict another incident of the action at the northern edge of town: "There was an Irishman named Burgoyne in the 9th

Confederate victims of first day's fighting

Louisiana . . . a typical son of the Emerald Isle, over six feet high in his stockings (when he had any), broad-shouldered and muscular, slightly bow-legged, and springy as a cat; as full of fire and fight and fun as he could hold; indeed, often a little fuller than he could hold, and never having been known to get his fill of noise and scrimmage. Whenever the 9th supported Hilary Jones, if the musketry fire slackened while the artillery was in action, Burgoyne would slip over to the nearest gun and take someone's place at the piece.

"Seeing us unlimber in the street . . . he had come over now for this purpose, seized the sponge-staff and rammed home the charge, and was giving vent to his enthusiasm in screams and bounds that would have done credit to a catamount. Standing on the other side of the gun, with his arms folded, was a Federal Irishman, a prisoner just captured—a man even taller than Burgoyne and somewhat heavier in frame, altogether a magnificent fellow. Catching Burgoyne's brogue, he broke out, 'Hey, ye spalpane! Say, what are yez doing in the Ribil army?' Quick as a flash, Burgoyne retorted, 'Be-dad, ain't an Irishman a freeman? Haven't I as good right to fight for the Ribs as ye have to fight for the damned Yanks?' 'O, yes!' sang out the Federal Irishman. 'I know ye now you've turned your ougly mug to me. I had the plizure of kicking yez out from behind Marye's Wall [during the Battle of Chancellorsville]. . . .' 'Yer a damned liar,' shouted our Pat, 'and I'll jist knock yer teeth down yer ougly throat for that same lie,' and suiting the action to the word he vaulted lightly over the gun, and before we had time to realize the extreme absurdity of the thing, the two had squared off against each other in the most approved style and the first blow had passed, for the Federal Irishman was as good grit as ours.

"Just as the two giants were about to rush to close quarters . . . I noticed that the right fist of the Federal gladiator was gory, and the next movement revealed the stumps of two shattered fingers, which he was about to drive full into Burgoyne's face. 'Hold!' I cried. 'Your man's wounded!' On the instant, Burgoyne's fists fell. 'You're a trump, Pat. Give me your well hand,' said he. 'We'll fight this out some other time. I didn't see ye were hurt.' "

For the civilians who resided in the central and southern parts of the town, knowledge of the Federal defeat, north and west, developed in stages. William McClean, a Gettysburg lawyer, explains: "My wife in the yard was dressing the hand of a New York soldier whose thumb had been shot off, when he observed some Union soldiers getting over [a] fence into . . . [a] vacant lot. . . . His experienced eye understood what that meant. The tide of battle had turned, and he said to my wife, 'Madam, I cannot wait. I must go to the rear.' And he left before his wounded hand had been fully dressed and bound. . . . Then the ambulances with the most seriously wounded . . . went out Baltimore Street [toward Cemetery Hill], and the shrieks and groans of the poor sufferers rent the air."

It wasn't long, according to Anna Garlach (the girl who had begun the day by stringing beans for her mother), before the defeated troops came on in a surge. "In front of our house the crowd was so great that I believe I could have walked across the street on the heads of the soldiers. The soldiers in retreat called to us, 'Go to the cellar! Go to the cellar!' Our cellar had a foot or more of water in it, and after we had been told several times to go to the cellar Mother took us to the next house up the street, where there was a ten-pin alley, and we went into the basement . . . and we were hardly there before the Rebels appeared . . . and began firing."

Returning to Attorney McClean: "My wife and little girls and a faithful domestic, Ann Leonard, and myself all crowded into a little narrow platform at the head of the cellar stairs, behind the door, as we did not know what was next to happen, when the first words we heard from the outside were, 'Don't touch that water; they have poisoned it!', referring to the buckets of water that we had taken out for our soldiers and which remained on the pavement. Imagine what emotions were wrought in the little flock huddled at the head of the stairs when they learned of such feelings being entertained toward us by the armed host on the street at our door!"

Among the other residents who took to their cellars at this time was a boy named Albertus McCreary. "We heard firing all around the house, over the porch where a few minutes before we had been handing out water, and over the cellar doors in the pavement. I heard a voice say, 'Shoot that fellow going over the fence!' The order was obeyed, and a shot rang out just by the cellar window. There were several small windows in the walls, and their light cast shadows on the opposite wall of men rushing back and forth. Those shadows filled all of us with horror. There was more and more shooting until the sound was one continuous racket. I peeped out one of the windows just in time to see a cannon unlimbered and fired down the street. What a noise it made, and how the dust did fly!

"After a time the noise grew less and less and farther and farther away. We were all waiting to see what would happen next, when suddenly the outer cellar doors were pulled open and five Confederate soldiers jumped down among us. We thought our last day had come. Some of the women cried, while others, with hands clasped, stood rooted to the spot with fear. Father stepped forward and asked them what they wanted and begged them not to harm his people. One fellow . . . with a red face covered with freckles, and very red hair, dirty and sweaty, with his gun in his hand, said, 'We are looking for Union soldiers.' 'There are none here,' Father answered. But the soldier said he would have to search, and that we could go upstairs, as the danger was over for a time.

"From that time on we had no fear of harm from individual soldiers. We all went upstairs, and the searchers found thirteen of our men hiding in all parts of the house, some under the beds, and one under the piano, and others in closets. The prisoners were brought into the dining room, where the officer in charge took down their names. . . . Now that they had stopped fighting, both sides seemed to be on the best of terms, and laughed and chatted like old comrades. We did not have to take to the cellar again."

Things were also better for Attorney McClean. "When we found that we were not to be hurt, we came out of our hiding place, and the tired Rebels seated themselves all along the curb of the pavement, and found recreation and amusement in opening the knapsacks of the soldiers who had retreated, and taking out and reading the letters they contained. A large, fine-looking officer, mounted, turned into our street, when a cheer went up from the men, and he stopped and addressed them with jubilation that they had met their foes, driven them back, and taken possession of the town. . . . My brave, fearless, pretty little oldest daughter, Mary, not then six years old, put her head out of the window and sung, in hearing of the Rebel soldiery, 'Hang Jeff Davis on a Sour Apple Tree!'

"While the Rebels were halting, resting, and rejoicing, the 1st and 11th Corps of the Army of the Potomac fell back upon Cemetery Hill and Culp's Hill, undisturbed in obtaining . . . these strong natural positions. . . . The enemy did not go on the flood tide that leads to fortune."

Confederate General James Longstreet explains: "As General Lee rode to the summit of Seminary Ridge and looked down upon the town he saw the Federals in full retreat and concentrating on the rock-ribbed hill that served as a burying-ground for the city. He sent orders to Ewell to follow up the success if he found it practicable, and to occupy the hill on which the enemy was concentrating. As the order was not positive, and left discretion with General Ewell, the latter thought it better to give his troops a little rest and wait for more definite instructions.

"I was following the 3rd Corps as fast as possible, and as soon as I got possession of the road [its congestion having eased] went rapidly forward to join General Lee. I found him on the summit of Seminary Ridge watching the enemy concentrate on the opposite hill. He pointed out their position to me. I took my glasses and made as careful a survey as I could from that point. After five or ten minutes I turned to General Lee and said, 'If we could have chosen a point to meet our plans of operation I do not think we could have found a better one than that upon which they are now concentrating. All we have to do is to throw our army around by their left, and we shall interpose between the Federal army and Washington. We can get a strong position and wait, and if they fail to attack us we shall have everything in condition to move back tomorrow night in the direction of Washington, selecting beforehand a good position into which we can place our troops to receive battle next day. . . . The Federals will be sure to attack us. When they attack we shall beat them . . . and the probabilities are that the fruits of our success will be great.' 'No,' said General Lee, 'the enemy is there, and I am going to attack him there.' "

Lee had no designs to renew the attack that day, but the Federals were not aware of this. According to "Bonaparte," a correspondent of the New York *World:* "Not without grief nor without misgiving did the officers and soldiers . . . contemplate the day's engagement and await the onset they believed was to come. Their comrades lay in heaps beyond the village whose spires gleamed peacefully in the sunset before them. Reynolds the beloved and the brave was dead. . . . Many field, and scores of line officers had been killed. The men of the 1st Corps alone could in few instances turn to speak to the ones who stood beside them in the morning without meeting with a vacant space. The havoc in that corps was so frightful as to decimate it fully one half, and that in the 11th Corps . . . was scarcely less great. [The latter unit's losses included perhaps 3,500 captured.] Yet the little army flinched not, but stood ready to fall as others had fallen, even to the last man."

There was a new top commander on the Federal field: Major General Winfield Scott Hancock, dubbed by newsmen "Hancock the Magnificent" because of his fine physique, his personal magnetism, and his proven talent for leadership. Hancock had been sent by Meade, who was still at Taneytown, both to assume general command and to size up the field. Hancock consulted with Oliver Howard (who had to be placated at being superseded by a man who was actually his junior), and the pair agreed that Gettysburg was indeed a good place to fight a battle. The organization of the new lines was pursued in earnest.

During the late afternoon and evening, elements of Daniel E. Sickles' 3rd Corps and Henry W. Slocum's 12th Corps began coming up from the south. Fifteen-year-old Tillie Pierce was a witness to the proceedings, and her involvement was ironic. Tillie's parents, fearing for her safety if she remained in the town, had sent her southward with a party seeking refuge at the Jacob Weikert farm, on the Taneytown Road just east of the Round Tops. Mr. and Mrs. Pierce had no idea that the farm was to be enveloped by the Union battle line. "It was not long after our arrival," Tillie relates, "until Union artillery came hurrying by. It was indeed a thrilling sight. How the men impelled their horses! How the officers urged the men as they all flew past. . . ! Now the road is getting all cut up. They take to the fields, and all is an anxious, eager hurry! Shouting, lashing the horses, cheering . . . they all rush madly on.

"Suddenly we behold an [accidental] explosion. It is that of a caisson. We see a man thrown high in the air and come down in a wheat field close by. He is picked up and carried into the house. As they pass by I see his eyes are blown out, and his whole person seems to be one black mass. The first words I hear him say are, 'Oh, dear! I forgot to read my Bible today! What will my poor wife and children say?' I saw the soldiers carry him upstairs. They laid him upon a bed and wrapped him in cotton. How I pitied that poor man. . . .

"After the artillery had passed, infantry began coming. I soon saw that these men were very thirsty and would go to the spring which is on the north side of the house. I was not long in learning what I could do. Obtaining a bucket, I hastened to the spring, and there, with others, carried water to the moving column until the spring was empty. We then went to the pump standing on the south side of the house, and supplied water from it."

Tillie's unexpected exposure to war conditions did not stop here. "Some of the wounded from the field of battle began to arrive. . . . They reported hard fighting, many wounded and killed, and were afraid our troops would be defeated and perhaps routed. The first wounded soldier whom I met had his thumb tied up. This I thought was dreadful, and told him so. 'Oh,' said he, 'this is nothing; you'll see worse than this

Winfield S. Hancock

before long.' 'Oh, I hope not,' I innocently replied. Soon two officers carrying their arms in slings made their appearance, and I more fully began to realize that something terrible had taken place.

"Now the wounded began to come in greater numbers, some limping, some with their heads and arms in bandages, some crawling, others carried on stretchers or brought in ambulances. Suffering, cast down and dejected, it was a truly pitiable gathering. Before night the barn was filled with the shattered and dying heroes of this day's struggle.

"That evening Beckie Weikert, the daughter at home, and I went out to the barn to see what was transpiring there. Nothing before in my experience had ever paralleled the sight we then and there beheld. There were the groaning and crying, the struggling and dying, crowded side by side while attendants sought to aid and relieve them as best they could. We were so overcome by the sad and awful spectacle that we hastened back to the house, weeping bitterly. As we entered the basement or cellar-kitchen of the house we found many nurses making beef tea for the wounded. Seeing that we were crying they inquired as to the cause. We told them where we had been and what we had seen. . . . They at once endeavored to cheer us by telling funny stories and ridiculing our tears. They soon dispelled our terror and caused us to laugh so much that many times when we should have been sober-minded we were not, the reaction having been too sudden for our overstrung nerves. . . .

"At this time a chaplain who was present in the kitchen stepped up to me while I was attending to some duty and said, 'Little girl, do all you can for the poor soldiers and the Lord will reward you.' I looked up in his face and laughed, but at once felt ashamed of my conduct and begged his pardon. After telling him what Beckie and I had seen, how the nurses had derided us for crying, and that I now laughed when I should not, being unable to help myself, he remarked, 'Well, it is much better for you and the soldiers to be in a cheerful mood.' "

In Gettysburg that evening, the streets were ribbons of Confederate gray. Professor Jacobs recounts: "That portion of [Major General Robert E.] Rodes' division which lay down before our dwelling . . . was greatly elated with the results of the first day's battle. And the same may be said of the whole Rebel army. They were anxious to engage in conversation—to communicate their views and feelings, and to elicit ours. They were boastful of themselves, of their cause, and of the skill of their officers, and were anxious to tell us of the unskillful manner in which some of our officers had conducted the fight which had just closed. When informed that General Archer and 1,500 of his men had been captured [the number was actually some hundreds fewer], they said, 'Tomorrow we will take all these back again; and, having already taken 5,000 (!) prisoners of you today, we will take the balance of your men tomorrow.' Having been well fed, provisioned, and rested, and successful on this day, their confidence knew no bounds. . . . To us it seemed as if the Rebels would really be able to accomplish their boasts. We were disheartened, and almost in despair."

Young Albertus McCreary witnessed one of the evening's sidelights. "A number of colored people lived in the western part of the town, and . . . a great many of them were gathered together by the Confederate soldiers and marched out of town. As they passed our house our old washerwoman called out, 'Goodby; we are going back to slavery.' Most of them were crying and moaning. We never expected to see 'Old Liz' again. . . . She was marched with the rest down the street, and there was such a crowd that when they were opposite the Lutheran Church, in the confusion [attendant on the hospital activities there] she slipped into the church . . . and climbed up into the belfry. She stayed there for . . . two days without anything to eat or drink." (After the Confederates left town, Old Liz went to the McCreary house and exclaimed as she walked in, "Thank God, I's alive yet!")

Lying among the Union wounded in one of the town's churches at the end of the first day was William J. Starkes, a junior officer in the 104th New York Volunteer Infantry. "About 8:00 o'clock P.M. the [Confederate] Provost Marshal came in. He approached the group of cots occupied by wounded officers and greeted us quite cheerily. 'Good evening, gentlemen,' he said. 'I trust none of you are seriously hurt. You have your own surgeons and men here, and they will not be disturbed.' We . . . soon began to ply him with questions. He was quite communicative. Lee's army was . . . flushed with victory. The Union army was very much demoralized. 'We shall walk over it tomorrow,' he said, and then he added something about the time they expected to arrive in Philadelphia. Now, the truth is I had always been rather an optimist in this matter of preserving the Union, and, although things certainly did look rather black, I somehow had no confidence in that trip to Philadelphia, and so I replied to the Colonel, 'I say, Colonel, if there should happen to be any just cause or impediment which prevents that walk-over, would you mind dropping in and telling us about it?' He laughed a little and said he would."

Anna Mary Young, who had spent the afternoon and evening in the cellar of her home at the northern edge of town, now emerged. "The moon was shining brightly in the heavens, while on the earth, scattered everywhere, were the dead, and the wounded moaning with pain. Our yard and house were full. I actually thought I had been transferred to some strange place, so different did it seem from the home I had seen in the morning. . . . The Rebels took their wounded from our house to the rear of their army; so we went to work . . . and tried to make our wounded as comfortable as possible. . . .

"We were in the center and near the front of the Rebel army. . . . The college . . . quite near us, was . . . taken as a hospital. From the cupola, there is a splendid view of the country for miles around; and there, under the protection of the hospital flag, stood General Lee, taking note [by the light of the moon] of both armies and sending dispatches all over the field.

"General Ewell and staff took tea with us [that] evening. We, being in their power, kept quiet as to our sentiments until they commenced the subject. We then very warmly expressed our feelings, and told them they were unwelcome guests. Many of them were handsome and intelligent, and all polite and accommodating. Seeing there were none but ladies in the house, the General gave us a guard to protect us. General Ewell wanted to make his quarters with us; but, as we could not, or, rather, would not put ourselves to any trouble to give him two private rooms, he went elsewhere to sleep."

With the coming of night, the Confederate army enjoyed a tighter concentration than that of the Union. A substantial fraction of the latter was still a good distance from the battlefield, whereas Lee's rearmost corps, that of Longstreet, was nearing on the Cashtown Road. Pickett's division, however, had not yet left its rear-guard position at Chambersburg. As for Jeb Stuart, he had spent the evening skirmishing with militia troops at Carlisle and had set fire to the United States Cavalry Barracks located there. With the flames serving them as a beacon in the dark, two of Stuart's staff officers, sent earlier on a search for the Confederate army, came galloping in from Gettysburg with orders from Lee for Stuart to report to him at once.

At Gettysburg that night, Union General Abner Doubleday and a part of his command found themselves encamped in the town cemetery, at the arched gateway of which was the following sign: ALL PERSONS FOUND USING FIREARMS IN THESE GROUNDS WILL BE PROSECUTED WITH THE UTMOST RIGOR OF THE LAW. Says Doubleday: "We lay on our arms that night among the tombs . . . so suggestive of the shortness of life and the nothingness of fame; but the men were little disposed to moralize on themes like these, and were much too exhausted to think of anything but much-needed rest."

In the town, as the hour grew late, things at last became quiet. "I lay down to sleep amid that stilled world," says Henry Jacobs, the professor's son (who, it will be recalled, lived in the northern outskirts), "when from the brooding silence, out where the battle had raged, I heard a wounded, forsaken soldier crying in his soft Southern voice, 'Wahter! Wahter!' He kept calling, calling; and that solitary cry, its anguish uplifted in the pitiless truce of the night, racked the very heart. But the law of the conquerors lay like iron on the town. No one might pass beyond the lines. They themselves made no response to their comrade's call. I fell asleep with his anguish wailing on my ear."

Rest was elusive for many of the overwrought people of the town. Sallie Broadhead, who had fled her home during the morning but was now back in its shelter, claims that she and her husband got no sleep at all. "Part of the time we watched the Rebels rob the house opposite. The family had left sometime during the day, and the robbers must have gotten all they left in the house. They went from the garret to the cellar, and, loading up the plunder in a large four-horse wagon, drove it off. I expected every minute that they would burst in our door, but they did not come near us."

Out in their rural area, Mrs. Bayly and her son Billy were able to go to sleep, but their rest was disturbed. "Sometime after midnight," Billy relates, "we were awakened by a knocking at the kitchen door, and Mother told me to follow her downstairs. At the door we found a little fellow in a gray uniform, hardly taller than I and only a couple of years older, who said he had been through the battle of the day before, that his company had been cut to pieces, that he was from North Carolina, was tired of fighting, and never wanted to see another battle. Would not Mother conceal him somewhere until the battle was over? He was given a suit of [civilian] clothes and sent to the garret where the featherbeds were stored for the summer and several old bedsteads not in use, told to find a bed, and in the morning change his gray uniform for the civilian attire." (The disguise was wholly effective, and when Lee's army left Gettysburg the boy remained behind and became a citizen of the area.)

14

Deploying for the Showdown

FEDERALS AND CONFEDERATES ALIKE were astir before dawn on July 2,
each side intent upon improving its position for the major fight that
everyone knew was now at hand. One of the witnesses to Lee's deployment was Colonel Arthur Fremantle, a British officer attached to the
Confederate army. At five o'clock the colonel and a companion climbed
into a tree on Seminary Ridge southwest of Gettysburg. "Just below us,"
Fremantle recounts, "were seated Generals Lee, Hill, Longstreet, and
[John B.] Hood in consultation, the two latter assisting their delibera-
tions by the truly American custom of whittling sticks. General Heth was
also present. He was wounded in the head yesterday, and, although not
allowed to command his brigade, he insists upon coming to the field.

"At 7 A.M. I rode over part of the ground with General
Longstreet. . . . The enemy occupied a series of . . . ridges, the tops of
which were covered with trees, but the intervening valleys between their
ridges and ours were mostly open and partly under cultivation. The
cemetery was on their right, and their left appeared to rest upon a . . .
rocky hill. The enemy's forces, which were now supposed to comprise
nearly the whole Potomac army, were concentrated into a space apparently not more than a couple of miles in length. The Confederates
inclosed them in a sort of semicircle, and the extreme extent of our
position must have been from five to six miles, at least. Ewell was on our
left, his headquarters in a church with a high cupola at Gettysburg; Hill
in the centre; and Longstreet on the right. Our ridges were also covered
with . . . woods at the tops and, generally, on the rear slopes. The artillery of both sides confronted each other at the edges of these belts of

trees. . . . The enemy was evidently intrenched, but the Southerners had not broken ground at all. . . . Only two divisions of Longstreet were present today—viz., [Lafayette] McLaws' and Hood's—Pickett being still in the rear.

"As the whole morning was evidently to be occupied in disposing the troops for the attack, I rode to the extreme right with Colonel [Peyton T.] Manning and Major [Thomas] Walton, where we ate quantities of cherries, and got a feed of corn for our horses. We also bathed in a small stream, but not without some trepidation on my part, for we were almost beyond the lines and were exposed to the enemy's cavalry."

On the Union side, General Carl Schurz stood on Cemetery Hill and studied the two armies as they marshaled for battle. "Neither of them was ready. But . . . the Confederates were readier than we were. There was a rumor that Lee's army was fully as strong as ours—which, however, was not the case—and, from what we saw before us, we guessed that it was nearly all up and ready for action. We knew, too, that to receive the anticipated attack, our army was, although rapidly coming in, not nearly all up. It was indeed a comforting thought that Lee, who, as rumor had it, had wished and planned for a defensive battle, was now obliged to fight an aggressive one against our army established in a strong position. Yet we anxiously hoped that his attack would not come too early for our comfort. Thus we watched, with not a little concern, the dense columns of our troops as they approached at a brisk pace on the Taneytown Road and the Baltimore Pike, to wheel into the positions assigned to them.

"It was . . . about eight o'clock when General Meade [who had ridden up from Taneytown during the night] quietly appeared on the cemetery on horseback, accompanied by a staff officer and an orderly. His long, bearded, haggard face, shaded by a black military felt hat, the rim of which was turned down, looked careworn and tired, as if he had not slept that night. The spectacles on his nose gave him a somewhat magisterial look. There was nothing in his appearance or his bearing— not a smile nor a sympathetic word addressed to those around him—that might have made the hearts of the soldiers warm up to him. . . . There was nothing of pose, nothing stagy about him. His mind was evidently absorbed by a hard problem. But this simple, cold, serious soldier with his businesslike air did inspire confidence. The officers and men, as much as was permitted, crowded around and looked up at him with curious eyes, and then turned away, not enthusiastic but clearly satisfied. With a rapid glance he examined the position of our army . . . nodded,

Looking across the valley of death, from little Round-Top.

Looking northward across the battlefield from Little Round Top. Cemetery Hill is in background on right

seemingly with approval. After the usual salutation I asked him how many men he had on the ground. . . . 'In the course of the day I expect to have about 95,000—enough, I guess, for this business.' And then, after another sweeping glance over the field, he added, as if repeating something to himself, 'Well, we may fight it out here just as well as anywhere else.' Then he quietly rode away."

According to Warren Lee Goss, a private from New England whose unit was stationed near the center of the Union lines, the day had begun with a cloudy sky, a heavy vapor hanging over the terrain between the armies. "By ten o'clock the threatening clouds vanished and the green meadows were bathed in sunlight, with here and there the shadow of transient clouds flitting across the sunlit valley and hills. Cattle were grazing in the fields below; the shrill crowing of chanticleer was heard from neighboring farmyards; tame pigeons cooed on the hillside, and birds sang among the trees. The crest, as far as the eye could see, glittered with burnished arms. On our right was the cemetery with its white monuments, among which shone the burnished brass pieces of artillery and the glittering bayonets of the infantry. Beyond this were seen the spires of the town, while farther to the right and rear was Culp's Hill. Running across our front, obliquely, was the Emmitsburg Road, while farther beyond was Seminary Ridge, on which the enemy was posted. On our left, over a mile distant, rose the sugar-loaf summits of the Round Tops.

"Our men were in their usual moods. To the observant eye there was perceptible beneath the mask of rough humor and careless indifference an undercurrent of anxiety and gloomy foreboding. The look of earnestness which gathers on soldiers' faces before a battle was, perhaps, now deepened by the thought that the impending battle was to be fought on our own soil, and of the consequences if we met defeat. This expression was no more obvious among the Pennsylvania regiments than those from the other states. At no time had there been such intense feeling shown among all ranks as then. It showed itself in earnest glances and tones of voice. The general feeling was well expressed by a sergeant of a Pennsylvania regiment who said, 'We've got to fight our best today or have those rebs for our masters!'

"Long lines of skirmishers were stretched out on our center and left, where in the green meadows the Blue and Gray confronted each other. Here and there along the line little puffs of smoke curling up and drifting away in thin blue vapor told that the skirmishers were firing upon each other. Occasionally a lightning-like glimmer on the opposite hills showed the reflection from the burnished arms of the enemy, who were moving into position. With a glass, the rebel soldiers, clad in butternut and gray, as well as the skirmish line in front, could be distinctly seen. The Confederate soldier wore a slouch hat, short jacket, and blanket strapped over his shoulder and under his arm. This light marching order, so invariably a characteristic of the Confederate, was one of the features of their army which made them so fleet of foot. Their poverty had its compensations. . . .

"Occasionally a shell would burst after hurrying over our heads from the opposite hills. At times the Confederate skirmishers would rush upon our lines with a yell, and then a shell from our batteries, in a curved line, would go spluttering and hoarsely whispering, like an absent-minded man talking to himself, and burst in a seeming exclamation of recognition on their front. In rushing thus upon our lines it was doubtless their intention to develop the position of our artillery."

Goss, who assembled his recollections some twenty years after the war, goes on to explain the overall strategic and tactical situation as he came to understand it: "Our prospects never looked darker than at the opening of this battle [on July 1]. Even the Government, in whose defense this army was to pour out its best blood, seemed to have conspired against it. The general commanding was untried in his position, having been appointed only three days previous. He had not been long enough in command to gather the reins of control into his hands, and could not, therefore, exercise that quickness of perception and readiness of decision so essential to success on the battlefield. On the other side, Lee had held command for thirteen eventful months, and, with victory upon victory, had won the supreme confidence and the enthusiastic devotion of his soldiers. He intimately knew the temper and composition of his battalions, and this knowledge and mutual confidence was in itself worth 40,000 men to him.

"The Union army on these hills was the only barrier between them and the large cities of the North. This battle was to decide not only the future character of the war but of the nation; whether the wave of invasion was to break upon this rocky barrier and recede across the border, or sweep unchecked over the fertile fields and rich cities of the North; whether we were to have an undivided country, vital with liberty in all its parts, or one broken into puny groups of states, warlike and despotic, fighting against each other. The common soldier recognized dimly that this was the pivotal battle of the war, and hence every man's hand was nerved to do his best.

"The wonder is that with 90,000 available men [both seasoned troops and rookie militia levies] inactive and useless at different posts, one-half or two-thirds had not been summoned to this army to make the overthrow of the invaders certain instead of doubtful.

"From the first this battle was an illustration of the superior directing power which men call Providence or Fate. The armies had met without design on the part of either of their commanders. If, on the 1st of July, the Union army had not been driven back, we should not have taken position on the line of heights which gave us so great an advantage. If, after a *victory*, we had fallen back on these lines, Lee would have stood on the defensive at Seminary Ridge, and Meade would have attacked and probably been defeated.

"It has been asked why Lee fought the battle under so many disadvantages. The answer is that fate or circumstances compelled him. The temper of his army was such, and its confidence in its ability to defeat the Yankees at all times and under all circumstances so great that Lee himself, with all his equipoise of character, caught something of this overconfidence. He [also] felt obliged to fight a battle to preserve his communications [with the South]. . . . After the victory of the 1st of July he was inclined to attack rather than await attack. He was subsisting on the country, and could feed his army only by scattering it, hence could not afford to delay. It was a necessity with him to deal the Army of the Potomac a decisive blow before his movement into the Free States could be converted into a positive invasion.

"It has been thought that Lee should have maneuvered Meade out of his strong position. Had he done so the Union general would have fallen back behind Pipe Creek, or some position equally strong. Delays would constantly strengthen Meade, while they would complicate Lee's problems of feeding a concentrated army. It was not so easy a task . . . to maneuver Meade out of his strong position. In order to do so Lee must have menaced [Washington], and this involved the abandonment of Gettysburg and its advantageous converging roads, just won at the expense of a battle, and a flank movement . . . southeast from Gettysburg. This movement, made in an open country, surrounded by numerous spies and a people unfriendly to his cause, would be revealed and perhaps defeated.

"Every consideration, therefore, impelled Lee to fight. . . . The Confederate army was posted . . . [so that] its wings almost encircled ours. . . . It will be seen at a glance that this concave line . . . made communication between its different parts difficult. The convex line of the Union army made it easy to reinforce one part of the line from another. In this position Lee, having marked out the work to be done by his corps commanders, could do little but wait, without personal supervision, for results. At this time when it was essential to [Confederate] success to be able to mass men at some one point to break the Union lines, their form of line presented a great impediment to such concentration."

Lee's plan for the day called for Longstreet, on the Confederate right, to storm the heights on the Union left while Ewell, on the Confederate left, made a diversionary attack on the Culp's Hill defenses. A. P. Hill was to demonstrate against the Union center in an effort to keep reinforcements from being sent to either flank. Jeb Stuart was now on his way toward a junction with Lee's left wing, but he would take no part in the day's attack.

While the two armies made their fateful preparations, Tillie Pierce, still at the Jacob Weikert house east of the Round Tops, was agog at the bustle on the Taneytown Road. "About ten o'clock many pieces of artillery and large ammunition trains came up, filling the open space to the east of us. Regiment after regiment continued to press forward. I soon engaged in the occupation of the previous day, that of carrying water to the soldiers as they passed.

"How often my thoughts were anxiously fixed on my dear ones [in the town] as the troops hurried along. . . . Were they well? Were they alive? Did I still have a home? These, with many other silent inquiries, sprang to my mind without any hope of an answer. It was impossible in the present state of affairs to expect any tidings from them."

Tillie's concern was warranted, since Gettysburg was enveloped by Lee's left wing. Some of the southern and eastern parts of the town, in fact, were an active part of the Confederate battle line. Streets had been barricaded, and the windows of upstairs rooms bristled with sharpshooters engaged in harassing the Federals on Cemetery Hill. At least one section of row houses had been subjected to a unique improvisation. Passageways had been cut through the upstairs walls so that the Confederates could pass from one house to another. There was an added reason, well known to young Albertus McCreary, why the town found the sharpshooters unwelcome. "Our house stood on the corner of Baltimore and High Streets, and we did not dare to look out of the windows on the Baltimore Street side. Sharpshooters from Cemetery Hill were watching all the houses for Confederate sharpshooters, and . . . from that distance they could not distinguish citizen from soldier."

The perils of the morning were ignored by Sallie Broadhead's husband, who, she says, "went to the garden and picked a mess of beans, though stray firing was going on all the time and bullets from sharpshooters or others whizzed about his head in a way I would not have liked. He persevered until he picked all, for he declared the Rebels should not have one."

At about this same time, another backyard was the scene of a different kind of drama. On the previous evening, Union General Alexander Schimmelfennig, while retreating before the Confederate surge through town, had lost his horse to a bullet, and, about to be cut off, jumped over a board fence and landed on the Garlach property, where he took cover behind a woodpile near a pigpen. There he had remained, and the Garlachs had learned of his presence. "It was remarkable," marvels Anna, "that he was not captured. The Rebels had torn down fences from Breckenridge Street southward through the yards, and there were Rebels on all sides of us, and any movement of his in daytime might have been seen from a number of points. On the second day, Mother made a pretense of going to the swill barrel to empty a bucket. In the bucket, however, was water and a piece of bread, and instead of these going into the barrel they went to the general in hiding. Mother was so afraid that she had been seen and the general would be found that she did not repeat this." (Schimmelfennig became very hungry, very thirsty, and very stiff, but he escaped detection to the end.)

On the battlefields north and west of Gettysburg, some of the wounded of both sides, Federals in the majority, lay yet unattended. That second morning Mrs. Bayly, on her farm northwest of the town, got news of this situation and decided to do something about it. "I packed a market basket full of bread and butter and wine, old linen and bandages and pins . . . and, mounting a family horse that had been blind for several years, with my niece . . . behind me, I started towards the town and scene of the first day's battle. When nearing the field of battle I met a Confederate officer who I was told later was General Jenkins; and, telling him my purpose, he told me to follow him. Before we had gone far a courier came for General Jenkins, and we never saw him again. But on I went. As far as I could see, there were men, living and dead, and horses and guns and cannon, and confusion everywhere. . . .

"Getting down into the valley I found our wounded lying in the broiling sun, where they had lain for twenty-four hours with no food and no water. A zigzag fence was standing on the side of the road, and in its angles were many who had taken shelter from the sun, and to avoid being trampled on. The very worst needed a surgeon's care; but, while my niece gave food to the hungry and wine to the faint, I looked after their wounds. I would cut open a trouser leg or coat sleeve until I found the wound, and then put on a fresh bandage. One of the first I touched was a poor fellow badly hurt in the back. I cut open his coat from the waist up and found that the cloth that he had put on the wound had become so dry with clotted blood that I could not loosen it—and had no water. A wounded comrade lying near said, 'Madam, there is a little tea in my canteen that I have been saving. Maybe you can loosen it with that.'

"I had been hearing the pitiful cry of 'Water, Water' all around me, and when I found that these men had none for twenty-four hours I rose up in my wrath and, turning to the rebels who were walking around me, I said, 'Is it possible that none of you will bring water to these poor fellows?' An officer heard me, and, finding that what I said was true, he ordered a lot of men to mount and to bring all that was necessary. They said that the wells at the nearest houses were pumped out; but in strong English—with stronger words thrown in—he sent them off with canteens strung over them, and I directed them where to find a good spring. Soon we had plenty of water.

"While busy at work a German surgeon came along, saying that he had been directed to look after the Union wounded. As he could not speak English, nor I German, I was content to hear his expressions of 'Goot! Goot!' when he examined the work I had done. He was as gentle as a woman in his touch, and it did me good to see how tenderly he handled those wounded men.

"On my way home . . . I saw a field full of men whom I found to be prisoners and that they expected to start south any hour. They swarmed around me like bees, begging me to take charge of letters to their friends. . . . When I got home . . . I found my family very anxious about me."

On the new battlefield between the long ridges south of town, only small quantities of blood had been shed, but Tillie Pierce, at the Weikert farm, got an indication of what was about to happen. "My attention was called to numerous rough boxes which had been placed along the road just outside the garden fence. Ominous and dismal as was the sight presented, it nevertheless did not prevent some of the soldiers from passing jocular expressions. One of the men nearby, being addressed with the remark that there was no telling how soon he would be put in one of them, replied, 'I will consider myself very lucky if I *get* one!'

"This forenoon another incident occurred which I shall ever remember. While the infantry were passing, I noticed a poor, worn out soldier crawling along on his hands and knees. An officer yelled at him, with cursing, to get up and march. The poor fellow said he could not, whereupon the officer, raising his sword, struck him down three or four times. The officer passed on, little caring what he had done. Some of his comrades at once picked up the prostrate form and carried the unfortunate man into the house. . . . He seemed quite a young man, and was suffering from sunstroke received on the forced march. As they were carrying him in, some of the men who had witnessed the act of brutality remarked, 'We will mark that officer for this.' It is a pretty well established fact that many a brutal officer fell in battle from being shot other than by the enemy.

"Shortly after this occurrence, and while still supplying water to the passing troops from the pump, three officers on horseback came riding up to the gate. The center one kindly requested me to give him a drink. . . . After he had drunk he thanked me very pleasantly. The other two officers did not wish any. As they were about turning away, the soldiers around gave three cheers. . . . The one to whom I had given the drink turned his horse about, made me a nice bow, and then saluted the soldiers. They then rode rapidly away. I asked a soldier, 'Who did you say that officer was?' He replied, 'General Meade.'

"Some time after this several field officers came into the house and asked permission to go on the roof in order to make observations. As I was not particularly engaged at the time and could be most readily spared, I was told to show them the way up. They opened a trapdoor and looked through their fieldglasses at the grand panorama spread out below. By and by they asked me if I would like to look. Having expressed my desire to do so, they gave me the glasses. The sight I then beheld was wonderful and sublime. The country for miles around seemed to be filled with troops; artillery moving here and there as fast as they could go; long lines of infantry forming into position; officers on horseback galloping hither and thither! It was a grand and awful spectacle. . . .

"Mrs. Weikert and her daughters were busy baking bread for the soldiers. As soon as one ovenful was baked it was replenished with new, and the freshly baked loaves at once cut up and distributed. How eagerly and gratefully the tired-out men received this food! They stated that they had not tasted such sweet bread for a long time. Perhaps it was because they were eating it once more on loyal soil.

"It was shortly before noon that I observed soldiers lying on the ground just back of the house, dead. They had fallen just where they had been standing when shot. I was told that they had been picked off by Rebel sharpshooters who were up in Big Round Top."

These sharpshooters, who had worked their way to the Union side of the arena at a time when all the rest of Lee's army was on Seminary Ridge, had taken advantage of a weakness in Meade's dispositions. There were no Federals on Big Round Top, the southern extremity of the Cemetery Ridge line, and there were only a very few on Little Round Top, across a valley to the north. Meade had been deploying his army southward from Cemetery Hill, and the Round Tops were at first neglected, although the left flank of Major General Daniel E. Sickles' 3rd Corps reached tentatively toward them.

On the Confederate side, James Longstreet deployed his corps in a deliberate manner, perhaps disinclined to hurry because he was still convinced that a flanking maneuver was in order. One of the units moving southward along Seminary Ridge was J. B. Kershaw's brigade of South Carolinians, the junior officers of which included Captain D. Augustus Dickert, who relates: "As we . . . marched we had little opportunity as yet to view the strongholds of the enemy on the opposite ridge, nor the incline between. . . . Occasionally a general would ride to the crest and take a survey of the surroundings. . . . Everything was quiet and still save the tread of the thousands in motion, as if preparing for a great review. Longstreet passed us once or twice, but he had his eyes cast to the ground, as if in a deep study, his mind disturbed, and had more the look of gloom than I had ever noticed before. Well might the great chieftain look cast down with the weight of this great responsibility resting upon him.

"There seemed to be an air of heaviness hanging around all. The soldiers trod with a firm but seeming heavy tread. Not that there was any want of confidence or doubt of ultimate success, but each felt within himself that this was to be the decisive battle of the war, and as a consequence it would be stubborn and bloody. Soldiers looked in the faces of their fellow-soldiers with a silent sympathy that spoke more eloquently than words an exhibition of brotherly love never before witnessed in the 1st Corps. They felt a sympathy for those whom they knew, before the setting of the sun, would feel touch of the elbow for the last time, and who must fall upon this distant field and in an enemy's country.

"About now we were moved over the crest and halted behind a stone wall that ran parallel to a country road, our center being near a gateway in the wall. As soon as the halt was made the soldiers fell down, and soon most of them were fast asleep. While here, it was necessary for some troops of Hill's to pass over up and through the gate. The head of the column was led by a doughty general clad in a brilliant new uniform, a crimson sash encircling his waist, its . . . heavy [tassels] hanging down to his sword scabbard, while great golden curls hung in maiden ringlets to his very shoulders. His movement was superb as he sat his horse in true knightly manner. On the whole, such a turn-out was a sight seldom witnessed by the staid soldiers of the 1st Corps.

"As he was passing, a man in Company D, 3rd South Carolina, roused up from his broken sleep, saw for the first time the soldier-wonder with the long curls. He called out to him, not knowing he was an officer of such rank, 'Say, Mister, come right down out of that hair,' a foolish and unnecessary expression that was common throughout the army when anything unusual hove in sight. This hail roused all the ire in the flashy general. He became as 'mad as a March hare,' and, wheeling his horse, dashed up to where the challenge appeared to have come from, and demanded in an angry tone, 'Who was it that spoke? Who commands this company?' And, as no reply was given, he turned away saying, 'Damned, if I only knew who it was that insulted me I would put a ball in him.' But, as he rode off, the soldier gave him a Parthian shot by calling after him, 'Say, Mister, don't get so mad about it. I thought you were some damn wagon master.'

"Slowly again our column began moving to the right. The center of the division was halted in front of Little Round Top. . . . Everything was quiet in our front, as if the enemy had put his house in order and awaited our coming. Kershaw took position behind a tumbled down wall to await Hood's movements on our right. . . . [He] was to open the battle by the assault on Round Top [i.e., by a move in the direction of the big hill]. The country on our right, through which Hood had to maneuver, was very much broken and thickly studded with trees and . . . under-growth, which delayed that general in getting in battle line."

As recalled by one of Hood's men, Private W. C. Ward, a member of E. M. Law's brigade: "At last the division was halted . . . and imme-diately the men lay down in line. From this position the hill [Seminary Ridge] declined rapidly into the valley along the foot of the [Round Tops], which was densely wooded. From this position on the [extreme] right we could see occasionally puffs of white smoke on both sides of the valley as pickets engaged in desultory firing. In front of us no living thing was to be seen. There was a small, low-roofed cottage near the foot of Round Top, and adjoining it there was a picket garden. Nearby was a stone fence about four feet high. Through this little valley slowly ran a stream of water that spread out some yards in width. . . .

"As we lay there making these mental notes, the soldiers overheard a comrade say, 'Boys, we are going to have a battle. There is Old Fairfax, Longstreet's fighting adjutant [Major John W. Fairfax, a Virginia aristocrat known for his daring in combat], and we never see him that we do not have a fight.' Looking over the shoulder to the rear, one saw a tall, very handsomely dressed officer in full uniform, mounted on a magnificent horse. In front of him there were gathered the division generals and the brigade generals, with members of their several staffs, making quite a company. This man was seen pointing in the direction of Little Round Top and to the right of it and [to the left of it] along the ridge, as if giving the position of the enemy."

It was now around 2 P.M., and the Union position indicated by Major Fairfax was about to undergo a radical change. General Daniel Sickles, a prewar politician who had gained his present rank largely through his connections in Washington, made an error in judgment. When he learned that the Confederates were moving to attack him in front and on his left flank, Sickles, discounting the importance of his proximity to the Round Tops, decided that his best response would be to go to meet the attack. In his front, about halfway between Cemetery and Seminary ridges, was a secondary ridge, which he ordered his corps to occupy.

Lieutenant Jesse Bowman Young, serving as an aide to one of Sickles' division commanders, Andrew A. Humphreys, describes the advance: "It was a brilliant sight—the march of the 3rd Army Corps, under Sickles, from its place in the line of battle near Little Round Top, half a mile toward the west and the southwest, to occupy a new position on the ridge in their front. Battle flags waved above the heads of the gallant soldiers; the bright gleam of their muskets flashed along their extended line; aides were to be seen galloping in every direction to execute the orders for the advance; bugles sounded out their stirring blasts, indicating the will of the corps commander . . . who, with his gayly decorated staff, some of them in showy Zouave costume, superintended the movement. While no engagement had yet taken place, yet the rapid 'crack, crack' of muskets beyond the [new ridge], all along the skirmish line, afforded signs of fast-approaching battle. . . . The cheers that went up as the general galloped across the field showed that the 3rd Corps believed in the intrepidity and skill of its impetuous leader. The men found the fences all down as they marched forward, the skirmishers having destroyed them in their advance, thus clearing the fields of barriers that might have impeded the movement. The line was soon formed, and a brief breathing spell was afforded."

Sickles' extreme left was now at a jumble of huge rocks, just west of Little Round Top, known as Devil's Den. From this spot, which was wooded, the line made a northwesterly swing past a wheat field toward the Emmitsburg Road, which pursued a northeasterly course to Gettysburg. Striking the road at a peach orchard, the line followed the road for a distance toward town. Sickles' northern flank was more than a mile from his southern. Many of the troops back on Cemetery Ridge, up toward Cemetery Hill, were astonished at the great change in the army's left wing, and some wondered whether a general order to advance had somehow failed to reach them.

Returning to Jesse Bowman Young: "It is half past three o'clock in the afternoon, and suddenly a cannon shot is heard, followed by another, a sign that something is going to happen. General Sickles has been at Meade's headquarters, half a mile away to the rear on the Taneytown Road, and the noise of the artillery brings him galloping to his corps, with General Meade following close behind, the two making a striking contrast, Sickles being a dashing and brilliant rider, while Meade, with his spare, spectacled figure . . . [had an] ungainly look. . . . It seems that Sickles had gone out far beyond the point that Meade had intended as the line of battle, several motives prompting the movement, one being the fear that the rebels might occupy the Emmitsburg Road and thence advance against the Union line and break it in pieces. He judged that the line he now occupied was better than the other which Meade had chosen.

"As the two generals sat on their horses for a moment not far away from where [I] was stationed, it could be clearly seen that both were in deep concern. Finally, after some discussion, Sickles said, 'Well, General, I will withdraw and resume my former position back yonder if you give the command.' General Meade, rightly divining the movement then in progress on the part of the enemy, said, 'The Confederates will not let you withdraw now.' And the words were hardly out of his lips when an exploding shell in the air almost over their heads showed that the battle was begun."

General Meade's horse, frightened into a frenzy, swung about and bolted toward the rear. This happened to be the direction in which Meade wanted to go, for he had to see that Sickles got the support he needed from the troops still on the original line. The dispositions were

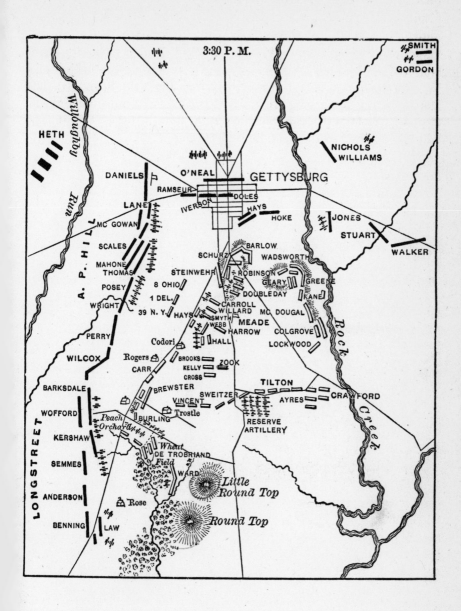

Second day at Gettysburg, about 3:30 P.M.

then as follows: George Sykes' 5th Corps had moved into a reserve spot a distance behind Sickles, its van on the part of Cemetery Ridge the impetuous general had abandoned; Winfield Hancock's 2nd Corps extended from Sykes' right to the approaches of Cemetery Hill; the Cemetery Hill–Culp's Hill "hook" was manned by three corps, John Newton's 1st (Meade had chosen Newton to replace the slain Reynolds, with Doubleday returning to his original post as a division commander), Oliver Howard's 11th, and Henry Slocum's 12th. John Sedgwick's 6th Corps had not yet reached the field, but was closing in.

15

A Near Thing at the Round Tops

ON THE CONFEDERATE SIDE, the outset of the battle found British observer Colonel Arthur Fremantle back in his tree near the center of the line. "Longstreet suddenly commenced a heavy cannonade on the right. Ewell immediately took it up on the left. The enemy replied with at least equal fury, and in a few moments the firing along the whole line was as heavy as it is possible to conceive. A dense smoke arose for six miles. There was little wind to drive it away, and the air seemed full of shells, each of which seemed to have a different style of going and to make a different noise from the others. The ordnance on both sides is of a very varied description.

"Every now and then a caisson would blow up—if a Federal one, a Confederate yell would immediately follow. The Southern troops . . . always yell in a manner peculiar to themselves. . . . The Confederate officers declare that the rebel yell has a particular merit, and always produces a salutary and useful effect upon their adversaries. A [unit] is sometimes spoken of as a 'good yelling regiment.'

"So soon as the firing began, General Lee joined Hill just below our tree, and he remained there nearly all the time, looking through his fieldglass—sometimes talking to Hill and sometimes to Colonel [A. L.] Long of his staff. But generally he sat quite alone on the stump of a tree. What I remarked especially was, during the whole time the [artillery] firing continued he sent only one message, and only received one report. It is evidently his system to arrange the plan thoroughly with the three corps commanders, and then leave to them the duty of modifying and carrying it out to the best of their abilities.

"When the cannonade was at its height, a Confederate band of music . . . began to play polkas and waltzes, which sounded very curious accompanied by the hissing and bursting of the shells."

Across the battle arena at the Jacob Weikert farm, Tillie Pierce and the Weikert family were taken unaware by the outbreak of the firing. "This was so terrible and severe that it was with great difficulty we could hear ourselves speak. It began very unexpectedly; so much so that we were all terror-stricken, and hardly knew what to do. Some of the soldiers suggested that we had better go to a farmhouse about one half a mile across the fields to the east; and, acting on their advice, we ran thither as fast as we could. On our way over, my attention was suddenly attracted, in the direction of the town, to what seemed a sheet of lightning. This bright light remained in the sky quite a while. The first thought that flashed upon my mind was, perhaps it is Gettysburg burning; and so expressed my fear to some of the soldiers we were then passing. One of the men, more bent on mischief than on sympathy, said, 'Yes, that is Gettysburg and all the people in it.' This made me cry, for I thought at once of the dear ones at home.

"When we reached the farmhouse, some of the soldiers who were about the place, seeing me in tears, were touched with compassion and asked the cause. I told them what had been said to me, and that my parents and sister were in the town. They assured me that in war the rule was, always to allow helpless and innocent citizens to get out of a place, and never to destroy them. I then felt comforted, and they further told me that the light I saw was some signal.

"Here we were permitted to remain but a few minutes, for hardly had we arrived at our supposed place of refuge when we were told to hurry back to where we came from; that we were in a great deal more danger, from the fact that the shells would fall just about this place, whereas at the house near Round Top the shells would pass over us. So there was no alternative but to retrace our steps about as fast as we came. . . .

"During the whole of this wild goose chase the cannonading had become terrible! Occasionally a shell would come flying over Round Top and explode high in the air overhead. Just before leaving [the Weikert place] so hurriedly, a baking had been put in the old-fashioned oven. When we came back we expected to find it all burned, but fortunately the soldiers had taken it out in good time. They doubtless had their eye on it as well as on the enemy."

About to attain a hero's status on the Union side at this time was

Brigadier General Gouverneur K. Warren, a former 5th Corps brigade commander who was now Meade's chief engineer. Warren relates: "Just before the action began in earnest . . . General Meade sent me to the left to examine the condition of affairs, and I continued on till I reached Little Round Top. There were no troops on it, and it was used as a signal station. I saw that this was the key of the whole position, and that our troops in the woods in front of it could not see the ground in front of them, so that the enemy would come upon them before they would be aware of it. The long line of woods on the west side of the Emmitsburg Road—which road was along a ridge—furnished an excellent place for the enemy to form out of sight, so I requested the captain of a rifle battery just in front of Little Round Top to fire a shot into these woods.

"He did so, and as the shot went whistling through the air the sound of it reached the enemy's troops and caused everyone to look in the direction of it. This motion revealed to me the glistening of gun barrels and bayonets of the enemy's line of battle, already formed and far outflanking the position of any of our troops, so that the line of his advance from his right to Little Round Top was unopposed. . . . The discovery was intensely thrilling to my feelings and almost appalling. I immediately sent a hastily written dispatch to General Meade to send a division at least to me."

It was a fortunate thing that the Union line some hundreds of yards in front of Warren—that part of Sickles' defense running from the Wheat Field to Devil's Den—was at this time being extended southward, far enough even to cover the western base of Big Round Top. This emergency thrust was thin, however, and could do no more than serve as a brief barrier to Hood's advance.

These were busy moments for Meade's chief of artillery, Brigadier General Henry J. Hunt, who traversed the lines on horseback inspecting the sites of the various batteries. While on the left flank, in the vicinity of Little Round Top, Hunt drew up and listened for the sound of Captain James E. Smith's 4th New York Light, which had been sent forward, supported by a regiment of infantry, to Devil's Den. No sound was forthcoming, and Hunt decided to investigate. "I dismounted and tied my horse to a tree before crossing the valley. . . . I was alone, a not infrequent and awkward thing for a general who had to keep up communications with every part of a battlefield and with the general-in-chief. On climbing to the summit [of Devil's Den], I found that Smith had just got his guns, one by one, over the rocks and chasms, into an excellent position. After pointing out to me the advancing lines of the

Gouverneur K. Warren

enemy, he opened, and very effectively. Many guns were immediately turned on him. . . .

"Telling him that he would probably lose his battery, I left to seek [additional] infantry supports, very doubtful if I would find my horse, for the storm of shell bursting over the place was enough to drive any animal wild. On reaching the foot of the [Devil's Den] cliff, I found myself in a plight at once ludicrous, painful, and dangerous. A herd of horned cattle had been driven into the valley between Devil's Den and Round Top, from which they could not escape. A shell had exploded in the body of one of them, tearing it to pieces; others were torn and wounded. All were stampeded, and were bellowing and rushing in their terror, first to one side and then to the other, to escape the shells that were bursting over them and among them.

"Cross I must, and in doing so I had my most trying experience of that battlefield. Luckily the poor beasts were as much frightened as I was, but their rage was subdued by terror, and they were good enough to let me pass through scot-free, but 'badly demoralized.' However, my horse was safe; I mounted, and in the busy excitement that followed almost forgot my scare."

On the Confederate side, General Hood saw very little of the attack he had launched. "I . . . rode forward with my line under a heavy fire. In about twenty minutes . . . I was severely wounded in the arm and borne from the field."

Confederate Private Ward of Law's brigade, on the right of Hood's line, tells how his regiment began its charge toward Plum Run, the north-south waterway in the valley between the Emmitsburg Road and the Round Tops: "The men sprang forward as if at a game of ball. The air was full of sound. A long line of Federal skirmishers, protected by a stone wall, immediately opened fire. [These troops were on the far side of Plum Run, near the western base of Big Round Top.] Grape and canister from the Federal battery [at Devil's Den, a fourth of a mile to the left] hurtled over us as we descended the hill into the valley. We rushed through our own battery while it was firing and receiving the fire from the enemy's guns. Men were falling, stricken to death. This soldier received on the left thigh a blow from a minie ball that was exceedingly painful, but for which he did not halt. The younger officers made themselves conspicuous by rushing to the front, commanding and urging the men to come on. . . .

"In the din of battle we could hear the charges of canister passing over us with the noise of partridges in flight. Immediately to the right,

Taylor Darwin, orderly sergeant of Company I, suddenly stopped, quivered, and sank to the earth dead, a ball having passed through his brain. There was Rube Franks, of the same company, just returned from his home in Alabama, his new uniform bright with color, the envy of all his comrades, his gladsome face beaming as if his sweetheart's kiss had materialized on his lips, calling to his comrades, 'Come on, boys; come on! The 5th Texas will get there before the 4th [Alabama]! Come on, boys; come on!' He shortly afterwards met the fatal shot. There was Billy Marshall, running neck and neck with this private soldier. . . . As we dashed into the slow-running water, Billy stopped, supporting himself on his left hand, without kneeling, holding his musket in his right hand, and drank as an animal might have done. I never saw him afterwards. His body was never found."

While the right wing of Hood's attack (with the division now commanded by Law) swung past the southern environs of Devil's Den, other regiments were ordered to make the bristling position their first objective. This element of the attack, according to Law, "continued to move forward, encountering, as it ascended the heights around the battery on the spur and to the right and left of it, a most determined resistance from the Federal troops, who seemed to be continually reinforced. [These supports were sent down from the Wheat Field.] The ground was rough and difficult, broken by rocks and boulders, which rendered an orderly advance impossible. Sometimes the Federals would hold one side of the huge boulders on the slope until the Confederates occupied the other.

"In some cases my men, with reckless daring, mounted to the top of the large rocks in order to get a better view and to deliver their fire with greater effect. One of these, Sergeant Barbee of the Texas brigade, having reached a rock a little in advance of the line, stood erect on the top of it, loading and firing as coolly as if unconscious of the danger, while the air around him was fairly swarming with bullets. He soon fell helpless from several wounds; but he held his rock, lying upon the top of it until the litter-bearers carried him off."

The defenders of Devil's Den managed to hold on as the fight to the south continued. Here the Federals behind the stone wall at the western base of Big Round Top were being pushed aside, some retreating northward between Devil's Den and Little Round Top, while others ascended Big Round Top. Law's right wing also divided itself, several regiments bearing leftward to the mouth of the valley between the Round Tops, while two, the 15th and the 47th Alabama, with Colonel William C. Oates in top command, followed the Federals who had retreated up the

The fighting at Devil's Den

mountain. Oates relates: "In places the men had to climb up, catching to the rocks and bushes and crawling over the boulders in the face of the fire of the enemy, who kept retreating, taking shelter and firing down on us from behind the rocks and crags which covered the side of the mountain thicker than gravestones in a city cemetery. Fortunately, they usually overshot us. We could see our foe only as they dodged back from one boulder to another, hence our fire was scattering."

By this time the request for troops that Union General Gouverneur Warren had dispatched from his position on Little Round Top had gained its initial response. Colonel Strong Vincent's brigade of Sykes' 5th Corps, awaiting orders on Cemetery Ridge, a half mile north of the threatened hill, was instructed to rush to its defense. One of Vincent's regiments was Colonel Joshua L. Chamberlain's 20th Maine, and one of the regiment's members was Private Theodore Gerrish, who recounts: "In a moment all was excitement. Every soldier seemed to understand the situation, and to be inspired by its danger. . . . Away we went, under the terrible artillery fire. It was a moment of thrilling interest. Shells were exploding on every side. . . . Up the steep hillside we ran, and reached the crest."

Vincent ordered the regiments to form an arc about Little Round Top's southwestern slopes, which overlooked the critical valley between the commanding hills. Private Gerrish continues: "We [of the 20th Maine] were on the left of our brigade, and consequently on the extreme left of all our line of battle. The ground sloped to our front and left, and was sparsely covered with a growth of oak trees which were too small to afford us any protection. Shells were crashing through the air above our heads, making so much noise that we could hardly hear the commands of our officers. The air was filled with fragments of exploding shells and splinters torn from mangled trees. But our men appeared to be as cool and deliberate in their movements as if they had been forming a line upon the parade ground in camp."

For the moment, Vincent's brigade went unmolested by anything but shellfire. But the Confederate regiments that had entered the mouth of the valley between the Round Tops were fast approaching the Federal position. Confederate Colonel Oates and his two regiments, meanwhile, had driven away their Federal tormentors and were nearing the summit of the larger mountain. "Some of my men," Oates discloses, "fainted from heat, exhaustion, and thirst. I halted [atop the summit] and let them lie down and rest a few minutes. . . . I saw Gettysburg through the foliage of the trees. Saw the smoke and heard the roar of battle which was then raging at the Devil's Den, in the Peach Orchard, up the Emmitsburg Road, and on the west and south of Little Round Top."

The fighting at Little Round Top had just begun, as the Confederates in the valley attacked Vincent in his rugged position. One of the attacking regiments was the 4th Alabama, and Private Ward was among those in the fore. "There was a long line of large boulders cropping out on the mountainside, forming a natural breastwork. Over and through this the line had to mount. The line had become broken because of the timber, and those of us in the front line, as soon as we were uncovered, received the first fire of the hidden Federals. A long line of us went down, three of us close together. There was a sharp, electric pain in the lower part of the body, and then a sinking sensation to the earth; and, falling, all things growing dark, the one and last idea passing through the mind was, 'This is the last of earth.'

"Over their fallen comrades the men rushed up the mountainside, and soon struck the main line of the enemy, for there was a crash of musketry at close range. Minie balls were falling through the leaves like hail in a thunderstorm. Consciousness had returned. Dragging himself along the stony earth, as a wounded snake might have done, this soldier took shelter under a boulder four or five feet in height."

Vincent's Federals at first had no great trouble holding off the attacking regiments, which were not yet reinforced by Colonel Oates, who was only now starting down the northern slope of Big Round Top. But by this time Devil's Den had fallen, which opened the way for a Confederate drive from the west. As these troops came on, headed for Vincent's right flank, Gouverneur Warren, still on Little Round Top, rode madly down the northeastern side of the hill for reinforcements. He shortly met Colonel Patrick H. O'Rorke's 140th New York Volunteers, of Stephen H. Weed's brigade, 2nd Division, 5th Corps. The regiment was following other units of the brigade toward the lines at the Wheat Field.

Riding with Colonel O'Rorke was his adjutant, Lieutenant Porter Farley, who narrates: "Warren came straight toward the head of the regiment. . . . He called out to O'Rorke, beginning to speak while still some eight or ten rods from us, that he wanted us to come up there; that the enemy were advancing unopposed up the opposite side of the hill down which he had just come, and he wanted our regiment to meet them. He was evidently greatly excited, and spoke in his usual impulsive style. O'Rorke answered, 'General Weed is ahead and expects me to

Union positions on Little Round Top

follow him.' 'Never mind that!' said Warren. 'Bring your regiment up here and I will take the responsibility.'

"It was a perplexing situation, but without hesitating O'Rorke turned to the left. . . . We . . . rushed along the wooded, rocky eastern slope of Little Round Top. . . . It was just here that some of the guns of [Charles E.] Hazlett's battery came rapidly up and plunged directly through our ranks, the horses being urged to frantic efforts by the whips of their drivers and [by] the cannoneers assisting at the wheels, so great was the effort necessary to drag the guns and caissons up the ragged hillside."

O'Rorke's regiment climbed to the crest and headed down the southwestern slope, making for Vincent's right flank, which had begun to crumble under the Confederate attack. Vincent had been mortally wounded, and his line was in momentary danger of being "rolled up," with the hill going to the assailants. Porter Farley continues: "We were moving with . . . not a musket . . . loaded, a fact which Warren of course knew nothing about when he rushed us up there. The enemy was coming from our right. . . . The order, 'On the right, by file into line,' would have brought us into proper position; but there was no time to execute it, not even time to allow the natural impulse which manifested itself on the part of the men to halt and load the instant we received the enemy's fire. O'Rorke did not hesitate a moment. 'Dismount,' said he to me, for the ground before us was too rough to ride over. We sprang from our horses and gave them to the sergeant-major.

"O'Rorke shouted, 'Down this way, boys!' and, following him, we rushed down the rocky slope with all the same moral effect on the rebels, who saw us coming, as if our bayonets had been fixed and we *ready* to charge upon them. Coming abreast of Vincent's brigade, and taking advantage of such shelter as the huge rocks lying about there afforded, the men loaded and fired; and in less time than it takes to write it the onslaught of the rebels was fairly checked, and in a few minutes the woods in front of us were cleared except of the dead and wounded. Such of the rebels as had approached so near as to make escape almost impossible dropped their guns, threw up their hands, and, upon a slight slackening of our fire, rushed in upon us and gave themselves up as prisoners, while those not so near took advantage of the chance left them and retreated in disorder.

"The firing for a few minutes was very rapid, and the execution on both sides was fearful. . . . O'Rorke exposed himself with the greatest gallantry, not taking the least advantage of the partial shelter which the rocks afforded. He was shot in the neck and dropped instantly dead without a word. [Two additional officers were killed, and three badly wounded. Of the enlisted men, twenty-five died, and some eighty were wounded.] . . . Our losses were much more severe than they would have been if our muskets had been loaded and if the regiment had been formed in proper line of battle. . . . This remark must not be construed as reflecting on anyone. Warren did not know that our guns were empty, and if he had known it, or if he or O'Rorke had halted the column for the purpose of loading, it would have caused a delay which might, and probably *would*, have been disastrous beyond all calculation. . . .

"Hazlett's battery, which was stationed on the crest above and behind us, had not been able to do any execution upon the force which actually assailed us, but it played upon the rebel masses who were driving Sickles' corps in the plain below. . . . Hazlett got his guns into position just at the time when Sickles' corps was falling back in great disorder . . . and it was against [the] advancing and for the moment victorious lines that he poured in an effective fire. Here, too, he met his death in a manner dramatic to the last degree. . . . When Warren detached and sent us up the hill, word was sent to our brigade commander . . . notifying him of the fact, he having gone at the head of the brigade directly to the front to the support of Sickles' corps. Upon receiving this word, Weed brought back the regiments with him as hastily as possible and put them in position to our right along the crest of Little Round Top, not, however, arriving till our bloody affair was over. But the sharpshooters [at Devil's Den] were . . . doing their best against Hazlett's gunners, and it was while standing among them that Weed received a mortal wound. . . . He was in the very act of committing his last messages to his friend Hazlett, who stooped over him, when there came the whiz and thud of another bullet as it sunk into Hazlett's brain, and that brave artilleryman fell a corpse across the body of his dying friend. . . .

"Up to that time in my life I had never felt grief so sharply, nor realized the significance of death so well, as then, when the wild excitement of our fight was over and I saw O'Rorke lying there so pale and peaceful. To me and all of us he had seemed so near the beau ideal of a soldier and a gentleman. All that he had been, and the bright promise of what he was to be, was so fresh in our minds; and now, in an instant, the fatal bullet had cut short the chapter of that fair life. I choked with grief as I stood beside his lifeless form."

The Federal success on the western slopes of Little Round Top played a major part in saving the hill, but there was an equally critical clash at the opposite end of the line that arced about the southern face.

This spot toward the east was the one that marked Meade's extreme left, where Colonel Joshua Chamberlain and his 20th Maine Volunteers had ensconced themselves. Confederate Colonel Oates and his two Alabama regiments had completed their descent of Big Round Top, and the 20th Maine was their objective.

In the words of Union Private Theodore Gerrish: "Our regiment mustered about 350 men. Company B, from Piscataquis County, commanded by the gallant Captain [Walter G.] Morrill, was ordered to deploy in our front as skirmishers. They boldly advanced down the slope and disappeared from our view. . . . The skirmishers must have advanced some thirty or forty rods through the rocks and trees, but we have seen no indications of the enemy. 'But look! Look! Look!' exclaimed half a hundred men in our regiment at the same moment; and no wonder, for right in our front, between us and our skirmishers, whom they have probably captured, we see the lines of the enemy. . . . They are rushing on, determined to turn and crush the left of our line. Colonel Chamberlain, with rare sagacity, understood the movement they were making and bent back the left flank of our regiment until the line formed almost a right angle, with the colors at the point. . . .

"How can I describe the scenes that followed? Imagine, if you can, nine small companies of infantry . . . in the form of a right angle, on the extreme flank of an army . . . put there to hold the key of the entire position. . . . Stand firm, ye boys from Maine, for not once in a century are men permitted to bear such responsibilities for freedom and justice, for God and humanity, as are now placed upon you.

"The conflict opens. I know not who gave the first fire, or which line received the first lead. I only know that the carnage began. Our regiment was mantled in fire and smoke. I wish that I could picture . . . the awful details of that hour—how rapidly the cartridges were torn from the boxes and stuffed in the smoking muzzles of the guns; how the steel rammers clashed and clanged in the heated barrels; how the men's hands and faces grew grim and black with burning powder; how our little line, baptized with fire, reeled to and fro as it advanced or was pressed back; how our officers bravely encouraged the men to hold on, and recklessly exposed themselves to the enemy's fire—a terrible medley of cries, shouts, cheers, groans, prayers, curses, bursting shells, whizzing rifle bullets, and clanging steel. . . .

"The enemy was pouring a terrible fire upon us, his superior forces giving him a great advantage. . . . The air seemed to be alive with lead. The lines at times were so near each other that the hostile gun barrels almost touched. . . . At one time there was a brief lull in the carnage, and our shattered line was closed up, but soon the contest raged again with renewed fierceness. . . . Many of our companies . . . suffered terribly."

The Confederates had not reached this point without having done their own share of suffering. Some of the companies, enfiladed by fire from Federal units on the right of the 20th Maine, had been driven from the field. Of those that remained (all belonging to the 15th Alabama), Oates has this to say: "My dead and wounded were then nearly as great in number as those still on duty. They literally covered the ground. The blood stood in puddles in some places on the rocks. The ground was soaked with the blood of as brave men as ever fell on the red field of battle." The colonel had experienced a personal loss: "Lieutenant John A. Oates, my dear brother . . . was pierced through by a number of bullets and fell mortally wounded."

Returning to Union Private Gerrish: "Our ammunition is nearly all gone, and we are using the cartridges from the boxes of our wounded comrades. A critical moment has arrived, and we can remain as we are no longer; we must advance or retreat. It must not be the latter, but how can it be the former? Colonel Chamberlain understands how it can be done. The order is given, 'Fix bayonets!' and the steel shanks of the bayonets rattle upon the rifle barrels. 'Charge bayonets! Charge!' Every man understood in a moment that the movement was our only salvation, but there is a limit to human endurance, and . . . for a brief moment the order was not obeyed, and the little line seemed to quail under the fearful fire that was being poured upon it. . . . Lieutenant H. S. Melcher, an officer who had worked his way up from the ranks . . . saw the situation and did not hesitate. . . . With a cheer and a flash of his sword that sent an inspiration along the line, full ten paces to the front he sprang—ten paces, more than half the distance between the hostile lines. 'Come on! Come on! Come on, boys!' he shouts. The color sergeant and the brave color guard follow, and with one wild yell of anguish wrung from its tortured heart, the regiment charged."

Chamberlain, who took a personal part in the charge, was surprised by what it effected: "Many of the enemy's first line threw down their arms and surrendered. An officer fired his pistol at my head with one hand, while he handed me his sword with the other. Holding fast by our right and swinging forward our left, we made an extended 'right wheel,' before which the enemy's second line broke and fell back, fighting from tree to tree, many being captured. . . . Meantime Captain Morrill with his skirmishers [who had not been captured, as feared, but had taken a flank position in concealment], with some dozen or fifteen ... U. S. Sharpshooters who had put themselves under his direction, fell upon the enemy as they were breaking, and by his demonstrations, as well as his well-directed fire, added much to the effect of the charge."

Oates admits that he and his men "ran like a herd of wild cattle." The colonel escaped the bullets that pursued the herd like angry hornets, but a private near him did not. "As we ran, a man named Keils ... who was to my right and rear had his throat cut ... and he ran past me breathing at his throat and the blood spattering. His windpipe was entirely severed." The wound was a mortal one, but the man would be hours in dying.

Colonel Chamberlain completes the tale: "Having thus cleared the valley and driven the enemy up ... Great Round Top ... I succeeded (although with some effort to stop my men, who declared they were 'on the road to Richmond') in getting the regiment into good order and resuming our original position."

After this repulse, the Confederates recessed their work against Little Round Top, and Meade's fears for his extreme left were eased. His right flank at Culp's Hill, where Ewell was supposed to be making his diversionary attack, was as yet menaced only by shellfire. In front of Cemetery Ridge, however, Union affairs were in mortal disarray. Simultaneously with the development and resolution of the issue at Little Round Top, the northerly sectors had been swept by a series of Confederate successes.

16

The Storm at the Salient

THE CHIEF WEAKNESS of Sickles' main line, which ran in a northwesterly direction from the Wheat Field to the Peach Orchard and then turned northeastward along the Emmitsburg Road, was that it formed a salient, or projection, that made it susceptible to pressure from two directions. Longstreet's first attack on the salient, begun soon after Hood started for the Round Tops, was made by McLaws' division, with Kershaw's brigade in the fore. Moving obliquely against the southwestern line, the brigade bypassed the Peach Orchard and headed for a belt of woods that shielded the Wheat Field.

In the words of Confederate Captain Augustus Dickert: "The men sprang to their work with a will and determination, and spread their steps to the right and left as they advanced. Kershaw was on foot, prepared to follow the line of battle immediately in rear, looking cool, composed, and grand, his steel-gray eyes flashing the fire he felt in his soul. The shelling from the enemy on [Cemetery Ridge] had, up to this time, been mostly confined to replying to our batteries, but as soon as this long array of bristling bayonets moved over the crest and burst out suddenly in the open, in full view of the cannon-crowned battlements, all guns were turned upon us. . . . The battery in the orchard began grapeing Kershaw's left as soon as it came in range. . . . Not a [musket on our side] was allowed to be fired either at sharpshooters that were firing on our front from behind boulders and trees in a grove we were nearing, or at the cannoneers who were raking our flank on the left. [The brigade's power was being saved for use at the closest range achievable.]

"Men fell here and there from the deadly minnie-balls, while great gaps or swaths were swept away in our ranks by shells from the batteries on the hills, or by the destructive grape and canister from the orchard. On marched the determined men across this open expanse, closing together as their comrades fell out. . . . When the brigade was near the woodland . . . a most deadly fire was directed towards the center of the 3rd [Dickert's regiment] both by the battery to our left and sharpshooting in the front. It was thought by some that it was our flag that was drawing the fire, four color guards having gone down. Someone called out, 'Lower the colors; down with the flag.' Sergeant Lamb, color bearer, waved the flag aloft; and, moving to the front where all could see, called out in loud tones, 'This flag never goes down until I am down.'

"Then the word went up and down the line, 'Shoot that officer! Down him! Shoot him!' But still he [the Union battery commander on the left] continued to give those commands, 'Ready, aim, fire!' and the grapeshot would come plunging into our very faces. The sharpshooters, who had joined our ranks as we advanced, now commenced to blaze away, and the cannoneers scattered to cover in the rear. This [Union] officer, finding himself deserted by his men, waved his sword defiantly over his head and walked away as deliberately as on dress parade, while the sharpshooters were plowing up the dirt all around him; but all failed to bring him down."

Kershaw's attack, backed by a second of McLaws' brigades, boded ill for the Federals at the Wheat Field, a single brigade commanded by Regis de Trobriand and belonging to David Birney's division. Birney had been obliged to weaken the unit by sending two of its regiments southward to help with the work against Hood. De Trobriand relates: "I had then but two regiments in line of battle, and a third prolonging my line as skirmishers, when the avalanche rolled upon me. Hold on there, hard and firm! There is no reserve. It was a hard fight. The Confederates appeared to have the devil in them. . . . On the other side, my men did not flinch. Like veterans, accustomed to make the best of every resource, they had sheltered themselves behind the rocks and trunks of trees which were on the line, and . . . their assailants . . . were received, at a distance of twenty yards, with a deadly volley, every shot of which was effective. . . . On both sides, each one aimed at his man, and, notwithstanding every protection from the ground, men fell dead and wounded with frightening rapidity.

"An aide [from the division commander] came through a hail of bullets to ask another regiment from me. 'Tell General Birney,' I replied to him, showing him my line, 'that I have not a man left who has not upon his hands all that he can do; and tell him that, far from being able to furnish reenforcements to anyone, I shall be in need of them myself in less than a quarter of an hour.'

"In fact, the persistent nature of the attack showed clearly that we had a contest with superior forces. If they had attacked us entirely with the bayonet, we would have been swept away. Happily, the nature of the ground broke their lines and enabled us to hold them at a distance by the rapidity and precision of our fire. I had never seen any [of our] men fight with equal obstinacy. One would have said that each believed the destiny of the Republic was attached to the desperate vigor of his efforts. So that we maintained our hold. But my line was melting away in its position. It seemed to me that nearly half were struck down. It remained to be seen how long the other half would hold out.

"At this moment . . . one of my aides told me that a brigade of the 5th Corps was lying in two lines behind us, awaiting the time to come into action. This was good news. But, as I went to assure myself of its accuracy, I saw these troops rise up and fall back hurriedly at the command of their officers. I galloped forward towards the nearest of them and asked them, 'Where are you going?' 'We do not know.' 'Who has given you orders to retire?' 'We do not know.' "

These 5th Corps troops backed off only a short distance, then moved forward around the north side of De Trobriand's position to fill a weak spot between the Frenchman's troops and those at the Peach Orchard. The maneuver was supportive of De Trobriand but not directly helpful. At this time, however, Brigadier General John C. Caldwell's division of Hancock's 2nd Corps was forming on Cemetery Ridge, its mission to advance to the Wheat Field. As recalled by one of the division's regimental commanders, Major St. Clair A. Mulholland: "There is yet a few minutes to spare before starting, and the time is occupied in one of the most impressive religious ceremonies I have ever witnessed. The Irish Brigade [composed of men from Massachusetts, New York, and Pennsylvania], which had been commanded formerly by General Thomas Francis Meagher, and whose green flag had been unfurled in every battle in which the Army of the Potomac was engaged . . . and now commanded by Colonel Patrick Kelly, and to which our regiment [the 116th Pennsylvania] was attached, formed a part of this division. The brigade stood in column of regiments closed in mass. As a large majority of its members were Catholics, the chaplain of the brigade, Reverend William Corby, proposed to give a general absolution to all the men before going into the fight. While this is customary in the armies of the

Catholic countries in Europe, it was, perhaps, the first time it was ever witnessed on this continent, unless, indeed, the grim old warrior, Ponce de Leon, as he tramped through the Everglades of Florida in search of the Fountain of Youth, or De Soto, on his march to the Mississippi, indulged in this act of devotion.

"Father Corby stood upon a large rock in front of the brigade. Addressing the men, he explained what he was about to do, saying that each one could receive the benefit of the absolution by making a sincere act of contrition and firmly resolving to embrace the first opportunity of confessing their sins, urging them to do their duty well, and reminding them of the high and sacred nature of their trust as soldiers and the noble object for which they fought, ending by saying that the Catholic church refuses Christian burial to the soldier who turns his back upon the foe or deserts his flag. The brigade was standing at 'order arms,' and as he closed his address every man fell on his knees, with head bowed down. Then, stretching his right hand toward the brigade, Father Corby pronounced the words of the general absolution. . . .

"The scene was more than impressive; it was awe-inspiring. Nearby stood Hancock, surrounded by a brilliant array of officers who had gathered to witness this very unusual occurrence; and while there was profound silence in the ranks of the 2nd Corps, yet over to the left . . . the roar of the battle rose and swelled and reechoed through the woods, making music more sublime than ever sounded through cathedral aisles. The act seemed to be in harmony with all the surroundings. I do not think there was a man in the brigade who did not offer up a heartfelt prayer. For some it was their last. They knelt there in their grave clothes. . . .

"The division moved off by the left flank and marched rapidly [southward]. We had hardly got under way when the enemy's batteries opened, and shell began falling all around us. . . . As we passed [a] road . . . north of the Wheat Field, General Hancock sat upon his horse looking at the troops. As Colonel [Edward E.] Cross . . . passed by, he said to him, 'Cross, this is the last fight you'll fight without a star.' [Hancock was promising the colonel promotion to brigadier.] Without stopping, Cross replied, 'Too late, general; this is my last battle.' "

Three of the division's brigades headed for deployment between the Wheat Field and Little Round Top. The fourth marched through the field toward De Trobriand's rear. The Frenchman's thin line had been driven from the skirting woods and was itself now in the field. De Trobriand recounts: "Our position was no longer tenable. Our ammu-

nition was nearly exhausted, and already some of the men were searching the cartridge boxes of the dead for ammunition, when, at last, a
brigade of the 2nd Corps came to relieve us. *They* did not lie down
behind us. They advanced in good order and with a resolute step. I had
only to show them my line, three-quarters demolished. They rushed
forward. I learned afterward that it was the brigade of General [Samuel
K.] Zook, who was killed among the first at the place where he relieved
me.

"However, the enemy, profiting by [my] movement in retreat, had
advanced into the Wheat Field, on the edge of which I rallied what
remained to me of the 5th Michigan and the 110th Pennsylvania. General Birney, who was near, immediately brought into line of battle the
17th Maine and a New Jersey regiment of [Colonel George C.] Burling's
brigade. I hastened to complete the line with what troops I had at hand,
and we charged through the Wheat Field, driving the rebels back to the
other side of [its] stone wall. It was the first charge of the day on that
ground which saw so many more before night. It was also the last effort
of my brigade. After the offensive return, I received orders to fall back."
Zook's brigade repaired the gap.

Union Major Mulholland's regiment was among the units that bypassed the Wheat Field on the side toward Little Round Top. The major
says that Colonel Cross and his men were also a part of this wing, and
that within ten minutes "the country lost one of the best soldiers in the
army. Cross was dead, shot at the head of his brigade leading them to the
charge. . . . Up to this moment, strange to say, not a shot was fired at our
regiment. . . . Suddenly someone in the ranks cried out, 'There they
are!' Sure enough, not forty feet from us, up towards [a] crest, behind
the trees and big rocks covering that ground, was the enemy. No orders
were given, but in an instant every musket on the line was at its deadly
work. The enemy having to rise to fire over the rocks, their shots for the
most part passed over our heads, but as they exposed themselves to our
men at such close quarters, armed with smooth-bore muskets firing 'buck
and ball'—one large ball and three buckshot—the effect of our fire was
deadly in the extreme, for, under such circumstances, a blind man could
not have missed his mark. The officers too joined in the fray, each one
emptying his revolver with effect. For ten minutes this work went on,
our men seeming to load and fire twice as fast as the enemy.

"Now the voice of Kelly is heard ordering the charge. With a cheer,
a few quick strides, and we are on the crest among the enemy. Here took
place a rather extraordinary scene. Our men and their opponents were

mingled together. In charging we had literally run right in among them. Firing instantly ceased, and we found there were as many of the enemy as there were of ourselves. Officers and men of both sides looked for a time at each other, utterly bewildered. The fighting had stopped, yet the Confederate soldiers stood there facing us, still retained their arms, and showed no disposition to surrender. At this moment I called out, 'Confederate troops lay down your arms and go to the rear!' This ended a scene that was becoming embarrassing. The order was promptly obeyed, and a large number of what I think were men of Kershaw's brigade became our prisoners. . . .

"In front of our brigade we found that the enemy had suffered much more than we had. When engaged, our line was below theirs as they stood on the crest of the hill. They fired down while our men fired upward, and our fire was more effective. On their line we found many dead but few wounded. They were nearly all hit in the head or upper part of the body. Behind one rock we counted five dead bodies. This was some of the most severe fighting our division had ever done."

For the moment at least, the southwestern sector of the Peach Orchard salient had been spared collapse. But now the Confederates on Seminary Ridge were preparing an advance on the Peach Orchard itself, held by a brigade of Federals under Charles K. Graham. (Longstreet's attack, begun at the Round Tops, continued to develop from south to north. Union General Sickles' right wing, on the Emmitsburg Road north of the Peach Orchard, was still relatively unmolested, its troops being occupied mainly with watching the awesome show to the south.)

The Confederates who had been chosen to move directly against the Peach Orchard—the Mississippi brigade of McLaws' division—were led by Brigadier General William Barksdale, once a member of the U.S. Congress known for his fiery speeches in favor of states' rights, and now an impetuous military champion of the Southern cause. It was an aide from McLaws, Captain G. B. Lamar, Jr., who brought Barksdale his orders to attack. The aide recalls: "I had witnessed many charges marked in every way by unflinching gallantry . . . but I never saw anything equal the dash and heroism of the Mississippians. . . . General Barksdale . . . was in front of his brigade, hat off, and his long white hair reminded me of the 'white plume of Navarre.' I saw him as far as the eye could follow, still ahead of his men, and leading them on."

Barksdale's advance, soon strongly supported, marked the beginning of Sickles' downfall. Observing from the Union right up the Emmitsburg Road, Jesse Bowman Young was appalled by the salient's fate. "Sickles and Birney made a brave struggle to keep their men in place and hold their line unbroken. Nevertheless, it was flanked and driven. Graham was wounded and captured in the Peach Orchard. And, without exception, all the organizations which had been stationed in front of Little Round Top were flanked, crowded back, and at last forced in more or less confusion toward the rear [i.e., toward the section of Cemetery Ridge extending northward from Little Round Top]. The artillery was thus left without infantry support, and in due time had to withdraw to evade capture. The literal truth is that the batteries at the Peach Orchard stood their ground until their horses were all disabled or killed, and then the men that were left saved their guns by 'firing with fixed prolonge' [i.e., with drag-ropes behind] as they withdrew to the rear, loading and firing as they retreated, the Confederates pursuing with yells and sweeping the field with fresh batteries brought to the scene from their rear."

Confederate Colonel E. Porter Alexander, who commanded six of the batteries involved, found the moment one of supreme exhilaration. "I believed that Providence was indeed 'taking the proper view' and that the war was nearly over. Every battery was limbered to the front, and . . . all six charged in line across the plain and went into action again at the position the enemy had deserted. . . . An artillerist's heaven is to follow the routed enemy, after a tough resistance, and throw shells and canister into his disorganized and fleeing masses. Then the explosions of the guns sound louder and more powerful, and the very shouts of the gunners ordering 'Fire!' in rapid succession thrill one's very soul. There is no excitement on earth like it. . . . Now we saw our heaven just in front and were already breathing the very air of victory. Now we would have our revenge and make them sorry they had stayed so long."

Revenge was soon inflicted on Sickles himself. The general, on horseback, was trying to pull things together from a position near the Trostle house, north of the Wheat Field. As told by a 3rd Corps staff officer: "I was within a few feet of General Sickles when he received the wound by which he lost his leg. . . . A terrific explosion seemed to shake the very earth. . . . This was instantly followed by another equally stunning, and the horses all began to jump. I instantly noticed that Sickles' pants at the knee was torn clear off to the leg, which was swinging loose. . . . As he attempted to dismount, he seemed to lose strength, half fell to the ground. He was very pale, and evidently in most fearful pain, as he exclaimed, 'Quick! Quick! Get something and tie it up before I bleed to death!' Those were the exact words. . . . He was carried to a

Alexander's batteries charging toward the front

nearby farmhouse [before his journey to the rear], coolly smoking a cigar, quietly remarking to a Catholic priest, a chaplain to one of his regiments, 'Man proposes and God disposes.' "

The collapse of Graham's brigade at the Peach Orchard brought an end to the immunity of the Union right. This division (Humphreys') was triply jeopardized: flanked on the south and open both to a frontal assault and a move against its exposed northern flank by fresh troops from Seminary Ridge. Anderson's division of Hill's corps, positioned on Longstreet's left, now entered the fight.

One of the Union regiments facing Anderson was that to which Captain Henry Blake belonged. "The regiment was formed upon the Emmitsburg Road and partially sheltered by the house and barn of Peter Rogers. . . . The skirmishers in our immediate front reported that the rebels were massing their brigades for an assault on the position held by the division, and the men . . . prepared to resist the onset. . . . The batteries and infantry [down at the Peach Orchard] were steadily driven . . . and were rapidly moving half of a mile in the rear of the division before the yells and bullets of the enemy showed that the long-expected line was advancing. . . .

"A snake that rustled through the grass at this exciting moment was promptly despatched by a squad whose minds were not discomposed by the perilous state of affairs. The skirmishers fell back to the main line, which was calmly resting in the road and holding its fire until the rebels should reach and attempt to climb a rail fence in front. The regular battery, planted upon the left of the regiment, decimated their ranks with terrible discharges of canister that swept the field again and again and caused clouds of dust; and all thought that the repulse might be decisive. When the musketry [of the enemy] riddled the house, a kitten, mewing piteously, ran from it, jumped upon the shoulders of one of the men and remained there a few minutes during the fight.

"Before [our] regiment could deliver its volley, the companies about-faced in pursuance of the orders of some stupid general, and executed a right half-wheel under a severe fire . . . and thus abandoned the advantages of the strong line of defense in the road. The 'stars and bars' of treason were visible when the infantry could not be seen, and the column which had been shattered by [our] battery appeared in front and began to shoot the gunners, who performed their duty with the utmost fidelity, and retired at last to escape the capture which seemed to be unavoidable.

"While the rebel standard-bearers waved their colors, the officers [leading the attack] beckoned with their drawn swords. The [oncoming] men . . . exultingly pointed to the divisions that were flying from [the Peach Orchard to Cemetery Ridge], and sought by their shouts and gestures to encourage the timid and quicken the march of the support; and the soldiers [in the fore of the attack] were constantly loading and aiming their rifles at the breasts of the members of the regiment. Orders were duly transmitted from a blockhead, termed upon the muster-roll a brigadier general, not to discharge a musket because they 'would fire upon their own men;' and the enemy was enabled in this way to cut down the ranks and diminish the effect of the first volley.

"Candor compels me to admit that this mistake was excusable upon this ground: that the officer from his standpoint, which was far in the rear, could not distinguish one line of battle from the other. The command was disregarded. The foe stood in groups of three or four, and the large number of gaps . . . revealed the extent of the slaughter; and the survivors . . . entered the road, sought the protection of a slight ridge, and their advance was entirely checked."

The check, of course, was momentary. Soon Humphreys' entire division was retrograding. Blake continues: "The troops were subjected in certain positions to volleys from three distinct points, and the men slowly retreated, foot by foot; while thousands, pierced by the deadly Minie balls or torn asunder by the explosion of the infernal shell-bullet, fell and saturated the plain with their blood. As soon as the bullets began to whistle, a general said to the orderly who carried the color of his brigade, which he supposed would attract notice and draw the fire of the enemy upon him, 'Take away that flag!' And the person who obeyed this direction remarked in [telling of the incident], 'Faith, an' I was as willin' to run with it to the rear as he was to have me.' The most demoralizing results would have occurred if the troops had been new when this event took place; but they were veterans, and the shameful misconduct of the officers who commanded them did not affect their constancy or firmness."

Adds Jesse Bowman Young: "The space occupied by the division of Humphreys by this time was the vortex of a caldron of fire, the crater of a volcano of destruction. . . . The batteries were surrounded, and one gun after another was captured by the enemy and turned against the Union forces, every horse having been killed and every man in the battery having fallen at his post. Against the weakened, struggling lines of Humphreys . . . regiments of heroic Confederates were pressing with eager yells, trampling the wounded Union men under their feet."

Slain artillery horses at the Trostle house

The sun was now dropping behind Seminary Ridge. Customarily mellow over these woods and farmlands, the waning rays were unable in many places to penetrate the alien screen of smoke and dust. The entire Union line, from north to south, was in retreat. Some valiant stands were made, one of the most notable by Captain John Bigelow's 9th Battery, Massachusetts Light, at the Trostle house in the Union center. These desperate acts helped cover the retreat and were costly to the Confederates. The aggressive, white-maned Barksdale himself went down, mortally wounded and left momentarily alone in the confusion. Says a Mississippian who was near: "I hear a weak hail to my right, and, turning to it, find General Barksdale; and what a disappointment when I hold my canteen to his mouth for a drink of water and found a ball had gone through it and let it all out. I took his last message to his brigade and left him."

Down at the Wheat Field, Union Major Mulholland and his comrades were subjected to the severest of tests. "We were in a trap. A line of the enemy was advancing on the Wheat Field from the south, and [Confederate General W. T.] Wofford's brigade, [a] column I had seen marching around the Peach Orchard and into our rear, was closing in from the north. We caught it from both sides. The slaughter here was appalling, but we kept on, the men loading and firing as they ran; and by the time we reached the middle of the field the two lines of the enemy were so close that for a few moments they ceased firing on us, as they fired into each other. . . .

"Passing through this alley of death . . . we got away with a large part of the division, but the loss was terrible. In the half hour we were under fire, 1,400 men were lost. . . . Some of the men who fell . . . and were forced to lie there between the two fires fared badly. One man of our regiment fell shot through the leg, and while he lay there was hit five or six times. . . . Our wounded, with visions of Belle Isle and Libby [prison camps] before them, begged piteously to be taken along—many of them keeping with us wholly unaided. . . .

"Until toward dark the fight had certainly gone against us, and the battle had extended along the line to the right almost halfway to the cemetery. The evening, and our prospects, grew dark together. The 3rd Corps had been driven back, broken and shattered, its commander wounded and carried from the field. The troops that had gone to its support fared no better, and every man felt that the situation was grave. However, all was not yet lost. Meade had again thought of Hancock; and, as yesterday he sent him to stop the rout of the 1st and 11th Corps,

Groups of dead on the Wheat Field

so today he orders him to assume command on the left. . . . A half hour of daylight yet remains, but it is long enough to enable him to rally some of our scattered troops, face them once more to the front, [and] gather reenforcements."

By this time the Union line had been forced back to its original position on Cemetery Ridge, and the reverse slope held a seething tangle of defeated men and trembling horses, along with equipment scattered in disarray. On the ridge itself, with the Union's northern wing, was a group of observers that included Lieutenant Frank A. Haskell, an aide to Brigadier General John Gibbon, one of Hancock's division commanders. Haskell recounts: "Men are dropping dead or wounded on all sides, by scores and by hundreds, and the poor mutilated creatures, some with an arm dangling, some with a leg broken by a bullet, are limping and crawling towards the rear. . . . A sublime heroism seems to pervade all [of those still in the fight], and the intuition that to lose that crest, all is lost. How our officers, in the work of cheering on and directing the men, are falling. . . . The fire all along our crest is terrific, and it is a wonder how anything human could have stood before it; and yet the madness of the enemy drove them on, clear up to the muzzle of the guns, clear up to the lines of our infantry—but the lines stood right in their places.

"General Hancock and his aides rode up to Gibbon's division, under the smoke. General Gibbon, with myself, was near, and there was a flag dimly visible, coming towards us from the direction of the enemy. . . . The flag was no more than fifty yards away, but it was the head of a Rebel column, which at once opened fire with a volley. . . . [Captain W.D.W.] Miller, General Hancock's aide, fell, twice struck, but the general was unharmed, and he told the 1st Minnesota, which was near, to drive these people away. That splendid regiment . . . swings around upon the enemy, gives them a volley in their faces, and advances upon them with the bayonet. The Rebels fled in confusion, but . . . many [Union] officers and men will never fight again. More than two-thirds fell."

It was at another spot toward the north that the attacking Confederates made their farthest advance. Brigadier General A. R. Wright's brigade of Anderson's division, Hill's corps, had charged across the Emmitsburg Road, shattering each line it encountered. "We were now," says Wright, "within less than 100 yards of the crest of the heights, which were lined by artillery, supported by a strong body of infantry, under protection of a stone fence. My men, by a well-directed fire, soon drove the cannoneers from their guns, and, leaping over the fence, charged up to the top of the crest, and drove the enemy's infantry . . . some 80 or 100 yards in rear of the enemy's batteries. We were now complete masters of the field, having gained the key, as it were, of the enemy's whole line. Unfortunately, just as we had carried the enemy's last and strongest position it was discovered that the brigade on our right had not only not advanced across the turnpike, but had actually given way and was rapidly falling back to the rear, while on our left we were entirely unprotected, the brigade ordered to our support having failed to advance.

"It was now evident, with my ranks so seriously thinned as they had been by this terrible charge, I should not be able to hold my position unless speedily and strongly reenforced. My advanced position and the unprotected condition of my flanks invited an attack which the enemy were speedy to discover, and immediately passed a strong body of infantry . . . upon my right and rear . . . while a large brigade advanced from [a] point of woods on my left . . . and . . . moved rapidly to meet the party which had passed around upon our right.

"We were now in a critical condition. The enemy's converging line was rapidly closing upon our rear. A few moments more and we would be completely surrounded. Still no support could be seen coming to our assistance, and with painful hearts we abandoned our captured guns, faced about, and prepared to cut our way through the closing lines in our rear. This was effected in tolerable order, but with immense loss. The enemy rushed to his abandoned guns as soon as we began to retire, and poured a severe fire of grape and canister into our thinned ranks. . . . In this charge my loss was very severe, amounting to 688 in killed, wounded, and missing, including many valuable officers."

General Meade played a personal part in Wright's dislodgment, riding at the head of a body of reinforcements, waving his hat and shouting, "Come on, gentlemen!" The general's audacity appalled his aides, and they soon hustled him to the rear.

"Such fighting as this," says Union Lieutenant Frank Haskell, "cannot last long. . . . The battle has gone on wonderfully long already. But if you will stop to notice it, a change has occurred. The Rebel cry has ceased, and the men of the Union begin to shout there, under the smoke, and their lines to advance. See, the Rebels are breaking! They are in confusion in all our front! The wave has rolled upon the rock, and the rock has smashed it. Let us shout, too!"

Actually, there remained a moment of uncertainty in the south. As explained by Union General Abner Doubleday: "The enemy . . . now swarmed in the front of our main line between the Wheat Field and

Little Round Top. General S. Wiley Crawford, who commanded a division composed of two brigades of the Pennsylvania Reserve Corps, was ordered to drive them farther back. This organization, which at one time I had the honor to command, were veterans of the Peninsula and were among the most dauntless men in the army. Crawford called upon them to defend the soil of their native state, and headed a charge made by [Colonel William] McCandless's brigade with the colors of one of the regiments in his hand. The men went forward with an impetus nothing could withstand. The enemy took shelter behind a stone fence on the hither side of the Wheat Field, but McCandless stormed the position, drove them beyond the field, and then, as it was getting dark, both sides rested on their arms."

Doubleday adds a comment about Sickles' original advance to the Peach Orchard line: "The movement, disastrous in some respects, was propitious as regards its general results, for the enemy had wasted all their strength and valor in gaining the Emmitsburg Road, which after all was of no particular benefit to them. They were still outside our main line."

It must not be supposed that the two armies were through with bloodshed for the day. In the words of Union Major Mulholland, who had been a part of the retreat through the "alley of death" in the Wheat Field: "As the fight was closing upon the left of our army, Ewell was striking . . . the right. As we reformed our division on the Taneytown Road—and we had some difficulty in getting things in shape after the rough handling we had received—we heard, away to the right and rear, the yells of Ewell's men. . . . This was the most anxious hour of all."

17

Lightning in the Twilight

EWELL'S CORPS FACED that part of the Union line forming a northerly arc
running from Cemetery Hill, just south of Gettysburg, to the eastern
face of Culp's Hill. About a mile in breadth, this was the "hook" joined
to Meade's Cemetery Ridge "shank." The northern sector was not strong,
for Meade had drawn heavily on its manpower to bolster his defense in
the south. On the plus side, the arc was well stocked with artillery, and
it was fortified with earthworks and with breastworks made of felled
trees. Also favoring the Union cause, Ewell did not get started until
night was near, and he was unable to muster among his troops the
coordination he needed to bring his entire corps into action. He managed to strike two blows, both at the same time: one on the eastern side
of Culp's Hill, the other on the east-west saddle between Culp's Hill and
Cemetery Hill.

Only one Union brigade—that of George S. Greene, Slocum's 12th
Corps—was in position to meet the attack on Culp's Hill. As related by
one of the brigade's junior officers, Jesse H. Jones: "Word was brought
from the officer in charge of our pickets that the enemy was advancing
in heavy force in line of battle, and, with all possible celerity, such dispositions as the case admitted of were made. The brigade was strung out
into a thin line of separate men as far along the breastworks as it would
reach. The intention was to place the men an arm's-length apart, but, by
the time the left of the brigade had fairly undoubled files, the enemy was
too near to allow of further arrangements being made. In a short time
the woods were all flecked with the flashes from the muskets of our
skirmishers. Down in the hollow there, at the foot of the slope, you could

catch a glimpse now and then, by the blaze of the powder, of our brave boys as they sprang from tree to tree and sent back defiance to the advancing foe. With desperation they clung to each covering. For half an hour they obstructed the enemy's approach.

"The men [on the heights] restrained their nervous fingers; the hostile guns flamed out against us not fifteen yards in front. Our men from the front [the skirmishers] were tumbling over the breastwork, and for a breathless moment those behind the breastwork waited. Then out into the night like chain-lightning leaped the zigzag line of fire. Now was the value of breastworks apparent, for, protected by these, few of our men were hit; and, feeling a sense of security, we worked with corresponding energy. Without breastworks our line would have been swept away in an instant by the hailstorm of bullets and the flood of men. The enemy worked still farther around to our right, entered the breastwork beyond our line, and crumpled up and drove back, a short distance, our extreme right regiment. They advanced a little way, but were checked by the fire of a couple of small regiments borrowed for the emergency from General James Wadsworth [of the 1st Corps, whose division held the northern face of Culp's Hill]."

The Union position on the saddle between Culp's Hill and Cemetery Hill was manned by elements of both the 1st and 11th Corps. In the words of General Carl Schurz: "It was already [growing] dark when we on Cemetery Hill were suddenly startled by a tremendous turmoil at the batteries of [Captain Michael] Wiedrich and [Captain R. Bruce] Ricketts, placed on a commanding point on the right of Cemetery Hill. General Howard and I were standing together in conversation when the uproar surprised us. There could be no doubt of its meaning. The enemy was attacking the batteries on our right, and if he gained possession of them he would enfilade a large part of our line toward the south as well as the east, and command the valley between Cemetery Ridge and Culp's Hill, where the ammunition trains were parked.

"The fate of the battle might hang on the repulse of this attack. There was no time to wait for superior orders. With the consent of General Howard, I took the two regiments nearest to me, ordered them to fix bayonets; and, headed by Colonel [Wladimir] Krzyzanowski, they hurried to the threatened point at a double-quick. I accompanied them with my whole staff."

The Confederate attack was made by Harry Hays' brigade of Louisiana Tigers, supported by a brigade of North Carolinians. Riding among the foot troops in the gathering dusk was cavalry officer Harry

Confederates at the foot of Culp's Hill

Gilmor, who had volunteered to accompany the mission because he liked
to fight. The bold horseman recounts: "There was a perfect network of
rifle pits to be taken before reaching the intrenchments; and, although
the brave boys fell in piles, they charged and took them one after another. On reaching the main works, the brigade [of Tigers] was a good
deal scattered, but still went bravely forward. I was the only mounted
man in the whole command, not caring to attempt the ascent on foot,
and I had no difficulty in leaping the trenches and keeping well up to the
front.

"There were fifteen guns mounted in those works, all pouring a
deadly avalanche of shell and canister down among the Louisianians,
who never quailed but pressed on until they scaled the works. . . . While
advancing on the main line . . . I saw one of our color-bearers jump on
a gun and display his flag. He was instantly killed. But the flag was seized
by an Irishman, who, with a wild shout, sprang upon the gun, and he too
was shot down. Then a little bit of a fellow, a captain, seized the staff and
mounted the same gun; but, as he raised the flag, a ball broke the arm
which held it. He dropped his sword and caught the staff with his right
before it fell, waved it over his head with a cheer, indifferent to the pain
of his shattered limb and the whizzing balls around him. His third cheer
was just heard, when he tottered and fell, pierced through the lungs."

Union General Schurz and his two regiments were now approaching from the rear. "Soon we found ourselves surrounded by a rushing
crowd of stragglers from the already broken lines. We did our best,
sword in hand, to drive them back as we went. Arrived at the batteries,
we found an indescribable scene of melee. Some rebel infantry had
scaled the breastworks and were taking possession of the guns. But the
cannoneers defended themselves desperately. With rammers and fence
rails, hand-spikes, and stones, they knocked down the intruders. In
Wiedrich's battery, manned by Germans from Buffalo, a rebel officer,
brandishing his sword, cried out, 'This battery is ours!' Whereupon a
sturdy artilleryman responded, 'No, dis battery is unser!' and felled him
to the ground with a sponge-staff.

"Our infantry made a vigorous rush upon the invaders, and, after a
short but very spirited hand-to-hand scuffle, tumbled them down the
embankment. Our line to the right [of the batteries], having been
reenforced by [Samuel S.] Carroll's brigade of the 2nd Corps, which had
hurried on in good time, also succeeded in driving back the assailants
with a rapid fire, and the dangerous crisis was happily ended."

In all of its zones, the effusively bloody contest of July 2 was finally

Ewell's attack on east slope of Cemetery Hill

over. "By 9 o'clock," says Confederate artillery officer E. Porter Alexander, "the field was silent. It was evident that we had not finished the job and would have to make a fresh effort in the morning. The firing had hardly ceased when my faithful little darkey, Charlie, came up hunting for me, with a fresh horse, affectionate congratulations on my safety, and, what was equally acceptable, something to eat. Negro servants hunting for their masters were a feature of the landscape that night."

Another feature of the landscape was its carpet of dead and wounded. Relates Union Colonel Theodore B. Gates, commander of a regiment of New Yorkers: "I took [the] opportunity to walk with some of my officers over that portion of the battlefield, in our immediate front, across which the 3rd Corps had retreated. The enemy's pursuit was pushed close up to our lines, and the dead and wounded of both sides mingled together and covered the ground. Our pickets for the night—the men who watch while the army sleeps—had been posted . . . some 600 yards in advance of our line of battle and embraced a portion of the field where the combat raged fiercest in the afternoon. . . . The low moans of the wounded . . . guided us in our search.

"We found among them men from almost every state, loyal and disloyal—the fierce, half-barbaric Texan, side by side with the cool, unimpassioned soldier from Maine—the Georgian and New Yorker—the Mississippian and Pennsylvanian—who, a few short hours before, thirsted for each others' lives. Now, softened by the anguish of wounds, and, still more, by the soothing spirit that pervades the night while its myriad stars are looking down upon you—all their fierce passions hushed, and all their rancor gone—these wounded men sought to comfort and to cheer one another.

"The stretcher-bearers, groping about for the wounded, moved noiselessly over the field, carrying their human burdens to the ambulances within our lines, and these conveyed them to the hospitals."

One of the hospitals was the Jacob Weikert farm, where Tillie Pierce remained. "The number of wounded brought to the place was indeed appalling. They were laid in different parts of the house. The orchard and space around the buildings were covered with the shattered and dying, and the barn became more and more crowded. The scene had become terrible beyond description. . . . In the house, I made myself useful in doing whatever I could to assist the surgeons and nurses. Cooking and making beef tea seemed to be going on all the time. It was an animated and busy scene. Some were cutting bread and spreading it, while I was kept busy carrying the pieces to the soldiers."

Close work at a Union battery

For the citizens of Gettysburg, the day had been one of anxiety and uncertainty. Says Billy Bayly, the farm boy who lived northwest of town: "I had stood during the day looking from a point of vantage over the battlefield, but the movements of the forces fighting there could not be distinguished, partly because of the distance, but more particularly, perhaps, because of the clouds of smoke that hung over the whole field. A flash of flame and the angry crack of guns a few seconds afterwards indicated where the opposing forces were engaged. But that was all the eye could distinguish save here and there a wagon train or reinforcements of artillery moving into position.

"Just before nightfall . . . I had the sensation of a lifetime. . . . There was a thunder of guns, a shrieking, whistling, moaning . . . of shells before they burst, sometimes like rockets in the air. . . . No results of the conflicts would be noted; no shifting of scenes or movement of actors in the great struggle could be observed. It was simply noise, flash, and roar, the roar of a continuous thunderstorm and the sharp angry crashes of the thunderbolt. . . . There were guns in action that evening, the reverberation from whose discharges shook the windows in the house. I did not know . . . where these guns were located, but I know that the windows rattled and the house shook. . . . As . . . the firing ceased . . . all was . . [as] uncanny in its silence as the noise had been satanic in its volume."

Adds Professor Jacobs: "To us . . . who were at the time within the Rebel lines, the result seemed doubtful, and gloomy forebodings filled our minds. . . . The unearthly yells of the exultant and defiant enemy had, during the afternoon, been frequently heard, even amidst the almost deafening sounds of exploding cannon, of screaming and bursting shells, and of the continuous roar of musketry; and it seemed to us, judging from the character and direction of these mingled noises, that the enemy had been gaining essentially on our flanks. . . . Intensely anxious to know, we had no means of finding out the relative condition of the two armies; and, like drowning men, we were ready to catch at straws.

"The Rebels returned again to our streets at 10 P.M. and prepared their supper; and soon we began to hope that all was not lost. . . . Some were heard to say, 'The Yankees have a good position, and we must drive them out of it tomorrow.' This assured us that our men had been able to hold their position, and that our lines were unbroken. There seemed now to be an entire absence of that elation and boastfulness which they manifested when they entered the town on the evening of the 1st of July. . . . One said to another, in tones of great earnestness, 'I am very much discouraged,' from which we learned that the results of the day were not in accordance with their high expectations, although they said [that] during the evening they had been driving us on our right and our left."

That night Sallie Broadhead wrote in her diary: "I have just finished washing a few pieces for my child, for we expect to be compelled to leave town tomorrow, as the Rebels say it will most likely be shelled. I cannot sleep, and as I sit down to write to while away the time, my husband sleeps as soundly as though nothing was wrong. I wish I could rest so easily, but it is out of the question for me either to eat or sleep under such terrible excitement and such painful suspense. We know not what the morrow will bring forth. . . . I think little has been gained by either side so far. 'Has our army been sufficiently reenforced?' is our anxious question. A few minutes since, we had a talk with an officer of the staff of General Early, and he admits that our army has the best position, but says we cannot hold it much longer."

William Starkes, the New York officer who lay with a group of Union casualties in one of Gettysburg's Confederate hospitals, had another interview with the enemy provost marshal. "It was late in the evening. . . . He smiled as usual when he approached us, though I fancied not as cheerily as before. 'It has been a terrible day,' he said. The Union army was all in front of Lee's now, and the fight had been raging with varied success . . . and had closed with the advantage all in favor of the South. He spoke of the [Union] position . . . as a very strong one, and said its capture was a necessity . . . [and that it] would be taken.

"We were in much improved spirit. We had had some experience, and knew that when hard fighting was the order . . . if the Army of the Potomac was not whipped very soon, it was not apt to be whipped at all. . . . As the colonel was about retiring, I called after him thus: 'I say, Colonel—that strong position of which you speak—that is a matter in which we have much interest, as you will concede. Would you mind calling or sending us word about the time you take it?' He laughed pleasantly again. 'You will see,' he said."

Out on Cemetery Ridge, General Meade called for a council of war to be held at his headquarters, a whitewashed cottage on the Taneytown Road south of Cemetery Hill. According to Lieutenant Frank Haskell, the meeting took place in a room of the humblest design. "Its only furniture consisted of a large, wide bed in one corner, a small pine table in the center, upon which was a wooden pail of water with a tin cup for drinking, and a candle stuck to the table by putting the end in tallow

General Meade's headquarters

melted down from the wick, and five or six straight-backed rush-bottomed chairs. The generals came in—some sat, some kept walking or standing, two lounged upon the bed, some were constantly smoking cigars.

"And thus disposed, they deliberated whether the army should fall back from its present position to one in rear which it was said was stronger, should attack the enemy on the morrow wherever he could be found, or should stand there upon the horseshoe crest, still on the defensive, and await the further movements of the enemy. The latter proposition was unanimously agreed to. Their heads were sound. The Army of the Potomac would just halt right there and allow the Rebel to come up and smash his head against it, to any reasonable extent he desired, as he had today. After some two hours the council dissolved, and the officers went their several ways."

Meade believed that Lee, having failed to crush the Union flanks, would make his next effort against the center. And that is exactly what the Confederate commander had in mind.

Jeb Stuart had reported to Lee that afternoon. The greeting was a somewhat severe, "Well, General Stuart, you are here at last." Stuart's attempt to explain his absence was met with a frown. But then Lee's face softened, and he waved the topic aside. Turning to matters at hand, he said, "Help me fight these people."

During the evening hours, Lee was smitten with the common but embarrassing and debilitating battlefield complaint of diarrhea. People in the vicinity of his headquarters tent saw the general, hobbling as though in pain, make trip after trip to the rear. Later, after the battle had been lost and it seemed that Lee had fought it with something less than his usual skill, there were Confederate officers who believed that his ailment had diminished him not only physically but also mentally.

On both sides of the battlefield, the night of July 2 remained a busy one throughout. Troops and guns were shifted hither and yon, supply wagons lumbered in all directions, and the wounded continued to be a problem of monstrous proportions. Augustus Buell, the Union cannoneer, was a member of a party sent southward from Cemetery Hill to find the reserve ammunition train and tap it for supplies, and he gives the details of the circuitous trip: "We went down the Taneytown Road till we came to the bivouac of the 6th Corps, and thence [eastward] to the Baltimore Pike by a crossroad, and [turning northward] found the reserve ammunition parked in a field some distance to the rear of General Meade's headquarters. . . . The route [i.e., along the Taneytown Road] ran close in the rear of the positions of the 2nd, 3rd, and 5th Corps, which had sustained the brunt of the main fight . . . and the whole way it was literally a solid field hospital. . . .

"As we passed slowly along the road we could see on every side in the fields in and around such farm buildings as had escaped the flames [kindled during the afternoon of fighting], and fairly lining both sides of the road, innumerable groups of wounded in all stages of misery; groaning, crying, swearing, begging for water or whiskey, or for food; entreating the surgeons and attendants to come to them; some in delirium, calling for their friends at home; some even begging someone to shoot them, to escape from their present pangs; and the whole scene fitfully lighted up by the flaring lanterns of the hospital forces, or the flickering fires of rails and boards here and there; the fields toward the front full of flitting lights from the lanterns of the stretcher parties busy bringing fresh additions to the wretched mass.

"Meantime the surgeons were at work as best they could, in the darkness and confusion, dressing wounds, administering stimulants, and all that sort of thing. In the course of this mile or so of road there must have been . . . not less than 8,000 wounded men, of whom, no doubt, 1,000 died during the night."

Among the Union wounded who spent the night on the battlefield was a Private Stowe of Bigelow's artillery battery, who had been shot through the body. "I was left between the picket lines. There I was all night with none but the dead, save now and then a ghoul in gray searching the dead and stripping them of their clothing. If seen by our pickets they were fired on and driven away. The night was long and dark to me. I thought, if the boys could, they would come for me. Toward morning a man in gray came near me. He appeared to be looking about, but not trying to strip any bodies. He stood looking at me, and I put out my hand and touched his foot. He jumped as if surprised; he probably thought me dead. On recovering, he stooped over, asked me where I was shot, if I was cold, and got a rubber blanket, placed it under me, and covered me with two of woolen. He sat by me some time, talking, till it began to be light, then gave me his canteen of water, saying he must get back to his post."

18

The Third Morning

ALTHOUGH IT WAS TRUE that the Confederates of Ewell's command who had attacked in the north the previous evening were checked, George Steuart's brigade of Johnson's division had made a lodgment in the Union works of the Spangler's Spring area, southeast of Culp's Hill, which marked Meade's extreme right flank. It was a part of Lee's plan for July 3 for Ewell to exploit this lodgment in support of the main attack from Seminary Ridge. But Ewell could not wait for the main attack to form. His work began at earliest dawn, when the Federals at Culp's Hill, strongly reinforced during the night, brought the lodgment under heavy artillery fire.

One of the Confederates involved at the spot where the morning's action was hottest was Randolph McKim, a junior officer in Steuart's brigade. "We had no means of replying [to the artillery fire], as our guns could not be dragged up that steep and rugged ascent. Then, a little after sunrise, their infantry moved forward in heavy force to attack us. They drove in our skirmishers, but could not dislodge us from the works we had captured, although these were commanded in part by the works on the crest of the hill to our right, whence a galling fire was poured into our ranks. Next a strong effort was made to take us in flank, and . . . at one time our line resembled three sides of a pentagon, the left side being composed of some other brigade, [the] center and right composed of our own brigade, which thus occupied the most advanced position toward the crest of the hill. About this time, I think, word came to General Steuart that the men's ammunition was almost exhausted. One of his staff immediately took three men and went on foot to the wagons, distant about a mile and a quarter, and brought up two boxes of cartridges. . . .

"It was now, I think, about half-past nine, and ever since four o'clock the fire of the enemy had been almost continuous, at times tremendous. . . . But all the efforts of the enemy failed to dislodge us. Unassisted, the 3rd Brigade held the position they had won the night before. . . .

"Then came General Ewell's order to assume the offensive and assail the crest of Culp's Hill, on our right. . . . Both General Steuart and General Daniel [Junius Daniel of Rodes' division], who now came up with his brigade to support the movement, strongly disapproved of making the assault. And well might they despair of success in the face of such difficulties. The works to be stormed ran almost at right angles to those we occupied. Moreover, there was a double line of entrenchments, one above the other, and each filled with troops. In moving to the attack we were exposed to enfilading fire from the woods on our left flank, besides the double line of fire which we had to face in front, and a battery of artillery posted on a hill to our left-rear opened upon us at short range. What wonder, then, if Steuart was reluctant to lead his men into such a slaughter-pen, from which he saw there could be no issue but death and defeat! But though he remonstrated, he gallantly obeyed without delay the orders he received, giving the command, 'Left face,' and afterwards, 'File right.' He made his men leap the breastworks and form in line of battle on the other side at right angles, nearly, to their previous position, galled all the time by a brisk fire from the enemy. Then, drawing his sword, he gave the command, 'Charge bayonets!' and moved forward on foot with his men into the jaws of death."

As recalled by one of Steuart's battalion commanders, Major W. W. Goldborough: "O God! What a fire greeted us, and the death-shriek rends the air on every side! But on the gallant survivors pressed, closing up the dreadful gaps as fast as they were made. At this moment I felt a violent shock, and found myself instantly stretched upon the ground. I had experienced the feeling before, and knew what it meant, but to save me I could not tell where I was struck. In the excitement I felt not the pain, and, resting upon my elbow, anxiously watched that struggling column. Column, did I say? A column no longer, but the torn and scattered fragments of one."

Returning to Randolph McKim: "The end soon came. We were beaten back to the line from which we had advanced with terrible loss and in much confusion, but the enemy did not make a counter charge. By the strenuous efforts of the officers of the line and of the staff, order

Federals at Culp's Hill on morning of third day

was restored, and we re-formed in the breastworks from which we had emerged, there to be again exposed to an artillery fire exceeding in violence that of the early morning. . . . Daniel's brigade remained in the breastworks during and after the charge, and neither from that command nor from any other had we any support. Of course, it is to be presumed that General Daniel acted in obedience to orders. We remained in this breastwork after the charge about an hour before we finally abandoned the Federal entrenchments and retired to the foot of the hill."

One of the Confederate soldiers who died on Culp's Hill was Gettysburg native Wesley Culp, who, before the war, had moved to Virginia, and, when the war came, had embraced the Southern cause. It was a strange turn of events that brought Wesley back to the hill, named after his family, on which he had spent a great part of his youth, and a stranger thing still that he died while assaulting the hill on behalf of his family's enemies.

It was about 11 A.M. when the Confederates retired. As the shooting stopped, the Federals on Culp's Hill raised a tremendous cheer. Over on the main battlefield, meanwhile, nothing much had been happening. The Federals strung along Cemetery Ridge had spent the morning listening, with considerable anxiety, to the uproar in their right-rear. The sound of the cheering brought both relief and joy. "Every man in the army," says Major Mulholland, "knew we were again in possession of Culp's Hill. Then came two hours of peace—a perfect calm. It was a warm summer day, and from Round Top to Culp's Hill hardly a sound was heard. . . . The men rested after the fighting of the previous evening. No troops were moving to or fro. The only activity seen was the stretcher-bearers taking the wounded to the field hospitals. But during those two hours we could see considerable activity along Seminary Ridge. Battery after battery appeared along the edge of the woods. Guns were unlimbered, placed in position, and the horses taken to the rear. Our men sat around in groups and anxiously watched these movements in our front and wondered what it all meant."

Lee had decided to hit the Union center with some ten or fifteen thousand men, the divisions of George Pickett, Henry Heth (under James Pettigrew; Heth had been wounded on July 1), and William Pender (under Isaac Trimble; Pender had been wounded on July 2). Jeb Stuart's cavalry, now stationed on Ewell's left, east of Gettysburg, was ordered to cooperate with the attack by swinging southwestward against the Union rear.

In charge of sending the infantry divisions forward from Seminary Ridge was a gloomy James Longstreet, who had lost another appeal to Lee that the Union position be flanked. The key figure in the chain of artillery command was E. Porter Alexander, who recounts: "It had been arranged that when the infantry column was ready, General Longstreet should order two guns fired by the Washington Artillery. On that signal all our guns were to open on Cemetery Hill and the ridge extending toward Round Top, which was covered with batteries. I was to observe the fire and give Pickett the order to charge.

"I accordingly took position, about 12, at the most favorable point ... with one of Pickett's couriers with me. Soon after, I received the following note from Longstreet: 'Colonel: If the artillery fire does not have the effect to drive off the enemy or greatly demoralize him so as to make our efforts pretty certain, I would prefer that you should not advise General Pickett to make the charge. I shall rely a great deal on your good judgment to determine the matter, and shall expect you to let General Pickett know when the moment offers.'

"This note rather startled me. If that assault was to be made on General Lee's judgment it was all right, but I did not want it made on mine. I wrote back to General Longstreet to the following effect: 'General: I will only be able to judge of the effect of our fire on the enemy by his return fire, for his infantry is but little exposed to view and the smoke will obscure the whole field. If, as I infer from your note, there is any alternative to this attack, it should be carefully considered before opening our fire, for it will take all the artillery ammunition we have left to test this one thoroughly, and, if the result is unfavorable, we will have none left for another effort. And even if this is entirely successful, it can only be so at a very bloody cost.'

"To this presently came the following reply: 'Colonel: The intention is to advance the infantry if the artillery has the desired effect of driving the enemy's off, or having other effect such as to warrant us in making the attack. When the moment arrives advise General Pickett, and of course advance such artillery as you can use in aiding the attack.'

"I hardly knew whether this left me discretion or not, but at any rate it seemed decided that the artillery must open. I felt that if we went that far we could not draw back, but the infantry must go too. General A. R. Wright, of Hill's corps, was with me looking at the position when these notes were received, and we discussed them together. Wright said, 'It is not so hard to *go* there as it looks; I was nearly there with my brigade

esterday. The trouble is to *stay* there. The whole Yankee army is there
1 a bunch.'

"I was influenced by this, and somewhat by a sort of camp rumor
rhich I had heard that morning, that General Lee had said that he was
oing to send every man he had upon that hill. At any rate, I assumed
hat the question of supports had been well considered, and that what-
ver was possible would be done. But before replying I rode to see
'ickett, who was with his division a short distance in the rear. I did not
ell him my object, but only tried to guess how he felt about the charge.
Ie seemed very sanguine, and thought himself in luck to have the
hance. Then I felt that I could not make any delay or let the attack
uffer by any indecision on my part. And, that General Longstreet might
now my intention, I wrote him only this: 'General: When our artillery
re is at its best I shall order Pickett to charge.' "

It was one o'clock in the afternoon when the battlefield's quiet was
udely broken by the boom of Longstreet's signal guns. Within mo-
nents, according to Union Major Mulholland, every soldier in Meade's
ines knew that a titanic move was afoot. Mulholland himself was posi-
ioned with Hancock's 2nd Corps just south of Cemetery Hill. "The
eadquarters wagons had just come up, and General Gibbon had invited
Iancock and staff to partake of some lunch. The bread that was handed
round—if it *was* eaten—was consumed without butter, for, as the or-
lerly was passing the latter article to the gentlemen, a shell from Sem-
nary Ridge cut him in two. Instantly the air was filled with bursting
hells. The batteries that we had been watching for the last two hours
;oing into position in our front did not open singly or spasmodically.
The whole hundred and thirty-seven guns which now began to play
ipon us seemed to be discharged simultaneously, as though by electric-
ty. . . .

"Streams of screaming projectiles poured through the hot air falling
nd bursting everywhere. Men and horses were torn limb from limb;
aissons exploded one after another in rapid succession, blowing the
;unners to pieces. No spot within our lines was free from this frightful
ron rain. . . . It was literally a storm of shot and shell that the oldest
,oldiers there—those who had taken part in almost every battle of the
var—had not yet witnessed. That awful rushing sound of the flying
nissiles which causes the firmest hearts to quail was everywhere."

News correspondent "Bonaparte" of the New York *World* gives this
picture as he saw it from a position on Cemetery Hill: "The storm broke

upon us so suddenly that soldiers and officers—who leaped as it began from their tents, and from lazy siestas on the grass—were stricken in their rising with mortal wounds, and died, some with cigars between their teeth, some with pieces of food in their fingers, and one at least—a pale young German from Pennsylvania—with a miniature of his sister in his hands. . . . The boards of fences, scattered by explosion, flew in splinters through the air. The earth, torn up in clouds, blinded the eyes of hurrying men; and through the branches of the trees and among the gravestones in the cemetery a shower of destruction crashed ceaselessly. As, with hundreds of others, I groped through this tempest of death for the shelter of [a] bluff, an old man—a private in a company belonging to the 24th Michigan—was struck scarcely ten feet away by a cannonball which tore through him, extorting such a low, intense cry of mortal pain as I pray God I may never again hear."

Adds Union Captain Samuel Fiske, another member of Hancock's corps: "It was touching to see the little birds, all out of their wits with fright, flying wildly about amidst the tornado of terrible missiles and uttering strange notes of distress. It was touching to see the innocent cows and calves, feeding in the fields, torn in pieces by the shells. . . . It was a nobler sight to see the sublime bravery of our gallant artillerists, serving their guns with the utmost precision and coolness . . . knowing they were the mark aimed at by an equally brave and skillful enemy, and clinging to their beloved pieces to the bitter end."

Meade's headquarters cottage, on the Taneytown Road behind Cemetery Ridge, took a particular beating. With a group of newsmen gathered there was Samuel Wilkeson (whose son, artilleryman Bayard Wilkeson, was mortally wounded on July 1). "Every size and form of shell known to British and to American gunnery shrieked, whirled, moaned, whistled, and wrathfully fluttered over our ground. As many as six in a second, constantly two in a second, bursting and screaming over and around the headquarters made a very hell of fire. . . . They burst in the yard, burst next to the fence on both sides, garnished as usual with the hitched horses of aides and orderlies. The fastened animals reared and plunged with terror. Then one fell, then another. . . .

"Through the midst of the storm of screaming and exploding shells, an ambulance, driven by its frenzied conductor at full speed, presented to all of us the marvelous spectacle of a horse going rapidly on three legs. A hinder one had been shot off at the hock. A shell tore up the little step of the headquarters cottage, and ripped bags of oats as with a knife. Another soon carried off one of its two pillars. Soon a spherical case burst opposite the open door. Another ripped through the low garret. The remaining pillar went almost immediately."

By this time Meade and his staff had headed for a safer spot. Returning to Union narrator Mulholland: "At this tumultuous moment we witnessed a deed of heroism such as we are apt to attribute only to the knights of the olden time. Hancock, mounted and accompanied by his staff . . . with the corps flag flying in the hands of a brave Irishman . . . started at the right of his line where it joined the Taneytown Road, and slowly rode along the terrible crest to the extreme left of his position, while shot and shell roared and crashed around him, and every moment tore great gaps in the ranks [of his units]. It was a gallant deed, and withal not a reckless exposure of life, for the presence and calm demeanor of the commander, as he passed through the lines of his men, set them an example which . . . bore good fruit and nerved their stout hearts."

This nerving might have been less successful had the men been aware that the enemy in their front was not their only concern. Unnoticed in the din at hand was the horse artillery beginning to sound in the right-rear, east of Gettysburg, where Jeb Stuart was operating. What the sound meant was that Stuart had encountered opposition from Meade's cavalry. Union trooper George Armstrong Custer was about to win special distinction. It was largely through his daredevil leadership in a brief but savage fight, which took place at the same time as Pickett's Charge, that Stuart was stopped and Meade's rear was rendered safe.

The punishment dealt by the Confederate guns on Seminary Ridge was roundly reciprocated. As recalled by Lieutenant G. W. Finley, a member of Pickett's division: "The most terrific cannonade any of us had ever experienced was kept up, and it seemed as if neither man nor horse could possibly live under it. Our gunners stood to their pieces and handled them with such splendid courage as to wake the admiration of the infantry crouching on the ground behind them. We could see nothing whatever of the opposing lines, but knew from the fire that they must have a strong position and many guns. Our loss was considerable under this storm of shot and shell; still there was no demoralization of our men in line. They waited almost impatiently for the order to advance, as almost anything would be a relief from the strain upon them."

Adds another of Pickett's men, Captain W. W. Wood: "The firing was so rapid and continuous that the report of a single gun could not be distinguished. Over the space intervening between the infantry and artillery passed some mounted officer and his staff—notably once General

Custer leading the fight against Stuart

Lee, and several times Generals Longstreet and Pickett. . . . When General Lee passed over the ground it was being swept with a deadly hail of every missile known to the nomenclature of artillerists. His appearance at a place of such eminent danger both thrilled and horrified the line, and men shouted to him to go away to shelter. Always regardless of himself when duty called, he had but one attendant with him. When the men yelled to him to go away, he took off his hat in acknowledgment of their affectionate solicitude, and then rode on, quickening the pace of his noble gray."

19

Pickett's Charge

NEW APPREHENSIONS HAD SEIZED Alexander, the Confederate artillery commander. "Before the cannonade opened I had made up my mind to give Pickett the order to advance within 15 or 20 minutes after it began. But when I looked at the full development of the enemy's batteries, and knew that his infantry was generally protected from our fire by stone walls and swells of ground, I could not bring myself to give the word. It seemed madness to launch infantry into that fire, with nearly three-quarters of a mile to go at midday under a July sun. I let the 15 minutes pass, and 20, and 25, hoping vainly for something to turn up. Then I wrote to Pickett: 'If you are coming [forward] at all, you must come at once, or I cannot give you proper support; but the enemy's fire has not slackened at all; at least 18 guns are still firing from the cemetery itself.'

"Five minutes after sending that message, the enemy's fire suddenly began to slacken, and the guns in the cemetery limbered up and vacated the position. We Confederates often did such things as that to save our ammunition for use against infantry, but I had never before seen the Federals withdraw their guns simply to save them up for the infantry fight. So I said [to an aide], 'If he does not run fresh batteries in there in five minutes, this is our fight.' I looked anxiously with my glass, and the five minutes passed without a sign of life on the deserted position, still swept by our fire, and littered with dead men and horses and fragments of disabled carriages. Then I wrote Pickett urgently: 'For God's sake, come quick. The 18 guns are gone. Come quick or my ammunition won't let me support you properly.'"

Alexander's first note had been enough to stir Pickett to action.

When the courier reached him, he had just finished writing a letter to his sweetheart, his "Sally of the sunset eyes," a letter he intended to give to Longstreet to mail. In a subsequent letter to Sally, one written the following day, Pickett explained that he was standing with Longstreet when Alexander's note arrived. "After reading it I handed it to him, asking if I should obey and go forward. He looked at me for a moment, then held out his hand. Presently clasping his other hand over mine without speaking, he bowed his head upon his breast. I shall never forget the look in his face nor the clasp of his hand when I said, 'Then, General, I shall lead my division on.'

"I had ridden only a few paces when I remembered your letter and (forgive me) thoughtlessly scribbled in a corner of the envelope, 'If Old Peter's nod means death, then good-bye and God bless you, little one,' turned back and asked the dear old chief if he would be good enough to mail it for me. As he took your letter from me, my darling, I saw tears glistening on his cheeks and beard. The stern old war horse, God bless him, was weeping for his men, and, I know, praying too that this cup might pass from them."

While Pickett went back for his division, Longstreet rode forward to Alexander's position. Alexander relates: "I explained the situation, feeling then more hopeful, but afraid our artillery ammunition might not hold out for all we would want. Longstreet said, 'Stop Pickett immediately and replenish your ammunition.' I explained that it would take too long, and the enemy would recover from the effect our fire was then having; and we had, moreover, very little to replenish with. Longstreet said, 'I don't want to make this attack. I would stop it now but that General Lee ordered it and expects it to go on. I don't see how it can succeed.'

"I listened, but did not dare offer a word. The battle was lost if we stopped. Ammunition was far too low to try anything else, for we had been fighting three days. There was a chance, and it was not my part to interfere. While Longstreet was still speaking, Pickett's division swept out of the wood and showed the full length of its gray ranks and shining bayonets, as grand a sight as ever a man looked on. Joining it on the left, Pettigrew stretched farther than I could see. General Dick Garnett, just out of the sick ambulance, and buttoned up in an old blue overcoat, riding at the head of his brigade, passed us and saluted Longstreet. Garnett was a warm personal friend, and we had not met before for months. We had served on the plains together before the war. I rode with him a short distance, and then we wished each other luck and a good-bye which was our last."

In the words of a Southern newsman, a representative of the Richmond *Enquirer:* "I stood upon an eminence and watched this advance with great interest. I had seen brave men [Wright's brigade] pass over that fated valley the day before. I had witnessed their death struggle with the foe on the opposite heights. I had observed their return with shattered ranks, a bleeding mass, but with unstained banners. Now I saw their valiant comrades prepare for the same bloody trial, and already felt that their efforts would be vain unless their supports should be as true as steel and brave as lions."

Switching to the Union side and to narrator Jesse Bowman Young: "Standing on the hill where the Union troops are posted, let us try to picture that almost matchless moment. A stone fence is immediately in our front, with batteries of artillery lining the slope. Look about you: here are bronzed and worn veterans in blue, with a set and dogged expression on their lips and in their eyes, line after line of them, massed on both slopes [of Cemetery Ridge] and on the crest of the ridge in support of the batteries. In front, toward the west, is the advanced line of Union troops [the skirmishers], and beyond them are pleasant fields rolling in beauty. The fences are mostly broken down. The road to Emmitsburg crosses the landscape [running] toward the southwest. And a mile away toward the region of the setting sun [is] Seminary Ridge, crested with woods and orchards. . . . Over this plain and against these batteries and upon this stone wall, more than 10,000 men are about to be led with a furious and indomitable courage not to be paralleled by any other martial achievement hitherto wrought by the Army of Northern Virginia. As we look with bated breath and quivering nerves on the landscape, we behold the shimmer of steel along the distant ridge, and then the flutter of banners, and then an advancing line of men."

Adds Northerner Edmund Rice, a junior officer of Gibbon's division, Hancock's corps: "A line of [Confederate] skirmishers sprang lightly forward . . . and, with intervals well kept, moved rapidly down into the open fields, closely followed by a line of battle, then by another, and by yet a third, almost a mile in length. Both sides watched this never-to-be-forgotten scene—the grandeur of attack of so many thousand men. Gibbon's division, which was to stand the brunt of the assault, looked with admiration on the different lines of the Confederates marching forward with easy swinging step, and our men were heard to exclaim, 'Here they come! Here they come! Here comes their infantry!' "

Longstreet's orders called for the dispersion of units to "dress on the center," using as a guide a small clump of trees at that point in the

Union lines where the attack was supposed to hit. Says Confederate Lieutenant Finley: "Where I marched through a wheat field that sloped gently toward the Emmitsburg Road, the position of the Federals flashed into view. Skirmishers lined the fences along the road, and back of them, along a low stone wall or fence, gleamed the muskets of the first line. In rear of this, artillery, thickly planted, frowned upon us.

"As we came in sight, there seemed to be a restlessness and excitement along the enemy's lines, which encouraged some of us to hope they would not make a stubborn resistance. Their skirmishers began to run in, and the artillery opened upon us all along our front. I soon noticed that shells were also coming from our right. . . . I discovered that they came from . . . the Round Tops. This fire soon became strictly enfilading as we changed the point of direction . . . to the left while on the march, and whenever it struck our ranks was fearfully destructive. One company, a little to my right, numbering thirty-five or forty men, was almost swept, to a man, from the line by a single shell. We had not advanced far beyond our [own] guns when our gallant Colonel [W. D.] Stuart fell mortally wounded. . . . We had no other field officer present, and the command devolved upon the senior captain."

Confederate artillery chief Alexander was providing as much support as he could muster. "I rode down the line of guns, selecting such as had enough ammunition to follow Pickett's advance, and starting them after him as fast as possible. I got, I think, fifteen or eighteen in all . . . and went with them. . . . The eighteen [Federal] guns were back in the cemetery, [adding to the] storm of shell . . . bursting over and among our infantry. . . . All of our guns—silent as the infantry passed between them—reopened over their heads when the lines had got a couple of hundred yards away, but the enemy's artillery let us alone and fired only at the infantry. No one could have looked at that advance without feeling proud of it.

"But, as our supporting guns advanced, we passed many poor, mangled victims left in its trampled wake . . . one with the most horrible wound that I ever saw. We were halted for a moment by a fence, and as the men threw it down for the guns to pass, I saw in one of the corners a man sitting down and looking up at me. A solid shot had carried away both jaws and his tongue. I noticed the powder smut from the shot on the white skin around the wound. He sat up and looked at me steadily, and I looked at him until the guns could pass, but nothing, of course, could be done for him."

Union General Carl Schurz, who watched the Confederates from a position on Cemetery Hill, was absorbed by the scene. "The alignment was perfect. The battle flags fluttered gaily over the bayonets glittering in the sunlight. . . . Through our fieldglasses we could distinctly see the gaps torn in their ranks and the ground dotted with dark spots—their dead and wounded. Now and then a cheer went up from our lines when our men observed some of our shells striking right among the advancing enemy and scattering death and destruction around. But the brave rebels promptly filled the gaps from behind or by closing up on their colors; and unshaken and unhesitating they continued their onward march. . . . So far not a musket had been discharged from behind the stone fences protecting our regiments."

Returning to Confederate Lieutenant Finley, of Pickett's division: "Still on, steadily on, with the [artillery] fire growing more furious and deadly, our men advanced. . . . As we neared the Emmitsburg Road, the Federals behind the stone fence on the hill [Cemetery Ridge] opened a rapid fire upon us with muskets. . . . Men were falling all around. . . . Cannon and muskets were raining death upon us. Still on and up the slope toward that stone fence our men steadily swept, without a sound or a shot, save as the men would clamor to be allowed to return the fire that was being poured into them."

By this time two regiments of Vermonters just south of the zone under assault had swung down the slope and were firing through the thickening smoke into Pickett's right flank. At the same time Pettigrew (supported by two brigades under Isaac Trimble), advancing abreast of Pickett's left, was being punished in a similar way by some Ohio troops on his left flank. The fire on the attack force as a whole was coming from three directions. Some of the fire was canister, and at the spots where these merciless balls cut their swaths, according to an unnamed Union officer, the Confederate lines "underwent an instantaneous transformation in a dense cloud of smoke and dust. Arms, heads, blankets, guns, and knapsacks were tossed in the air, and the moan from the battlefield was heard amid the storm of battle."

It was toward Union General Alexander Webb's brigade of Gibbon's division of Hancock's corps that the spearhead of the Confederate attack was pointed. Although reduced to a fraction of its original size, its flank supports fighting simply to survive (and a brigade of reinforcements from across the valley entering upon a similar plight), the spearhead retained an incredible sharpness. "When we were about seventy-five or one hundred yards from that stone wall," says Confederate Lieutenant Finley, "some of the men holding it began to break for the rear, when,

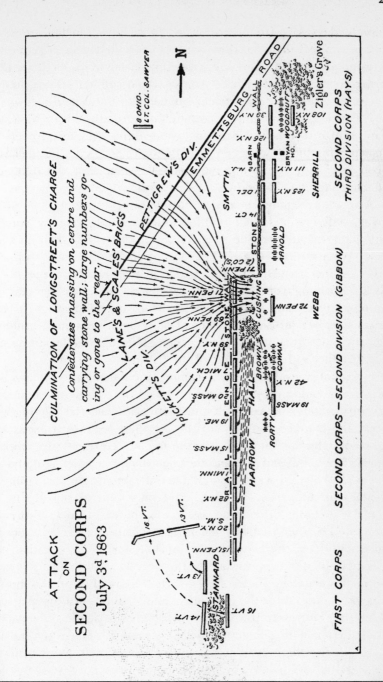

Pickett's Charge

without orders, save from captains and lieutenants, our line poured
volley or two into them, and then rushed upon the fence. . . . The Fed
eral gunners stood manfully to their guns. I never saw more gallar
bearing in any men. They fired their last shots full in our faces and s
close that I thought I felt distinctly the flame of the explosion."

A Union gun commander mortally wounded at this time was Lieu
tenant Alonzo H. Cushing. Standing by one of his weapons with a han
clutched to his midriff, a section of his intestines exposed, Cushing cried
"Webb, I will give them one more shot!" As the shot was fired, th
lieutenant shouted, "Good-bye!" and fell dead.

Among the Union officers on horseback behind Webb's lines wa
Gibbon's aide Frank Haskell, who was wondering how long the battere
Confederates would be able to maintain the offensive, when he got
shock. "Were my senses mad? The larger portion of Webb's brigade–
my God, it was true—there by the group of trees and the angles of th
wall, was breaking from the cover of their works, and, without orders o
reason, with no hand lifted to check them, was falling back, a fea
stricken flock of confusion! The fate of Gettysburg hung upon a spider
single thread! A great magnificent passion came on me at the instant. . .
My sword, that had always hung idle by my side, the sign of rank only i
every battle, I drew, bright and gleaming, the symbol of command. . .

"All rules and proprieties were forgotten; all considerations of pe
son, and danger, and safety despised; for, as I met the tide of thes
rabbits, the damned red flags of the rebellion began to thicken an
flaunt along the wall they had just deserted. . . . I ordered these men t
halt and face about and fire, and they heard my voice and gathered m
meaning and obeyed my commands. On some unpatriotic backs of thos
not quick of comprehension the flat of my saber fell not lightly. . .
General Webb soon came to my assistance. He was on foot, but he wa
active. . . . The men that had fallen back, facing the enemy, soon re
gained confidence in themselves and became steady."

The Confederate spearhead had been reduced to only a few hun
dred men, Lieutenant Finley among them. "Just as I stepped upon th
stone wall I noticed for the first time a line of troops just joining upo
our left. . . . They were from Archer's Tennessee brigade and a part c
Heth's division. This gallant brigade had been terribly cut up in the fir
day's fight, and there was but a fragment of them left. Some of then
with us, seized and held the stone wall in our front. For several minute
there were no troops in our immediate front, but to our left the Feder
line was still unbroken. This fact was impressed upon my mind by my . .

eeing our brave Brigadier General Garnett . . . riding to our left, just in my rear, with his eyes fastened upon the unbroken line behind the stone ence and with the evident intention of making such disposition of his men as would dislodge it.

"At that instant, suddenly a terrific fire burst upon us from our ront, and, looking around, I saw close to us, just on the crest of the idge, a fresh line of Federals attempting to drive us from the stone ence; but, after exchanging a few rounds with us, they fell back behind he crest, leaving us still in possession of the stone wall. Under this fire, s I immediately learned, General Garnett had fallen dead. Almost simultaneously with these movements General [Lewis A.] Armistead, on oot, strode over the stone fence, leading his brigade most gallantly, with is hat on his sword, and calling upon his men to charge. A few of us ollowed him until, just as he put his hand upon one of the abandoned ;uns, he was shot down."

Union General Hancock, conducting the critical defense on horse-back, was himself wounded in this fighting, a bullet striking his saddle and damaging his thigh. The injury was a severe one, but the general emained on the field. Hancock and Armistead had been the warmest of riends before the war, and Armistead, whose wounds were fatal but not immediately so, made a request that Hancock be given his personal effects for delivery to his family.

Panting and shouting, Union reinforcements in large numbers con-erged at the scene of the breakthrough. Meanwhile, there had been no etup in the fighting on the flanks that bent raggedly toward the Emmitsburg Road. Pandemonium was everywhere the rule. "Men fire nto each other's faces, not five feet apart," says Union newsman Charles Carleton Coffin. "There are bayonet thrusts, saber strokes, pistol shots; cool, deliberate movements on the part of some—hot, passionate, des-perate efforts with others; hand-to-hand contests; recklessness of life; enacity of purpose; fiery determination; oaths, yells, curses, hurrahs, houtings; men going down on their hands and knees, spinning round ike tops, throwing out their arms, gulping up blood, falling—legless, armless, headless. There are ghastly heaps of dead men. Seconds are centuries; minutes, ages. . . .

"The Rebel column has lost its power. The lines waver. The soldiers of the front rank look round for their supports. They are gone—fleeing over the field, broken, shattered, thrown into confusion by the remorse-ess fire. . . . The lines have disappeared like a straw in a candle's flame. The ground is thick with dead, and the wounded are like the withered

Repelling Pickett's Charge

leaves of autumn. Thousands of Rebels throw down their arms and give themselves up as prisoners.

"How inspiring the moment! How thrilling the hour! It is the high-water mark of the Rebellion—a turning point of history and of human destiny!"

To the Union soldiers on Cemetery Ridge, it was simply a spectacular success—something they were not accustomed to. According to Jesse Bowman Young: "Cheer after cheer rose from the triumphant boys in blue, echoing from Round Top, reechoing from Cemetery Hill, resounding in the vale below, and making the very heavens throb." Carl Schurz adds that "here and there the men began to sing, 'John Brown's soul.' The song swept weirdly over the bloody field." As for General Meade, he reacted to the moment with a fervent "Thank God!," which he followed with a somewhat subdued "Hurrah!"

The Confederate force had not been annihilated, but it had been monstrously damaged. Fewer than half the participants got off safely. Pickett himself escaped unhurt; Pettigrew was wounded; Trimble was wounded and captured.

For Confederate General James Longstreet, the sight of the exhausted survivors making their return was not only discouraging but also worrisome. "I fully expected to see Meade ride to the front and lead his forces to a tremendous countercharge. . . . The Federals were advancing a line of skirmishers which I thought was the advance of their charge. As soon as the line of skirmishers came within reach of our guns, the batteries opened again, and their fire seemed to check at once the threatened advance. After keeping it up a few minutes the line of skirmishers disappeared, and my mind was relieved of the apprehension that Meade was going to follow us."

British observer Arthur Fremantle says that Longstreet maintained a calm and cheerful demeanor during this trying time. "He asked for something to drink. I gave him some rum out of my silver flask, which I begged he would keep in remembrance of the occasion. He smiled, and, to my great satisfaction, accepted the memorial. . . . Soon afterwards I joined General Lee, who had in the meanwhile come to the front on becoming aware of the disaster. If Longstreet's conduct was admirable, that of General Lee was perfectly sublime. He was engaged in rallying and in encouraging the broken troops, and was riding about a little in front of the wood, quite alone—the whole of his staff being engaged in a similar manner further to the rear. His face, which is always placid and cheerful, did not show signs of the slightest disappointment, care, or annoyance; and he was addressing to every soldier he met a few words of encouragement. . . . He spoke to all the wounded men that passed him. . . . I saw many badly wounded men take off their hats and cheer him.

"He said to me, 'This has been a sad day for us, Colonel—a sad day; but we can't expect always to gain victories.' He was also kind enough to advise me to get into some more sheltered position. Notwithstanding the misfortune which had so suddenly befallen him, General Lee seemed to observe everything, however trivial. When a mounted officer began licking his horse for shying at the bursting of a shell, he called out, 'Don't whip him, captain, don't whip him. I've got just such another foolish horse myself, and whipping does no good.'

"I happened to see a man lying flat on his face in a small ditch, and I remarked that I didn't think he seemed dead. This drew General Lee's attention to the man, who commenced groaning dismally. Finding appeals to his patriotism of no avail, General Lee had him ignominiously set on his legs by some neighboring gunners.

"I saw General [Cadmus] Wilcox—an officer who wears a short round jacket and a battered straw hat—come up to him and explain, almost crying, the state of his brigade. General Lee immediately shook hands with him and said cheerfully, 'Never mind, general; all this has been *my* fault; it is *I* that have lost this fight, and you must help me out of it in the best way you can.'

"In this manner I saw General Lee encourage and reanimate his somewhat dispirited troops, and magnanimously take upon his own shoulders the whole weight of the repulse. It was impossible to look at him or to listen to him without feeling the strongest admiration; and I never saw any man fail him except the man in the ditch."

Even while the last of the Confederate survivors were returning to the lines at Seminary Ridge, there was a flurry of action on Lee's extreme right flank as several waves of Union General Judson Kilpatrick's troopers galloped against it. These ill-advised attacks were smartly stopped. Their only result was to add a good many names to the afternoon's casualty list. Among the fatalities was the newly appointed Union brigadier, Elon Farnsworth.

"The battle was now over," says Northerner Jesse Bowman Young, "but nobody knew it! The repulse of Pickett's charge was really the defeat of the Army of Northern Virginia, but . . . the two armies stood at bay, glaring like two wild beasts which had fought one another almost to death, watching for a stroke or a motion, and listening for a growl that

might indicate a further continuance of the struggle. General Meade
hardly durst venture out against the Confederates after the defeat of
Pickett, and General Lee was too weak to undertake any further movement except in retreat, unless he should be attacked. . . .

"There have been few such sights and circumstances as those amid
which the two armies found themselves at Gettysburg when the fight was
over on Friday afternoon, July 3, 1863. . . . Thousands of men were
lying unattended, scattered over the field, mingled with broken gun
carriages, exploded caissons, hundreds of dead and dying horses, and
other ghastly debris of the battlefield. At once the poor victims of shot
and shell nearest our lines were brought in; others farther out were in
due time reached; and the surgeons and nurses . . . kept up their work
of ministering to and caring for the wounded. . . .

"It was possible, as night came on, to make a bit of a fire, here and
there in the rear, and boil water for a cup of coffee, which was a boon to
be grateful for. While the boys sat or lay on the ground, eating a bite of
hardtack, and eagerly, in their hunger, devouring the succulent salt
pork, which was about the only nourishment to be secured, relays of
men with stretchers, and hundreds of others helping the wounded to
walk to the rear, passed back and forth with their bloody freight, now
and then a groan or a suppressed shriek telling the story of suffering
and heroic fortitude.

" 'Listen, boys!' was the shout of one of [the] men as they lay on the
ground. . . . 'The fight must be over—listen! There is a band in the rear
beginning to tune up. . . .' It was a sight and a situation long to be
remembered. The field was covered with the slain; the full moon looked
down with serene, unclouded, and softened luster on the field of
Gettysburg, trodden down for miles by the two great armies; surgeons
were cutting off limbs, administering whisky, chloroform, and morphine
to deaden pain; hundreds of men were going back and forth from the
fields where the actual fighting had occurred, to the rear, with the mangled bodies of the wounded; and about 100,000 men—the survivors who
were left out of 160,000 in the two armies [the original number, all arms
included, was probably closer to 175,000, and the casualties came to
about 43,000, the Federals suffering 23,000 and the Confederates
20,000]—were waiting to see what would come on the morrow, when
suddenly a band of music began to play in the rear of the Union line of
battle, down somewhere on the Taneytown Road. . . .

"Down the valley and up the hill and over the field, into the ears of
wounded and dying men, and beyond our line into the bivouac of the

Residual scene at point of Pickett's breakthrough

eaten enemy, the soft, gentle and melting tune . . . 'Home, Sweet, Sweet Home' was . . . breathed from the brazen instruments."

In the Confederate ranks, there was deep dejection over Pickett's repulse. According to Napier Bartlett, a cannoneer from Louisiana, many of the men, afraid for their dream of liberty from the Union, were moved to tears. Bartlett adds, however: "When we were permitted at length to lie down under the caissons, or in the fence corners, and realized that we had escaped the death that had snatched away so many others, we felt too well satisfied at our good fortune—in spite of the enemy still near us—not to sleep the soundest sleep it is permitted on earth for mortals to enjoy."

Not all of the Confederates slept. Among the wakeful was Brigadier General John D. Imboden, commander of an independent brigade of Lee's cavalry. Imboden and his troopers, who had seen no action at Gettysburg, were encamped in a meadow a mile behind the lines, and Imboden was awaiting orders. "We all knew that the day had gone against us, but the full extent of the disaster was only known in high quarters. . . . Our army was not in retreat, and it was surmised in camp that with tomorrow's dawn would come a renewal of the struggle. All felt and appreciated the momentous consequences to the cause of Southern independence of final defeat or victory on that great field. . . .

"About 11 P.M. a horseman came to summon me to General Lee. I promptly mounted, and, accompanied by an aide on my staff, and guided by the courier who brought the message, rode about a mile toward Gettysburg to General Lee's headquarters. On inquiry, I found that he was not there but had gone to the headquarters of General Hill, a mile further south. When we reached the place indicated, a flickering candle visible from the road through the open front of a common wall-tent exposed to view Generals Lee and Hill seated on camp stools with a map spread upon their knees. Dismounting, I approached on foot. After exchanging the ordinary salutations, General Lee directed me to go back to his headquarters and wait for him. I did so, but he did not make his appearance until about 1 A.M., when he came riding alone at a slow walk, and evidently wrapped in profound thought.

"When he arrived, there was not even a sentinel on duty at his tent, and no one of his staff awake. As he approached and saw us under a tree, he spoke, reined in his jaded horse, and essayed to dismount. The effort to do so betrayed so much physical exhaustion that I hurriedly stepped forward to assist him, but before I reached his side he had succeeded in alighting, and threw his arm across the saddle to rest, and, fixing his eyes upon the ground, leaned in silence and almost motionless upon his equally weary horse. . . . The light from a close-by campfire shone full upon his massive features and revealed an expression of sadness that I never had before seen upon his face.

"Awed by his appearance, I waited for him to speak until the silence became embarrassing, when, to break it and change the silent current of his thoughts, I ventured to remark, in a sympathetic tone and in allusion to his great fatigue, 'General, this has been a hard day on you.' He looked up and replied mournfully, 'Yes, it has been a sad, sad day to us,' and immediately lapsed into his thoughtful mood and attitude. Being unwilling again to intrude upon his reflections, I said no more. After perhaps a minute or two, he suddenly straightened up to his full height and, turning to me with more animation and excitement of manner than I had ever seen in him before, for he was a man of wonderful equanimity, he said in a voice tremendous with emotion, 'I never saw troops behave more magnificently than Pickett's division did today in that grand charge; and if they had been supported as they were to have been—but for some reason not fully explained to me, were not—we would have held that position, and the day would have been ours.' After a moment's pause he added in a loud voice, in a tone almost of agony, 'Too bad! Too bad! OH! TOO BAD!' "

Lee soon was in control of himself and told Imboden, "We must now return to Virginia. As many of our poor wounded as possible must be taken home. I have sent for you because your men and horses are fresh and in good condition to guard and conduct our train back to Virginia." Lee had already sent orders for Ewell's corps to withdraw from the town and the Culp's Hill area for a junction with Longstreet and Hill on Seminary Ridge.

20

Concluding Scenes

OR THE CITIZENS of Gettysburg, the whole of July 3 had been heavy with
nxiety and uncertainty. Late that night Sallie Broadhead summed up
he day in her diary: "The battle opened with fierce cannonading before
o'clock A.M. Shortly after the battle began we were told to leave this end
f the town, for likely it would be shelled. My husband declared he
vould not go while one brick remained upon another, and, as usual, we
etook ourselves to the cellar, where we remained until 10 o'clock [A.M.],
vhen the firing ceased. We could not get breakfast on account of our
ears and the great danger. During the cessation we managed to get a
old bite.

"Again, the battle began with unearthly fury. Nearly all the after-
oon it seemed as if the heavens and earth were crashing together. The
ime that we sat in the cellar seemed long, listening to the terrific sound
f the strife. More terrible never greeted human ears. We knew that with
very explosion, and the scream of each shell, human beings were hur-
ied, through excruciating pain, into another world, and that many more
vere torn and mangled and lying in torment worse than death, and no
ne able to extend relief. The thought made me very sad, and feel that,
f it was God's will, I would rather be taken away than remain to see the
nisery that would follow.

"Some thought this awful afternoon would never come to a close.
Ve knew that the Rebels were putting forth all their might, and it was a
lreadful thought that they might succeed. Who is victorious, or with
vhom the advantage rests, no one here can tell. It would ease the horror
f we knew our arms were successful. Some think the Rebels were de-

feated, as there has been no boasting as on yesterday, and they look uneasy and by no means exultant. . . . I fear we are too hopeful. We shall see tomorrow."

To the experienced ear of William Starkes, the officer with the group of Union wounded in one of Gettysburg's Confederate hospitals, the sounds of the afternoon had seemed indicative of an enemy attack that had been hurled back. Starkes waited impatiently for the nightly visit of the Confederate provost marshal. "The colonel was late in making his appearance, and there was no smile in response to our eager greetings. 'Yes, the charge has failed. There has been a dreadful loss.' He lingered but a little while, and was reticent. He said, however, that another charge was to be made at four o'clock in the morning, and the position would be taken. 'Do not fail to notify us, Colonel,' I said. 'No, I will not. Good night.' 'That is good-bye,' I said to an officer on a stretcher beside me. Our sleep was rather of the desultory character, and we were all wide enough awake at four o'clock, but there was no sound indicating a charge."

The narrative is assumed by Union soldier Jesse Bowman Young, who later made his home in Gettysburg and studied all aspects of the battle, both military and civilian. "The next morning was the Fourth of July, but it seemed at the time to those who were at Gettysburg a somber and terrible national anniversary, with the indescribable horrors of the field, as yet hardly mitigated by the work of mercy, before the eye in every direction. The army did not know the extent of the victory; the nation did not realize as yet what had been done. The armies were still watching each other, although the Confederates had withdrawn [during the night] from the town of Gettysburg and concentrated their troops on Seminary Ridge.

"The people in the village came out of their cellars and other places of refuge, and as the day broke upon them opened their doors. They had been under a reign of terror [although there had been only one civilian fatality, a young woman named Jennie Wade, hit by a stray bullet while baking bread in the kitchen of her home]. . . . During the night they had suspected a movement of Lee's troops, for they had noted in their places of concealment occasional hurried sounds as of men, wagons, and cannon passing through the streets; but whether these betokened withdrawal or preparations for another attack on the Union lines it was impossible for them to tell. Now, as they came out of doors, they cherished new hopes, for they could see no rebel soldiers. All had emingly disappeared, except, now and then, indeed, a straggler hurrying away after his fellow-rebels toward the west, or hiding in an alley r outhouse to escape further service in the 'lost cause.'

"It is almost daybreak, and some of the citizens venture to stand out n the pavements to watch for the development of events and note what going to take place. They see a squad of men coming toward them own the main street from the south, bearing a banner. It is too dark at rst to tell whether they wear the blue or the gray, whether the Conderates have returned to capture the place, or whether the boys in blue re advancing from Cemetery Hill. The watchers hold their breath in suspense, until in a moment the dawning light reveals to their longing yes the glorious flag which the advancing troops are carrying, the Stars nd Stripes, torn with the marks of battle, stained with blood, but reathed and crowned with victory.

"On that very morning, the nation's birthday, the Fourth of July, 863, while the troops of Meade planted their triumphant banner on the ecaptured heights of Gettysburg, a similar scene of victory was dislayed a thousand miles away to the southwest. There, in front of beaguered Vicksburg, a great chieftain . . . was waiting to receive the urrender of the army of [Confederate General John C.] Pemberton. . . . rant at Vicksburg that glorious day beheld 20,000 prisoners [actually o,ooo], with vast stores of guns and appliances of war becoming the roperty of the Union, while at the same hour . . . Meade rejoiced in the awn of the glorious truth . . . that the victory of Gettysburg was the ecisive battle of the war. . . .

"But nevertheless, among the troops themselves, that Fourth of uly, 1863, at Gettysburg was a wretched, dismal, and foreboding day, a ay of uncertainty and suspense for both armies, which still faced each ther. Each had thrown up fortifications and strengthened its line of efense, and was watching to find out what the other would do. Neither Meade nor Lee, just at that time, was anxious to bring about a renewal f the fight, and the time was occupied in caring for the wounded and urying the dead.

"A heavy rainstorm set in about noon, which made the roads and elds in the course of a few hours a sea of mud. Without tents, with ardly shelter even for the wounded, of whom there were still thousands n the reeking earth to be cared for, and amid the beating tempest that vept the whole region round about, the situation of the two armies was orlorn enough. . . . The day passed without any alarm or movement.

Federals reclaiming Gettysburg on July 4

All sorts of rumors, however, were flying here and there from mouth to mouth throughout the army. . . .

"When the day was over, the soldiers, anxiously and in discomfort, lay . . . on the soaking earth, trying almost in vain to keep up the smoldering fire at their bivouacs. And then, when the night had gone and Sunday morning arrived, July 5, there was news indeed. Before daylight the rumors spread far and wide, and they were verified by advance of the skirmish lines all along our front. 'The rebels have retreated back toward the Cumberland Valley!' "

Tillie Pierce, still at the Jacob Weikert house in the Union lines, was thrilled by the volume of the cheering. "On the summits, in the valleys, everywhere we heard the soldiers hurrahing for the victory that had been won. The troops on our right, at Culp's Hill, caught up the joyous sound as it came rolling on from the Round Tops on our left, and soon the whole line of blue rejoiced in the results achieved. . . . We were all glad that the storm had passed and that victory was perched upon our banners. But, oh, the horror and desolation that remained!"

The chief horror was the bloated and putrefying remains of men and horses, made more loathsome by the multitudes of flies that hummed about them and cavorted upon them. As for the stench of the field, it made men sick and it pervaded the town, impelling people to keep their doors and windows closed regardless of the summer heat.

The retreating Confederates, of course, had their own set of problems. Their train, escorted by John Imboden's cavalry at Lee's order, was seventeen miles long, and it was overburdened with packed ambulances. Imboden found the night of July 5 a special trial. He had remained at the rear of the train as it began its trip westward from Cashtown, and now, in the darkness, he began to make his way toward the front. "My orders had been peremptory that there should be no halt for any cause whatever. If an accident should happen to any vehicle, it was immediately to be put out of the road and abandoned. The column moved rapidly, considering the rough roads and the darkness, and from almost every wagon for many miles issued heart-rending wails of agony.

"For four hours I hurried forward on my way to the front, and in all that time I was never out of hearing of the groans and cries of the wounded and dying. Scarcely one in a hundred had received adequate surgical aid, owing to the demands on the hard-working surgeons from still worse cases that had to be left behind. Many of the wounded in the wagons had been without food for thirty-six hours. Their torn and bloody clothing, matted and hardened, was rasping the tender, inflamed, and still-oozing wounds. Very few of the wagons had even a layer of straw in them, and all were without springs. The road was rough and rocky from the heavy washings [by the rain] of the preceding day. The jolting was enough to have killed strong men, if long exposed to it.

"From nearly every wagon as the teams trotted on, urged by whip and shout, came such cries and shrieks as these: 'O God! Why can't I die?' 'My God! Will no one have mercy and kill me?' 'Stop! Oh, for God's sake, stop just for one minute. Take me out and leave me to die on the roadside.' 'I am dying! I am dying! My poor wife, my dear children, what will become of you?'

"Some were simply moaning; some were praying, and others uttering the most fearful oaths and execrations that despair and agony could wring from them; while a majority, with a stoicism sustained by sublime devotion to the cause they fought for, endured without complaint unspeakable tortures, and even spoke words of cheer and comfort to their unhappy comrades of less will or more acute nerves. Occasionally a wagon would be passed from which only low, deep moans could be heard.

"No help could be rendered to any of the sufferers. No heed could be given to any of their appeals. Mercy and duty to the many forbade the loss of a moment in the vain effort then and there to comply with the prayers of the few. On! On! We *must* move on. The storm continued and the darkness was appalling. There was no time even to fill a canteen with water for a dying man; for, except the drivers and the guards, all were wounded and utterly helpless in that vast procession of misery. During this one night I realized more of the horrors of war than I had in all the two preceding years."

General Meade set his columns in pursuit of the retiring Confederates, but he moved with caution. He was well aware that the Army of Northern Virginia was still a highly dangerous instrument, blunted edges notwithstanding. The Union general was satisfied with what had been accomplished. President Lincoln, however, felt strongly that the victory should be followed with an all-out effort to destroy Lee's army as it retreated. When Meade announced that his aim was merely "to drive from our soil every vestige of the presence of the invader," Lincoln cried, "My God, is that all?"

That was indeed all. The Confederates were permitted to cross the Potomac safely during the night of July 13. Lincoln soon softened toward Meade, grateful after all that Lee's alarming invasion of the North

Lee's retreat to Virginia

had been repelled and that the battle, together with Grant's success at Vicksburg, was clearly a turning point in the war. But later the President told Meade somewhat ruefully that his pursuit of the Confederates reminded him ever so much of "an old woman trying to shoo her geese across a creek."

Epilogue

WRITING IN 1888, Tillie Pierce—now Mrs. Tillie Alleman—ventured these thoughts on Gettysburg's ultimate meaning: "Years have come and gone. . . . Instead of the clashing tumult of battle, the groans of the wounded and dying, the mangled corpses, the shattered cannon, the lifeless charger, and the confusion of arms and accoutrements, a new era of joy and prosperity, harmony, and unity prevails. Where once the bloody hand of Mars blighted and killed the choicest of Nature's off-spring, there Peace, with her smiles and arts, has transformed the desolation into a paradise of beauty and bloom. Where once I saw a terrible chaos, I now behold a pleasing order.

"The struggle between human bondage and universal freedom . . . no more blurs our fair land. On the very spot where in their blindness they shed the blood of fratricide, I have seen the Blue and the Gray clasp hands, and in the presence of their fellow countrymen and before High Heaven, pledge their devotion to each other, and to a renewed and purified government. On this memorable ground I have seen Generals Longstreet, Gordon . . . and Sergeant Jones—who bore the colors of the 53d Virginia in Pickett's charge, being thrice wounded ere he fell—with many others of the Gray, standing together with Generals Sickles, Slocum . . . and others of the Blue; and like men and true patriots freely forgive and mourn the past. I have heard them, as representatives of different parts of our land, unitedly raise their voices in thanking God that we were once more a united people with one common cause. . . .

"The present appearance of the battlefield . . . must be seen and studied to be appreciated. Whoever can, should not fail to visit the place.

Annually it is becoming more and more beautified. The positions of the several corps and regiments are marked by the finest sculpture of which art and science are capable. Avenues are opened so that the visitor can pass all along the line of the terrible conflict, and at the same time learn from the inscriptions on the beautiful monuments, who were engaged, and at what period of the battle.

"The National Cemetery, wherein repose the heroic dead, has become a marvel of loveliness. Baptized with the blood of patriots, dedicated in the immortal words of Lincoln, nurtured and guarded by a grateful people, this spot, for all time to come, cannot be other than the nation's shrine of American virtue, valor, and freedom."

Quotation Sources

Alleman, Tillie Pierce. *At Gettysburg; What a Girl Saw and Heard of the Battle.* New York: W. Lake Borland, 1889.

Angle, Paul M., and Miers, Earl Schenck. *Tragic Years, 1860–1865,* vol. 2. New York: Simon and Schuster, 1960.

Annals of the War. Philadelphia: The Times Publishing Company, 1879.

Battles and Leaders of the Civil War, vol. 3. Robert Underwood Johnson and Clarence Clough Buel, eds. New York: The Century Co., 1884.

Bayly, Mrs. Joseph. *Personal Stories of the Battle.* Typescript in Library of Gettysburg National Military Park. Originally published in Gettysburg *Compiler.*

Bayly, William Hamilton. *Personal Stories of the Battle.* Typescript in Library of Gettysburg National Military Park. Originally published in Gettysburg *Compiler.*

Bigelow, John. *The Peach Orchard, Gettysburg.* Minneapolis: Kimball-Storer Co., 1910. Butternut and Blue reprint, 1984.

Blake, Henry N. *Three Years in the Army of the Potomac.* Boston: Lee and Shepard, 1865.

Broadhead, Sarah M. *Diary of a Lady of Gettysburg, Pennsylvania from June 15 to July 15, 1863.* Self-published. Undated.

Buell, Augustus. *The Cannoneer; Recollections of Service in the Army of the Potomac.* Washington, D.C.: The National Tribune, 1890.

Caldwell, J.F.J. *The History of a Brigade of South Carolinians.* Philadelphia: King & Baird, 1866. Facsimile edition by Morningside Bookshop, Dayton, Ohio, 1974.

Casler, John O. *Four Years in the Stonewall Brigade.* James I. Robertson, Jr., ed. Dayton, Ohio: Morningside Bookshop, 1971. Facsimile of 1906 edition.

Coffin, Charles Carleton. *The Boys of '61.* Boston: Estes and Lauriat, 1884.

Commager, Henry Steele. *The Blue and the Gray.* Indianapolis and New York: The Bobbs-Merrill Company, Inc., 1950.

Cooke, John Esten. *Wearing of the Gray*. New York: Kraus Reprint Co., 1969. Reprint of 1867 edition.

Dickert, D. Augustus. *History of Kershaw's Brigade*. Dayton, Ohio: Morningside Bookshop, 1976. Facsimile of 1899 edition.

Doubleday, Abner. *Chancellorsville and Gettysburg (Campaigns of the Civil War, vol. 6)*. New York: Charles Scribner's Sons, 1882.

Early, Jubal Anderson. *War Memoirs*. Bloomington, Ind.: Indiana University Press, 1960. Reprint of 1912 edition.

Fiske, Samuel. *Mr. Dunn Browne's Experiences in the Army*. Boston: Nichols and Noyes, 1866.

Gates, Theodore B. *The War of the Rebellion*. New York: P. F. McBreen, 1884.

Gerrish, Theodore. *Army Life; A Private's Reminiscences of the Civil War*. Portland, Me.: Hoyt, Fogg, & Donham, 1882.

Gilbert, J. Warren, ed. *The Blue and Gray; A History of the Conflicts During Lee's Invasion and Battle of Gettysburg*. Publisher not named. 1922.

Gilmor, Harry. *Four Years in the Saddle*. New York: Harper & Brothers, 1866.

Glazier, Willard. *Battles for the Union*. Hartford, Conn.: Dustin, Gilman & Co. 1875.

Gordon, John B. *Reminiscences of the Civil War*. New York: Charles Scribner's Sons, 1904.

Goss, Warren Lee. *Recollections of a Private*. New York: Thomas Y. Crowell & Co. 1890.

Greeley, Horace. *The American Conflict*, vol. 2. Hartford, Conn.: O. D. Case & Company, 1867.

Hale, Edward E., ed. *Stories of War Told by Soldiers*. Boston: Roberts Brothers, 1879.

Haskell, Frank Aretas. *The Battle of Gettysburg*. Wisconsin History Commission, 1908.

Hopkins, Luther W. *From Bull Run to Appomattox*. Baltimore: Fleet-McGinley Co. 1908.

Jacobs, M. *Notes on the Rebel Invasion of Maryland and Pennsylvania, and the Battle of Gettysburg*. Gettysburg: G. E. Jacobs, 1888.

Jones, John B. *A Rebel War Clerk's Diary*. Earl Schenck Miers, ed. New York: Sagamore Press, Inc., 1958. First published in 1866.

Lee, Fitzhugh. *General Lee of the Confederate Army*. London: Chapman and Hall, Ltd., 1895.

Longstreet, James. *From Manassas to Appomattox*. Millwood, N.Y.: Kraus Reprint Co., 1976. First published in 1896.

McClellan, H. B. *The Life and Campaigns of Major General J.E.B. Stuart*. Boston: Houghton, Mifflin & Company, 1885.

Miers, Earl Schenck, and Brown, Richard A. *Gettysburg*. New Brunswick, N.J.: Rutgers University Press, 1948.

Moore, Frank, ed. *The Rebellion Record*, vols. 7, 8, 10. New York: D. Van Nostrand, 1864, 1865, 1867.

Neese, George M. *Three Years in the Confederate Horse Artillery*. New York and Washington: The Neale Publishing Company, 1911.

Nicholson, John P., ed. *Pennsylvania at Gettysburg; Ceremonies at the Dedication of the Monuments.* 2 vols. Harrisburg, Pa.: E. K. Meyers, State Printer, 1893.

Norton, Oliver Willcox. *The Attack and Defense of Little Round Top.* New York: The Neale Publishing Company, 1913.

Oates, William C. *The War Between the Union and the Confederacy.* New York: The Neale Publishing Company, 1905.

Opie, John N. *A Rebel Cavalryman with Lee, Stuart, and Jackson.* Dayton, Ohio: Morningside Bookshop, 1972. Facsimile of 1899 edition.

Our Women in the War. Charleston, S.C.: The News and Courier Book Presses, 1885.

Owen, William Miller. *In Camp and Battle with the Washington Artillery.* Boston: Ticknor and Company, 1885. Second edition by Pelican Publishing Company, New Orleans, 1964.

Pickett, George E. *The Heart of a Soldier.* New York: Seth Moyle, Inc., 1913.

Robert L. Brake Collection. A treasury of early Gettysburg items in transcript: letters, diaries, book excerpts, magazine articles and newspaper clippings, many of the last from the Gettysburg *Compiler.* United States Army Military History Institute, Carlisle, Pennsylvania.

Stevens, George T. *Three Years in the Sixth Corps.* New York: D. Van Nostrand, 1870.

Stiles, Robert. *Four Years Under Marse Robert.* New York and Washington: The Neale Publishing Company, 1903.

Stine, J. H. *History of the Army of the Potomac.* Philadelphia: J. B. Rogers Printing Co., 1892.

Tenney, W. J. *The Military and Naval History of the Rebellion.* New York: D. Appleton & Company, 1865.

Trobriand, P. Regis de. *Four Years with the Army of the Potomac.* Boston: Ticknor and Company, 1889.

Under Both Flags: A Panorama of the Great Civil War. Chicago: W. S. Reeve Publishing Co., 1896.

Von Borcke, Heros. *Memoirs of the Confederate War for Independence,* vol. 2. New York: Peter Smith, 1938. Reprint of 1866 edition.

Walker, Francis A. *History of the Second Army Corps in the Army of the Potomac.* New York: Charles Scribner's Sons, 1886.

Wallace, Francis B. *Memorial of the Patriotism of Schuylkill County in the American Slaveholder's Rebellion.* Pottsville, Pa.: Benjamin Bannan, 1865.

The War of the Rebellion: A Compilation of the Official Records of the Union and Confederate Armies, Series I, Volume 27. 3 vols. Washington, D.C.: Government Printing Office, 1889.

Wheeler, Richard. *Voices of the Civil War.* New York: Thomas Y. Crowell Company, 1976.

Young, Jesse Bowman. *What a Boy Saw in the Army.* New York: Hunt & Eaton, 1894.

Supplementary References

Blackford, W. W. *War Years with Jeb Stuart*. New York: Charles Scribner's Sons 1945.

Catton, Bruce. *The Army of the Potomac: Glory Road*. Garden City, New York Doubleday & Company, Inc., 1952.

——. *Gettysburg: The Final Fury*. Garden City, New York: Doubleday & Company, Inc., 1974.

——. *Never Call Retreat*. Garden City, New York: Doubleday & Company, Inc. 1965.

Coffin, Charles Carleton. *Marching to Victory*. New York: Harper & Brothers 1889.

Cooke, John Esten. *Robert E. Lee*. New York: D. Appleton & Company, 1871

Davis, Burke. *Jeb Stuart, the Last Cavalier*. New York and Toronto: Rinehart & Company, Inc., 1957.

Evans, Clement A., ed. *Confederate Military History: A Library of Confederate State. History, in Twelve Volumes, Written by Distinguished Men of the South*. New York: Thomas Yoseloff, 1962. Reprint of edition by the Confederate Publishing Company, 1899.

Forney, John W. *Life and Military Career of Winfield Scott Hancock*. Philadelphia J. C. McCurdy & Co., 1880.

Guernsey, Alfred H., and Alden, Henry M. *Harper's Pictorial History of the Grea Rebellion*, vol. 2. Chicago: McDonnell Bros., 1866.

Hancock, Mrs. A. R. *Reminiscences of Winfield Scott Hancock*. New York: Charles L Webster & Company, 1887.

Hansen, Harry. *The Civil War*. New York: Bonanza Books, 1961.

Johnson, Rossiter. *Campfires and Battlefields*. New York: The Civil War Press 1967. First published in 1894.

Long, E. B., with Barbara Long. *The Civil War Day by Day*. Garden City, New York: Doubleday & Company, Inc., 1971.

Lossing, Benson J. *Pictorial Field Book of the Civil War*, vol. 3. New York: T. Belknap & Company, 1868.

Nichols, G. W. *A Soldier's Story of His Regiment.* Kennesaw, Georgia: Continental Book Company, 1961. Reprint of 1898 edition.

Page, Thomas Nelson. *Robert E. Lee, Man and Soldier.* New York: Charles Scribner's Sons, 1911.

Paris, Comte de. *History of the Civil War in America,* vol. 3. Philadelphia: Jos. H. Coates & Co., 1883.

Pennypacker, Isaac R. *General Meade.* New York: D. Appleton and Company, 1901.

Pollard, Edward A. *The Early Life, Campaigns, and Public Services of Robert E. Lee; with a Record of the Campaigns and Heroic Deeds of his Companions in Arms.* New York: E. B. Treat & Co., 1871.

_____. *The Lost Cause.* New York: E. B. Treat & Co., 1866.

_____. *The Second Year of the War.* New York: Charles B. Richardson, 1864.

Smart, James G., ed. *A Radical View: The "Agate" Dispatches of Whitelaw Reid, 1861–1865,* vol. 2. Memphis, Tenn.: Memphis State University Press, 1976.

Stackpole, Edward J. *They Met at Gettysburg.* New York: Bonanza Books, 1956.

Swinton, William. *Campaigns of the Army of the Potomac.* New York: Charles Scribner's Sons, 1882.

Taylor, Walter H. *Four Years with General Lee.* New York: D. Appleton and Company, 1878.

Thomas, Emory M. *Bold Dragoon; the Life of J.E.B. Stuart.* New York: Harper & Row, 1986.

Thomason, John W., Jr. *Jeb Stuart.* New York and London: Charles Scribner's Sons, 1930.

Urban, John W. *Battle Field and Prison Pen.* Edgewood Publishing Company, 1882.

Williams, T. Harry. *Lincoln and His Generals.* New York: Alfred A. Knopf, Inc., 1952.

Wood, William. *Captains of the Civil War.* New Haven, Conn.: Yale University Press, 1921.

Young, Jesse Bowman. *The Battle of Gettysburg.* Dayton, Ohio: Morningside Bookshop, 1976. Facsimile of 1913 edition.

Index

(Page numbers in **boldface** denote illustrations)